Management
of
Information Systems
Technology

Management
of
Information Systems
Technology

by

Janice Burn
Eveline Caldwell

Department of Computing Studies,
Hong Kong Polytechnic, Kowloon,
Hong Kong

VNR VAN NOSTRAND REINHOLD
New York

PUBLISHED BY
ALFRED WALLER LTD
Orchards, Fawley, Henley-on-Thames,
Oxfordshire RG9 6JF

First published 1990
Copyright © 1990
Janice Burn and Eveline Caldwell

ISBN 0-442-30478-1

Published in the U.S.A. by
Van Nostrand Reinhold
115 Fifth Avenue
New York, N.Y. 10003

Distributed in Canada by
Nelson Canada
1120 Birchmount Road
Scarborough, Ontario M1K 5G4

British Library Cataloguing in Publication Data

Burn, Janice
  Management of information systems technology.
  1. Organisations. Information systems. Management
  I. Title   II. Caldwell, Eveline
  658.4′038

Editorial and Production Services by
Fisher Duncan, 10 Barley Mow Passage, Chiswick, London W4 4PH

Printed in Great Britain by
Antony Rowe Ltd, Chippenham, Wiltshire

6-4-92

Contents

Part I Strategic modelling

Part II Strategies for information systems development

Part III The management of information technology

Part I   Strategic modelling

The first part of the book introduces readers to the idea of thinking about a system. It stresses the role of strategic framework for corporate planning. It intends to show that there is no unitary approach, system or technology and gives readers a broad understanding of a number of approaches which can fit into a contingency model. In so doing it provides a number of examples from simple to complex and concludes with a simple case study.

The overall aim is to show readers that although there is much to learn there is a model which can be applied to help them through the maze.

1   Strategic planning for information systems and technology

1.1   Introduction to strategic planning

Recently, we were asked to collaborate on a major government project. We received a telephone call from a man who identified himself as the manager in charge of strategic planning for information technology in an area of government. We arranged to meet him and looked forward to learning in detail how a large organization approached this problem.

He explained that until recently the government had been reactive rather than proactive to developments in information technology (IT) but was determined to change that. In future all developments using information technology should relate directly to the organizational 'mission'. His initial task was to develop a model which could be applied to all strategic planning for IT-related projects in government departments over the next 10 years. He suggested that we look at the overall plan and produced the dataflow modelling diagram, reproduced in fig. 1.1.

This shows the following five stages identified as headings at the top of the diagram:

External environment   This requires extensive analysis of the current social, economic, political, technological and cultural environment, both local and international, and a forecast of changes to be made in any of these areas. This data will be input to stage 2.

Impact of external environment   The scenario construction basically requires the development of a model which can simulate this 'real world' environment and then, for various projected scenarios, analyze the impact on government and hence the opportunities and threats which this may present. For each of these situations, the information needs are then identified and fed into the forward planning model in stage 3.

Information needs   The current information needs to satisfy the 'mission' of each department within government must be identified. This will involve deliberation over such issues as: What business are we in? What are our key

3

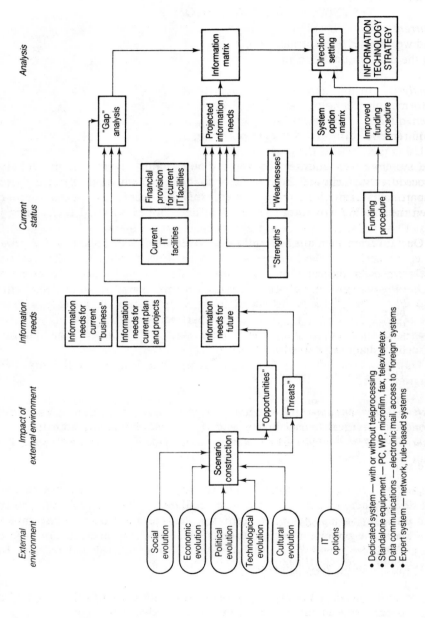

Fig. 1.1 Formulation of information technology (IT) strategy: methods of modelling.

External environment

Social evolution
Economic evolution
Political evolution
Technological evolution
Cultural evolution

IT options

Impact of external environment

Scenario construction

"Opportunities"
"Threats"

Information needs

Information needs for current "business"
Information needs for current plan and projects

Information needs for future

Current status

Financial provision for current IT facilities
Current IT facilities

"Strengths"
"Weaknesses"

Funding procedure

Analysis

"Gap" analysis

Projected information needs

Information matrix

System option matrix
Improved funding procedure

Direction setting

INFORMATION TECHNOLOGY STRATEGY

• Dedicated system — with or without teleprocessing
• Standalone equipment — PC, WP, microfilm, fax, telex/teletex
• Data communications — electronic mail, access to "foreign" systems
• Expert system — network, rule-based systems

results areas? What objectives should we achieve? This must be repeated for a 3- to 5-year development plan, and again for 5- to 10-year plan. From this a model can be derived of the current status.

Current status   This covers information technology, funding, and strengths and weaknesses of information provision. It will involve a mass correlation of all the data produced so far before entry into the final stage of the model.

Analysis   In the 'gap' analysis the difference between current provision of information technology and that required for future needs is identified and then quantified in terms of specific technology, funding and information requirements.

Using these results the government can assess the various IT options against the system needs and set the IT direction, whilst improving the funding procedures to facilitate this. The aim is to give much more freedom to the departments in the long term so that once their strategy has been approved then the funding will automatically be generated to match this.

Our government manager explained some of his problems:

> 'My major difficulty is in the "gap" analysis. Do you have any figures I can use — such as the requisite number of computer workstations per head or the recommended level of expenditure on information technology? I have no idea how to start quantifying the exact requirements for technology because I have found no definitive statistics on their usage. I have found an article suggesting a level of one workstation per four staff but I don't know whether this would apply to our situation.
>
> There is another area where I would like your help.
>
> How can I go about setting up a model of the environment in the earlier stages of the model? I have been reading some computer journals but I just don't have time to read them all. Surely, someone must already have done some research in this area?'

We said:

> 'You mean that at present you can't see your way to developing stages 1 and 2 because you are unfamiliar with the processes of setting up an environmental model; nor can you progress with stages 4 and 5 because of lack of knowledge of evaluation and quantification measurements in IT? What about stage 3? Are you applying a rigorous methodology such as Business Systems Planning (BSP) or Critical Success Factors (CSF) to determine the information needs?'
>
> 'Well, something like that except it is our own government method. But it is quite detailed and we will end up with a highly complex information matrix.'

At this point the situation seemed salvagable although not necessarily solvable. We said:

> 'We understand your problem and we have been doing some work in these areas which may help in the longer term. We suggest that you continue work on stage 3 which will be extremely time consuming, while we examine our data and see how these can be made useful to you. Do you have a specific timescale?'

> 'Perhaps I should explain, I used to work in the data processing department as an analyst and I have been seconded to this position to advise the government on the way we should implement our strategic planning. I need to present my final report in January.'

January was 3 months away.

At this point the situation not only became unsalvagable but also became a comic tragedy so typical of strategic planning efforts by organizations to date. It did, however, have one saving grace, in that it allowed us to use a true story to illustrate both the scope of strategic planning and some of the many problem areas therein. The story is a classic example of an organization which realises the need for strategic planning but has no understanding of the complexities, expertise or time involved. We would assume that a team of planners working on this project would require a minimum of 2 years and considerable research back-up. Instead, a single systems analyst was raised to the status of strategic planning manager for a period of 6 months (it had taken the first 3 months for him to begin to realise what a problem he faced).

1.2   Issues in strategic planning

This introduction to strategic planning was chosen because it provides a very good framework from which to explore the major issues.

This model in fig 1.1 has five stages and in itself is a reasonable, if simplistic, view of part of the strategic planning process. The first two stages are concerned with the development of an organizational model which will include an analysis of the external environment and its impact on the organization. Why is the model necessary? Is one organization not broadly the same as another? The answer is that organizations have only one certain thing in common: organizational problems! They may differ in structure, culture, size, age, ownership, business area, management models, role, job definitions, span of control, and technology; thus organizations will always differ in their information needs. This is why a model of each organization is so important: by defining specific information flow and usage patterns we can begin to understand some of the information requirements. We can also, at this stage, begin to appreciate the particular constraints which apply to the specific organization and the environmental issues which impact upon its overall operation.

Once a model has been conceptualized and the objectives of the organization clarified, it is possible to explore the specific information people need to make decisions in line with the overall objectives. This is normally identified by an examination of certain levels of management roles, such as strategic, planning or operational, or by examining functional areas such as accounting, personnel or purchasing. A comprehensive methodology such as BSP or CSF can be applied to provide a matrix of information needs mapped against functional areas and the specific level of decision making involved. This can be seen as the specific, detailed refinement of model 1.

The next stage in the process in fig. 1.1 is 'current status' which implies that some mammoth steps have been taken. In other words, it suggests the translation of these information needs into effective information-providing systems through the utilization of information technology. A great deal of work must be done here which is concerned with information systems development methods and tools; information technology evaluation and selection; information resource management. Effective strategic planning must cover all these issues and must be able constantly to measure and review the impact on performance.

This brings us to the last stage on the diagram, the analysis stage. Planning is all about the future, about being proactive rather than reactive. It must however, relate to the past, to other experience, for example in a similar organization, and to future expectations. We need to be able to judge the effectiveness of past performance in order to produce a measure for the future. This requires detailed cost–benefit evaluation of information system development and information technology usage; which must be constantly re-evaluated against system and organization performance. Using this we are likely to come up with meaningless statistics such as the number of terminals per employee, but we may become much more efficient at estimating costs involved at certain levels of information service provision — and so be able in the long term to give funding guidance and in the shorter term to evaluate specific facilities and implementation options for information technology.

This plan does, however, leave a great deal to be desired. It is a 'start-up and stop dead' kind of plan. It provides a model for arriving from the current position where there is no strategy to a position of defined IT strategy, and then stops short. There is no contingency for updating and maintenance. It also assumes the existence of many other such planning systems providing us with knowledge of strengths and weaknesses, opportunities and threats. Nowhere, however, does it specifically relate to the overall organizational, strategy which must be central to IT strategy. The impression we get from this plan is that it is back to front. Strategic direction should lead our IS/IT developments and stem from the overall organizational strategy. How can we go about developing a sensible strategy? Let us take a much simpler look at the basis of a strategic plan as shown in fig. 1.2.

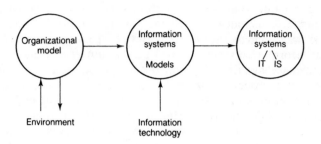

Fig. 1.2   The basis of a strategic plan.

There are at least two other stages surrounding and extending this process. Both relate specifically to information. Before we can start to model the environment and the organization we must have a clear understanding of what information is, and the way human beings interact with it. Humans use information to guide the actions of cooperating social groups — information is the lifeblood of the organization. It is necessary, therefore, to build a general model of information and how it behaves before we can build our model of the organization and the environment. Without the general model we will be unable to identify the specific information required from the environment or the level of usage of information required from the environment or the level of usage of information within the organization. This study is often referred to as information science and probably for that reason has found limited acceptance. It is now, however, widely accepted that more attention must be paid to the specific characteristics of information and their value to a particular organization.

This idea of value needs also to be applied at the final stage, not just in an evaluation of system performance but also in an evaluation of organizational productivity and profitability related directly to the provision of information services. Again this can be addressed from two directions. It is possible to perform a detailed study of managers' system usage and subsequent additional value-added services. By this we mean the extra services he is able to perform and the increased effectiveness of his decisions. It is also possible to examine the organization as a single system with inputs of IT and IS expenditure being matched against outputs on profit and loss, service, market share etc. Within the firm this would be matched against the strategic plan for targeted investment on information systems and technology. Much of the work in this area is still highly subjective but it is essential. Too many surveys have shown that the level of investment in IT has little or no correlation with profitability or productivity increases. It is not enough just to provide information; it needs to be information which improves the performance of the organization. Particularly in business, people are coming to realise that in information they have a major competitive weapon.

The extended model that we would apply to strategic planning is shown in fig. 1.3; note that it includes a major feature missing from the earlier process — feedback and control. Strategic plans are not static. They are active management information systems which should allow for variance tracking of actual performance against expected performance. They are also 'real life' which means the model cannot assume perfection: continual iteration, refinement and review must be built in to the process as an adaptive system with the ability to apply heuristic learning principles.

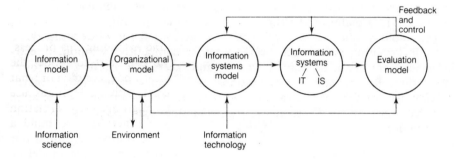

Fig. 1.3 An extended model of a strategic plan including feedback and control.

This model does still not, however, consider a major issue raised earlier: the need to include the organizational strategic plan.

1.3 The need for strategic planning

So far we have discussed the concept of strategic planning for information systems and technology without exploring the issue of why we do it at all? It is frustrating to see people who spend their life planning and never effecting. It is harmful to an organization when a major effort is required to produce plans and then no effort is made to implement them — so don't do it if you won't use it.

However, without planning you run the risk of failing to develop:

Systems with a strategic impact on your organization
Effective cost control over IT investment
Information services which give quantifiable added value

Let us look at some of the reasons why.

1.3.1 Strategic use of information technology

During the last decade we have witnessed a remarkable technological revolution which shows no sign of decreasing momentum. The computer invades every part of our working lives, domestic situations and social experiences. Electronic communication has advanced to the extent that the whole pattern of our lives has changed — there is now far less need for physical contact to exchange information; while this may have a depressing impact on our social life it has considerably expanded organizational horizons. This organizational impact is very much multi-dimensional. Ways of working and managing must also be altered when new technology is introduced. This has been particularly well explored in recent research with respect to the implementation of office automation systems. In order to exploit the benefits resulting from technological innovation, organizational innovation is also necessary. This really means that the strategic plan for information systems and technology must be an implicit part of the overall corporate strategy.

An information system can act as a major competitive weapon, directly influence the organizational structure and act as a catalyst to foster innovation. By including considerations of information technology in the development of corporate strategy, and by effectively managing information resources through an IT strategy, the technology can make its maximum contribution.

1.3.2 Cost of information services

Anyone examining the historical growth of information technology will become instantly aware of the massive reductions in the cost of hardware in relation to processing power. For example, at the time of writing, a Million Instruction Per Second (MIPS) performance rate on a large IBM mainframe machine costs about US$185 000, about US$120 000 on a DEC mini-computer, and less than US$10 000 on a PC and is dropping even further. This does mean that far less investment in technology is required to capitalize on information services. What it does not mean, however, is that the cost of information provision has been reduced overall. Quite the opposite.

The proliferation of technology and the information services which can be provided has created a huge growth industry. Porat (1977) at New York University showed that the total information sector spurted from 17% of the US economy in 1950 to 58% in 1980. whilst over the same period the industrial segment plummeted from 65% to 27%. These statistics highlight a profound change to national economies and to organizations. They also show that people must be spending more to acquire information both externally and internally. A survey conducted by us in 1988 of 125 organizations showed in all cases that the percentage of increased spending on information resources within the company (— technology, systems and services —) greatly exceeded that of other resource costs and in the majority of cases also exceeded that of turnover and profit. This enormous cost (in the case of information service industries — the major one) needs to be justified and controlled. Too often systems are justified on the basis of an individual department's needs or the 'Who shouts loudest' philosophy. In many organizations chief executives are allowed to give top priority to their pet hobby horses although frequently unsupported by in-depth knowledge of the application area or the technological support. The resulting situation is often worse than before. Uncoordinated systems cannot then be integrated into a management information system or related to corporate strategies. Control and coordination can only be effected if a clear strategy exists and is applied to all information systems developments.

This still does not mean, however, that the information produced will be of real benefit to the organization.

1.3.3   Measuring benefits of information services

The benefits from increased spending on information services are not always realised by managers. In a study by Lucas & Turner (1981) at the New York Center for Research on Information Systems, it was reported that the president of a medium-sized manufacturing company had remarked 'I receive about the same information today as was provided 30 years ago, before computers. Only now I spend millions to get it.'

A further study by Turner (1983) addressed the issue of whether organizational performance was influenced by how a firm made use of information resources. Unexpectedly, no relationship was found to exist between organizational performance and the relative proportion of resources allocated to data-operating cost and the intensity of data-processing use. These findings raise questions about the extent of benefits obtained from a data-processing intensive strategy and the effeciency with which firms convert capital and labour into application systems. Finding the answers to these questions is further complicated by the difficulties inherent in investment appraisal of information systems. This is a complex issue at the best of times but the innovative potential of new technologies means that not all the outcomes can be predicted. Sencker (1984), at the University of Essex, UK, suggests four main reasons for wild inaccuracies:

> The duration of the learning honeymoon drastically underestimated
> Equipment utilization rates frequently optimistic
> Adaptations to other equipment and systems underestimated
> Effort to promote commitment to change overlooked

For reasons such as this one can argue that much investment in this area has to be an act of faith. Boddy & Buchanan (1986) do suggest, however, that it is possible to make the act of faith more systematic by the use of cost/benefit analysis linked to the strategic objectives, and lend further support to the ideas that a strategic plan for IT is critical. Effectiveness of IT investments requires a yardstick and this will be provided by a well maintained strategy which is not blind to new opportunities, for example innovations in technology.

Figure 1.4 is an attempt to highlight these issues rather than address them all.

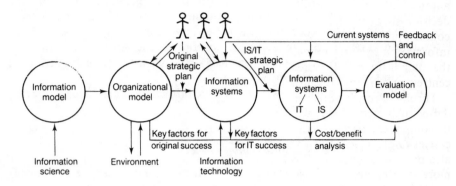

Fig. 1.4   Some of the issues facing the strategic planner.

It specifically introduces a very necessary component in terms of people who interact with the model and make the final decisions, based, it is to be hoped, on better information. The model is still highly generalized and simplistic, and does not necessarily cover all strategic issues. This is as it should be: too often we try to apply fixed scientific processes to problems of human information processing, and the result is fixed, non-adaptive solutions which in themselves promote greater problems.

1.4   Summary

This chapter has dealt with the role of strategic planning for information systems and technology. It has identified a model to be used to develop such plans and introduced the major stages of development and the issues of concern. The rest of the book will examine these issues in detail.

In Part I we will be concerned with conceptual models which can be applied to assist our understanding of the real requirements for information and supporting systems in an organization. An overview of the information technology which can be used to support information services will be presented and some of the public and private information network services introduced.

Part II will consider the strategies which can be adopted to develop appropriate information systems which fully exploit the available information technology. In particular, it will look at approaches to: requirements analysis definition; systems development methodologies; and evaluation, selection and distribution of information technology.

Part III is concerned with the management of IT and relates the previous sections to specific application of information technology in the business environment. These areas include: strategic information systems; office automation and management support systems; small business systems; decision-support and expert systems. Major developments and issues for concern are identified. We end this section by examining the whole issue of information resource management from a strategic viewpoint. This will cover: the management of systems development; information centres and data centres; and human resources and information technology.

Throughout this book an effort is made to present strategies rather than to define rules. Specifically we advocate an adaptive approach to the solution and its component parts. At the end of each part there is a summary and a short case example which draws together the concepts presented in that section. We also provide pointers to further study by highlighting research in some of the more exciting areas.

2   Information modelling

2.1   What is information?

The question 'what is information' may appear to be naive. Nevertheless, it has given rise to many answers by the information research community. Consider a few of the earlier definitions.

> 'Information is recorded experience that can or shall be used in decision making.' Churchman (1979)

> 'The distinction between data and information is simple. Information is associated data, that is to say, data items which have been processed in some way so that we can identify each item by associating it with other items.' Grindley (1975)

> 'Information is digested data. The same data can be processed in a variety of different ways to produce different pieces of information which are useful in different circumstances'. Martin (1981)

Clearly, 'information' is a term open to a variety of interpretation. Should we concern ourselves over a problem that is basically only semantic? Is the problem only semantic? Read any report from an investment newsletter or magazine. The report will contain *information*. What we need to ask is whether you find the information meaningful, useful or valuable.

Let us examine some possible options.
1.   *I do not find it meaningful because:*
     I do not understand the terminology; the references; the context
2.   *I do not find it useful because:*
     of 1; I have no interest in investment; it is not relevant to my portfolio
3.   *I do not find it valuable because:*
     of 1 and 2; I have already made use of this information; I do not believe it; it is out of date.

If any or all of these are true do we still have any information? Possibly only if we suggest that you can now make a value judgement concerning the quality of investment advice; literary style of investment writers or financial interests of the author. Information, therefore, is extremely specific to the needs of the recipient.

It will consist of data that has been processed into a *meaningful* form

It will *add* to a representation, by being relevant and new or confirmatory

It *reduces* uncertainty for future decision making.

Its overall value has been described by Tricker (1982) as the AhHa! factor — the surprise reaction to learning something relevant and new.

In chapter 1 we stated that information is the lifeblood of any organization. It informs decision makers at all levels about those variables which represent the state of the organization and about those which represent changes, or rates of change, in variables affecting the organization. This means that it is necessary both to define specific information needs and also to define the information flow and the interconnections. Information science has tried to address these issues and its influence is assessed in the next section.

2.2 Information science

2.2.1 Problem of complexity

The strategic planning model developed in chapter 1 had constant interaction with the environment at a highly complex level. The issues related to social, cultural, political, economic and technological developments are many and diverse: how does one know what information to collect and input as data to the organizational model? Obviously, we will build up a detailed specification of the requirements at later stages in the study, but initially we must gain a conceptual understanding of information models and specifically how to proceed when information systems become sufficiently complex. One suggested approach, based on information theory, resorts to heuristic learning or other adaptive approaches. A simple diagram (fig. 2.1) illustrates this approach.

In this diagram, part (a) has precise rules for defining the outputs from the environment. There is a clear and fixed definition of the information we will collect and the way we will use this combined set of information to evaluate the effect of the environment. In the case of large-scale strategic planning this can only be achieved by oversimplification of the information needs or overcomplication of the information processing. Using the model presented in fig. 1.1, even if we restricted the number of possible environmental outputs to six per evolutionary factor, giving 30 in all, this would give us a possible scenario of thousands of different cumulative affectors and would require a comprehensive analysis of the effect of each (detector) on the organizational model. This is a gross simplification but it should still be possible to see the extent of the problem; by applying a sophisticated 'game play' technique it would be possible to come up with winning strategies, although this would be a complex and time-consuming task. As a consequence, it would be many years

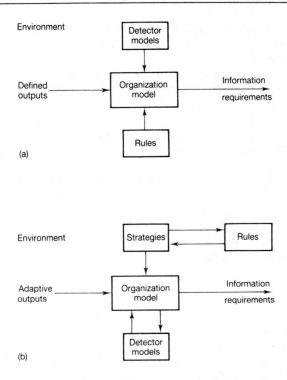

Fig. 2.1 Information models: (a) fixed control system; (b) adaptive system.

before the rule base and detector models could be set up and applied to overall strategy.

In part (b) you have to discover which rules are governing the impact on the adaptive system and then apply them to a winning strategy. Thus the detector model is built up within the adaptive system over time. This does eliminate some of the prerequisite cause-and-effect analysis of model (a) but still leaves us with the problem of what the significant, adaptive output message which we receive from the environment should be. The efficient detection of information has been the subject of considerable study in other branches of information science.

2.2.2 Theories of communication

Research in the general area of information theory started in the mid-1940s. The basic theory was established with the work of Shannon & Weaver (1962). This theory covers the transmission of messages over a channel, independent of meaning and whilst specifically concerned with technical communication problems, Weaver also identified three levels of information as follows:

Technical: how accurately can information be transmitted?

Semantic: how precisely do the transmitted symbols convey the desired meaning?

Effectiveness: how suitable is the message as a motivation of human action?

A very important part of the theory and an area which has given rise to much controversy, relates to the basic model of a communication system as shown in fig. 2.2. This communication system is one where messages are transmitted through some form of communication channel — for example a telecommunications system sending messages from one workstation to another where errors and distortions are introduced by the apparatus. The problem for the scientist is to reconstruct the original message.

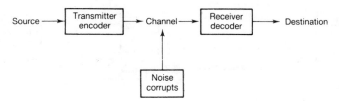

Fig. 2.2   Basic model of a communication system.

In addressing this problem Brillouin (1964) developed a scientific version of the model (fig. 2.3). Here, the scientist accumulates sufficient error-laden messages to reconstruct the correct ones and can plug those corrected values into a standard procedure to test this hypothesis.

A major flaw in these theories, apart from their limited consideration of the whole issue, lies in their presumption that channel noise will result in a received signal which is ambiguous only between a number of logically possible messages and that the primary vehicle for reducing this range is clever coding, redundancy and possibly inspired filtering. What they do not address is which messages are allowed to enter the system and how many possible messages are eliminated.

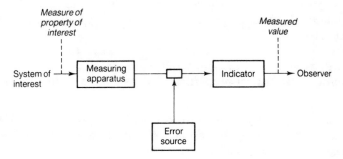

Fig. 2.3   Scientific model of a communication system.

Suppe (1977) at the University of Illinois examined this problem and developed a refinement of the model (fig. 2.4) which exploits the ways in which science controls its inputs, measures and corrects messages, and evaluates and reconstructs hypotheses. This suggests that the definition of information from a source such as the environment in our strategic model must be subject to rigorous experimentation.

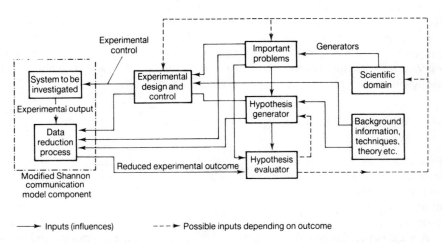

Fig. 2.4   Refined scientific model of a communication system showing the relationship between science and information.

2.2.3   Study of semiotics

Semiotics is the study of signs and sign processes and we can look at this concept to provide us with another model of the communication process (fig. 2.5.) where broadly, the following meanings apply:

> *Sign*: something which stands to somebody for something in some respect or capacity;
> *Pragmatics*: signs and behaviour as used by people (pure rhetoric);
> *Semantics*: signs and what they mean as the relation of data to reality (logic proper);
> *Syntactics*: structural arrangement of signs, to store and process regardless of what they signify (pure grammar);
> *Empirics*: a statistical properties of signs related to the transmission of data.

Researchers in this area are concerned with the precision with which the transmitted symbols convey the desired information and therefore relate to the ambiguous notion of relevance.

We can say that there are three meanings to every message:

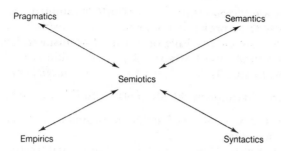

Fig. 2.5 Semiotics provides another model of the communication process.

> What the sender intended it to mean,
> What is actually contained in the message,
> What the recipient understands it to mean.

Few instances of 'perfect communication' are ever achieved in the first instance. Human perception will naturally try to organize a message into something meaningful, consistent with expectations, and consistent within itself, and the perceptual norms which are used to resolve these will vary enormously.

A major problem is that there are no signs which fall neatly into the category of purely semantic, syntactic or pragmatic in nature. Every sign process involves all three aspects and, in general, these dimensions are not independent. There is an enormous breadth of knowledge required to begin to deal with these problems and the extreme importance, therefore, of building a highly adaptive information system which can interact with users consistent with their level of expectation and perceptions.

2.2.4 Effectiveness of communication

The third level of information deals with the effectiveness of information: how information, once received and understood, is utilized. This, of course, implies that the level 3 model is embedded in the decision-making environment since that is how information is used. All sorts of attempts have been made to define a measure of effectiveness or pragmatic information. However, none of these efforts address the whole problem. This requires information measures, decision maker's effectiveness measures, system performance measures and probably profitability and productivity measures. Some useful research work has taken place which attempts to consider information in the domain of decision-making and a conceptual decision-maker. This uses a general model of information flow and analysis.

The model is dynamic in nature and the decision maker learns about his environment as follows:

He makes a decision on the basis of information.
He predicts some probable outcomes.
He compares actual resulting observables against predicted observables.
He updates total model as a result.
He returns to step 1.

For any problem environment he attempts to fulfill two main objectives:

To choose the best course of action according to some criteria (given his state of knowledge).
To learn the most about the total existing situation from the decision-making process.

The situation described above is very much a scientific approach using a monitoring and measurement approach to all observables. But does this ever happen in a real life situation? The answer now is yes. We have specifically drawn attention to this study because the principles suggested are very much those employed in the development of computer-based decision support systems, expert systems and artificial intelligence. With the help of a computer-based information system we can begin to measure the effectiveness of individual decision-making.

This does not necessarily, however, help an organization determine overall whether it is making effective use of information since an expert model of organizational decision-making is a very much more complex task. To do this we would have to extend the strategic model developed in chapter 1 to cover all decision-making in the organization and then develop a computer simulation model with 'intelligent' capabilities — not a practical or even highly feasible solution given our current level of understanding as to how organizations work.

How then can an organization attempt to apply practical measurement? This is a question which is raised more and more as organizations become conscious of the need to justify expenditure on information services by evidence of improved profitability and/or productivity. Two worthwhile efforts in this direction deserve more than a passing mention; both originated in computer-manufacturing organizations.

The first is the 'Four layer measurement methodology' piloted in IBM. As suggested by its name, it has four stages of measurement:

user-generated benefits, usage statistics, shift in pattern of activity and realized benefits.

On the basis of a questionnaire and interviews, the users' subjective impressions of where benefits and problems arise are gathered. This starts about 6 months after the system goes live, when users are asked to identify on a percentage scale what benefit they would assign to particular activities. From this a view of the users' perception of the system is developed and monitored regularly over time.

The next step is to monitor how perceptions compare with actual usage. The system automatically generates statistics on time spent by each user on each major function. Discrepancies are investigated.

The third stage focuses on changes to work practices and again uses questionnaires where users are asked to complete logs on time spent on various activities. Two categories of activities are used: first, opportunity areas such as reducing time spent looking for people or information; second, necessary evils such as travelling or trying to telephone someone. The logs are completed before and after installation and then as necessary.

The final step is to assess what gain the company has made. Each senior manager sets objectives expected to be achieved and indicators of performance to be used in assessing actual results. They are interviewed in depth before and after installation.

Using this methodology IBM, UK have assessed the effectiveness of their office information system and come up with specific figures of increased productivity gains. They have also assessed potential gains if the system were improved — particularly in response time, reliability and ease of use.

An alternative approach was developed by Strassman (1985). He advocates a value-added approach also but applies rather different measurements. Value-added analyses are used by many companies to evaluate capital investment. The basic value-added measure is obtained by subtracting total costs of purchases of goods and services from the company's turnover. The higher the value-added percentage compared to purchase costs, the better is the return on management (ROM).

Strassman uses this to calculate the return on IT investment by subtracting capital costs of IT from the total value-added, leaving the value-added for labour. This is divided into operations and management and all costs associated with them also subtracted. This leaves a net value-added figure and the relationship of this to the cost of management is the ROM. For a company to be successful, the ROM should be greater than 1.

Of course, there is much more to the calculations than this. Strassman typically uses studies of resource-freeing benefits of IT and uses of freed time as his base for measures. He then applies a specific calculation for ROM depending on the organization's allocation of costs.

Ranked resource-freeing potential	*Ranked new uses of managers*
Meetings	Long range planning of work
Reports and writings	New products and services
Planning and communicating	Training and development of staff
Unnecessary assignments	Training and development of self
Waiting for decisions	Improving recruitment
Random interruptions	Setting and tracking goals
Unnecessary travel	Improving management methods
Missed communications	Automation and computerization

Telephone	External, non-customer activity
Evaluation of projects	Meeting with customers
Administrative tasks	
Rewriting	
Clerical tasks	

These are just two methods which try to put theory into practice and they are very much concerned with measuring information value which results from the organization's information systems.

2.2.5 Knowledge versus information

Messages may contain data, information and/or knowledge. *Data* can be defined as raw facts and opinions formed from groups of characters. *Information* is data that has usefulness (value) in a current decision situation (evaluated facts). *Knowledge* requires experience, understanding and a stored body of information and can be defined as information with a potential use retained in some organized manner for reference in future decision making.

The real power of information processing systems can be enjoyed through the development of such knowledge based systems (KBS). IKBS (the intelligent version), AI (artificial intelligence) and expert systems are all variations on this theme where the theory of information science is an implicit part of the system construction. Figure 2.6 shows a highly simplified model of the IKBS process.

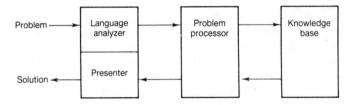

Fig. 2.6   Simplified model of the Intelligent version of a Knowledge Based System (IKBS).

2.3   Summary

This chapter has concentrated on the first stage of our strategic planning model and looked at some of the many different facets of information. In particular, we have explored the communications process from a mathematical, semiotic and effectiveness perspective. We have tried to show that, whilst much of the work that exists is theoretical, it does have very wide implications and growing practical application. Many of the problems which arise in organizations are basically problems of communication and are as likely to be caused by misinterpretations of information as by lack of it.

An area of increasing interest relates to the study of artificial intelligence where the information process is central to the development of knowledge based systems. This aspect is discussed in detail along with decision support systems in chapter 12.

In chapter 1 brief mention was made of the growth of the information sector and the emergence of a society where information processing occupies more of the work force than industrial processing. This is only the first step in an evolutionary process. The next step is to improve the effectiveness of information by both improving the quality of information transfer and the impact this has on organizational life. A further step in the process may come when we examine the way it can be systematized and organized to transfer knowledge. Both of these areas are currently the subject of much debate and research and the results will inevitably improve the quality of future information processing system developments.

3   Organizational change

3.1   Introduction

This brief chapter provides an introduction to the second stage of the model —
organizational modelling.

3.2   Tides of fortune

In 1987, *Computing* reported on several companies that were in a process of
great change.

3.2.1   Personal Computers

Computing reported PC dealer Personal Computers as having made good
profits, up 64%, unlike some others in the industry. Turnover too had
increased dramatically by 117%. Share earnings had doubled as had staff
levels.

Personal Computers claimed that the figures were due to 'a number of
sound business activities but, obviously, Big Bang played a significant part
in it'. There were plans to grow either by acquisition or by opening new
offices in other parts of the country. It was possible that Personal
Computers might expand its IBM product range upwards from PCs.

Here is a company which is enjoying the fruits of growth. The company is
changing: in size — doubling workforce; in location — acquiring new premises
or new companies; market area — expansion from small to middle market
range. These changes are all the result of natural growth but will affect the
future operation of the company since the same personnel policies may not
work with a larger employee force or with a distributed environment. The
same things may be true of marketing strategies, investment priorities,
management philosophies and the way the company is run. Undoubtedly, it
will affect the information that is needed to operate as effectively in the
proposed expanded model.

3.2.2 Acorn

Computing also reported on Acorn in 1987. It said that development and early promotion costs for the Archimedes micro helped to push Acorn's finances back into the red and send its shares into a nosedive. The latest 6 monthly figures showed a net loss of £1.38 million for the half year, compared with a profit of £300 000 for the same period in 1986.

Acorn said that the Master series were continuing to sell well but that promotion of the new Archimedes range had led to a slowdown in sales while customers evaluated the new machine, which is based on reduced instruction set technology (risc). Additionally, manufacturing and start-up costs, as well as research and development expenditure, were heavy in the first half.

Acorn is a company which was a major force in the home computer market prior to 1984 when the UK saw mass sales to the parents of computer-mad children. Unfortunately, computer games palled as children switched to new crazes and parents realized that the educational potential of home computers might not be so great as they had believed. Furthermore, there was an obvious limit to the market potential in size. After the Christmas 1984 slump many computers were on sale at less than half the price. A major change in their product and market has since meant increased expenditure on Research & Development but also a need for advance remarketing of Acorn as a company. Customer caution in evaluating the new products means slower sales and the nature of the new risc machine and its operating system may mean even longer term evaluation of market readiness and need.

3.3 Summary

Change may be generated from within the organization and forced from without. One particular agent for change is technology itself. It is perhaps easy to recognize the implications of technology on tasks and processes within an organization. It is less easy to identify the changes it may effect on decision-making, communication patterns, political control.

Information systems can also, however, act as innovators by changing the way companies are run and facilitating the exchange of new ideas and regular cross-fertilization of ideas.

Organizations must be capable of surviving change and the most successful organizations will plan to manage change and capitalize on it. For this to happen, information systems must not only be capable of responding to change but should themselves be capable of initiating change.

The organization that is successful at the management of change will have a thorough understanding of organizational models and the impact of information systems on this model. These are the issues explored in the following two chapters.

4 Organizational models

4.1 Introduction

In the previous chapter we described the changing situation in two companies. For you to analyze this in greater detail you would need considerably more information about the organizations:

How many years have they been in business?
How many employees do they have?
How is the organization managed?

At this stage you might search for some kind of organization chart similar to fig. 4.1 and from this begin to develop your views although it will still not tell you why one organization has chosen to move in a particular direction or why two organizations respond entirely differently to similar market conditions.

Fig. 4.1 A simple organization chart.

There is a great deal more to be learned before you can say how a company works — or how decisions are made. Providing a picture of the information flow which is required to support decision-making in an organization may involve an examination of some very complex issues relating to:

Company profile: size, age, ownership, business and sector.

Organization: structure, communication channels, control procedures.

Management: culture, role and jobs definition, span of responsibility.

Tasks: technology, development methods, functional units.

Environment: historical, political, social.

For example, a recent survey by Lind *et al.* (1989) shows that both size and structure of an organization had a significant impact on their adoption of microcomputers. Depending on the nature of the company any number of other issues might be relevant. In order to identify these we must first gain a thorough understanding of organizational and management theories and then apply these to the results of a detailed investigation into both formal and informal systems within the organization. The sections which follow highlight some of the major influencing theories in the field.

4.2 Organizational theories

It is clear that organizations do not 'just happen.' They are the consequences of specific decisions, normally made at management level. In the previous chapter we saw two companies each pursuing individual lines of development and hence displaying individual characteristics. Organizational theory attempts to provide a framework for characterizing organizations in such a way as to allow us to understand how the interaction of the many variables will produce certain models of organizations. A number of theories exist which proffer different views of an organization.

4.2.1 Views of an organization

One of the earliest and most widely used views comes from the work of Leavitt (1964) and his four-component description, refined by Burn & O'Neil (1987) as shown in fig. 4.2.

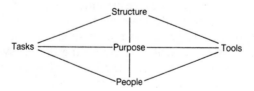

Fig. 4.2 Four-component description of an organization.

The interactions among these variables is essentially a system of communications and work flow whereby any change in one of the variables is likely to impact on all the others, either by compensation or retaliation. A technological change providing new tools will affect the tasks which have to be performed and the people who perform them. As a result the structure of the organization may have to adapt and a shift in its purpose may result.

Using the classical view of organizations, the business environment will essentially be hierarchical in nature and this 'chain of command' will shape the way by which individuals communicate both formally and informally.

When viewed in this manner (fig. 4.3) the organizational hierarchy looks comprehensive. A clear command structure exists with a well defined scope at each level and a direct reporting system to only one individual in the system, so fitting the Weberian view.

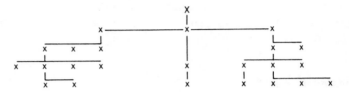

Fig. 4.3   Organizational hierarchy: the chain of command.

Figure 4.4 shows a different 'view' of the same structure. Here the pyramid is viewed as building blocks which highlights the 'gaps' in the structure. It shows the extent to which differentiation may exist between the organizational subunits and the need for interdepartment communication. There may be no-one assigned to cover that responsibility. Many organizations appoint an intermediate management line, Divisional Heads, to provide mechanisms for subunit integration and so try to overcome this problem. But there may still be much within the organization which is not controlled by the direct line of command. The more levels which are introduced (fig. 4.5) the more complex life becomes and the more people try to bypass certain lines or develop their own informal structures.

The issue of centralization or decentralization of decision-making and authority may not necessarily resolve the situation. This type of structure may be applied regardless of the physical distribution of the organization. Several centralized groups with a multiplicity of formal and informal systems in operation may present more problems than a single centralized authority.

Any information system modelled solely on the formal system as shown in fig. 4.5 is bound to become a disaster, the informal system must, at the very least, be acknowledged and any formal procedures related to their informal setting.

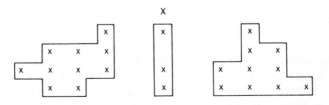

Fig. 4.4   Organizational hierarchy: there may be a need for communication between subunits.

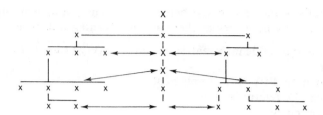

Fig. 4.5   Organizational hierarchy: the introduction of new levels of command can result in an overcomplicated structure.

4.2.2   Formal and informal systems

Formal systems are required in an organization to provide for information entering and leaving the organization on a regular routine basis. External factors such as institutional practices (government, law), customary commercial practices and technical requirements all encourage highly formalized communication. Internal motivators relate to accuracy, structure and permanence of information as well as the basic need to communicate at an understandable level using similar norms and perceptions as described in chapter 2.

The question is: Where is the dividing line between formal and informal information. Figure 4.6 provides a rough dividing line between what can be called *indicative* information on one side and *affective* information on the other, separating those messages which can best be handled formally from those that are best transmitted informally. Information can also be divided between descriptive and prescriptive information, where the latter influences actions under prescribed rules as opposed to mere description.

	Descriptive	Prescriptive
Indicative	Objective Facts	Rules Policy
Affective	Subjective Feelings	Persuasion Threats

Fig. 4.6   The dividing line between indicative (objective) and affective (subjective) information.

Formal systems only deal with indicative information and, therefore, only half the information value may be present. The informal organization largely consists of primary work groups. They derive both stability and individuality from the formation of norms of behaviour, agreed and sustained within the group by the communication of affective messages which may relate to language, body signs, monetary benefits etc. Such informal information systems can be very necessary as there are disadvantages to formal systems:

> They often provide information which is of very little use to the decision maker
> They can be difficult to implement
> They can be relatively slow
> They are costly
> It is impossible to formalize some information
> Formal information systems can become too costly
> Innovation may be stifled by formality — it may even produce a reactionary effect
> Interpretations of formal systems may vary and act as a source of misunderstanding

Formal systems can also produce useless information and problems are caused if they are routinely ignored so that occasional useful information is also ignored in preference to informal information.

Informal systems are, of course, always present but will not reflect the policy priorities of the organization as a whole. Some of the major problems which they present are:

> They have insufficient structure, they may be divisive, they can promote resistance to change, they allow information to be witheld.

Information is power and informal information may be seen as the key to obtaining power to whatever extent in an organization. Generally, informal systems are likely to be found at lower status levels within the organization where disaffection exists with the formal system imposed at higher levels. Around 50% of the total information requirements of an organization arise at senior management level and the informal system can be seen as a small threat. Two aspects of the informal organization which have received consistent attention in the literature (Bariff & Galbraith, 1978; Nadler & Tushman, 1977) are:

> The degree to which the norms for intergroup interaction are cooperative or competitive
> The evenness of the horizontal distribution of power across groups in the organization

An analysis of these will be necessary to build up a structural view overall of the organization. This model will still be highly simplified unless enlarged to take account of the environmental considerations.

4.2.3   The environment

This can be characterized in a variety of ways but several researchers have found the degree to which the environment is stable and predictable to be a particularly important attribute. Unfortunately, environments which appear stable and almost preordained by nature are still subject to cycles of depression outside individual control. Classic examples are the 50-year Kondratieff cycle based on the inherent dynamics of technology: every 50 years a long technological wave crests and for the last 20 years of the period the growth industries of the last technological advance appear to be doing remarkably well as record profits replace repayments of capital in industries with nowhere to grow. Suddenly, crisis occurs followed by panic and stagnation over a further 20-year cycle during which new emerging technologies generate insufficient jobs to make a growth economy. Petroleum, automobiles, steel, coal are all industries affected by this cycle after World War II. Individual organizations can often do little to avoid the backwash from the wave and many organizations outside the mainstream suffer indirectly.

Another similar theory is the Elliot Wave Theory which is related to stock market depressions and which has proved remarkably accurate in forecasting trends which reoccur in 30-year cycles. Indeed, the forecasts may be accused of setting up a feedback control mechanism which inspires these trends since so much faith is placed on them by market speculators.

The theory of global cycles over such a long period may be difficult to apply to individual companies in their immediate environment. Porter's (1985) five-forces model attempts to analyze a particular competitive environment. He describes the determination of the degree of competition and the profit potential of the market as an outcome of the interaction of the five major forces, namely

buyers, industry competitors, substitute products, potential new entrants and suppliers.

It is possible for organizations to provide an analysis of these and input them to a model of their organization to test the potential impact, as discussed in the development of a strategic plan in chapters 1 and 2.

A major force in research on environmental issues has been the idea of *contingency*. Theorists would suggest that there is a need for different structures in a changing environment and this has been related to market diversity, technology, tasks and people. This emphasis on environmental influences leads naturally into a system view of organizations, where a closed, stable, mechanistic organization will have far more routine information needs than an open, dynamic, organistic company requiring an adaptive support system.

One further special condition applies in the case of extreme hostility. This inevitably forces all four types to centralize regardless of the prior state of decentralization.

Environmental factors can, therefore have a profound impact on the whole organization and specifically on the structure which primarily exists to shield the operational factors from the effects of direct exposure to environmental influences. The factors described so far go some way towards identifying the reasons for organizational differences. We have, however, all experienced organizations with very similar structures which operate in entirely different ways. Classic examples are educational institutions, hospitals and even, to some extent, government bodies, although their similarities in the latter case can greatly outweigh their differences. Differences may well arise from the management approaches discussed in the next section.

4.3 Management theories

A large amount of available literature explores the concerns and approaches of management. This section examines some of the major management models, the interaction of management with structural models and the impact of technology and in particular, information technology on the management role.

4.3.1 Management models

Historically, the most important influence on managerial theory was the classical school. This includes Taylor, Fayol Gulick and Urwick and also influences the work of many of our modern day theorists. Their work set the scene to describe the active basic management functions

planning, organizing, coordinating, commanding and controlling

which have been further expanded to seven (known as POSDCORB)

planning, organizing, staffing, directing, coordinating, reporting and budgeting.

This school places great emphasis on detailing managerial activities but in reality does little to assist an understanding of management except to emphasize the confusion that may exist. The commonly heard jibe 'If you can't *do* you teach and if you can't *teach* you manage' could be described as a fundamental reaction from common sense to the POSDCORB theory which after all tells us nothing at all. Later theories looked far more at behavioural issues and related the role of management to the motivation needs of staff and leadership roles. Figure 4.7 shows Maslow's (1954) famous hierarchy of needs which has not only had an impact on management theory but has had a lasting effect on American education where the self-actuated child is a highly prized specimen!

Leadership, at one time, especially after World War II, a dirty word, has gained pre-eminence over the years and falls roughly into the Leader Effectiveness school, the Leader Power school, the Leader Behavioural school and the Entrepreneurial school. Some of the more famous theories in these respective categories are described below.

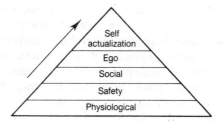

Fig. 4.7 The hierarchy of needs.

Blake & Mouton (1964) exemplify the Leader Effectiveness school. Figure 4.8 shows their leadership grid where attention was focused on the humanist approach and the particular style of leadership required was related to a number of situational factors such as reward structures, nature of work, power of position, skills and personality etc.

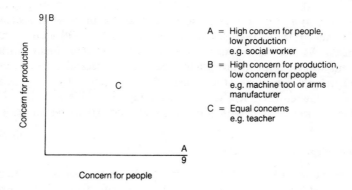

Fig. 4.8 A leadership grid showing how the 'people' aspect of a job can be compared with the 'production' aspect.

The Leader Power school owes much to Machiavelli and certainly to military training schools and political studies. It highlights the need for managers to understand their sources of power and the extent to which they have control over their own jobs. This has been explored in greater depth with regard to power in organizations with five different power styles prevalent with any central system:

> reward power, coercive power, referent power, legitimate power and expert power.

Whilst referent and expert power could produce informal leaders most formal leaders rely on reward, coercive or legitimate power structures.

The Leadership Behaviour school is really an amalgamation of theories which we have lumped together simply because they do not have a unifying theme. Some of the theories in the School are attempts to describe the behaviour of managers. Descriptions can be of managerial reactions in highly specialized situations or of the personalities themselves when they are somewhat unusual. General Motors must hold the corporate record for this, by producing two such 'great men': Alfred Sloan and Lee Iacocca. Their biographies are essential reading for the would-be car executive, although the DeLorean theory might give greater food for thought. Alternatively, the theories can be an analysis of managerial perceptions of their jobs, as in the Ohio State leadership studies over the last three decades.

A singular extension of the Leader Behaviour school is the Entrepreneurial school. This owed much in early days to Schumpeter but has its most recent flag borne by Drucker (1985) whose 'Innovation and Entrepreneurship' is a seminal work on the practice and principles. Drucker argues that innovation is the specific tool of entrepreneurs, the means by which they exploit change as an opportunity for a different business or a different service. This follows from an earlier (but not at all opposing) Drucker theory on management by objectives (MBO) as the only realistic style to adopt in large organizations.

Some or all of these theories have fed into the Contingency school of management. As the name suggests this implies that a specific model of management will be appropriate under specific situational circumstances.

Recent theory supports the idea that a particular organizational environment will require specific related managerial skills and that these will be completely inter-related with the organizational structure.

4.3.2   Organizational configurations

The culture theory developed by Handy (1985) postulates that organizations can be classified according to the nature of work, age, technology, people and other affectors of sets of values and beliefs.

These classifications result in four varieties of organization culture reflected in a structure and a set of systems: power culture which is control-centred, as shown in fig. 4.9; role culture which is bureaucratic, as shown in fig. 4.10; task culture which is project oriented, as shown in fig. 4.11; and person culture which is individualistic, as shown in fig. 4.12. Each of these are appropriate models in particular situations. Furthermore, several may be appropriate over the lifetime of an organization.

Mintzberg (1979) provides five structural configurations developing from a basic structural model (fig. 4.13) which in itself has five parts: the strategic apex (the people charged with overall responsibility for an organization); the operating core (those who perform basic work related to the production of goods or services); the middle line (the management hierarchy); the technostructure (analysts, planners and trainers); and support staff. The

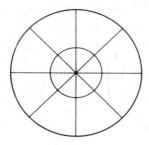

Fig. 4.9   Organizational culture: power culture is control centred.

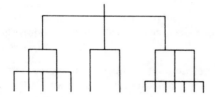

Fig. 4.10   Organizational culture: role culture is bureaucratic.

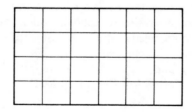

Fig. 4.11   Organizational culture: task culture is project orientated.

Fig. 4.12   Organizational culture: person culture is individualistic.

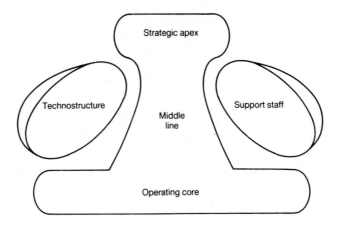

Fig. 4.13   A basic structural model can be divided into five component parts.

configurations are defined as: simple structure, machine bureaucracy, professional bureaucracy, divisionalized form and adhocracy.

And for each of these there is a unique prime coordinating mechanism, key part of organization and type of decentralization.

Most organizations experience pulls from all five constituent parts. However, to the extent that conditions favour one over the others, the organization is drawn to structure itself as one of the configurations.

Research such as this into the nature of organizations is implicit to the development of an organizational model which accurately reflects an organization's information needs. Both sets of configurations consider the role of technology but, in themselves do not examine the impact of information technology and the systems it supports on the organization. Before we look at the information flows required we need to briefly examine this technological role.

4.3.3   The impact of technology

In 1985 Handy suggested that the impact of technology on organizations required companies to re-evaluate certain of their traditional assumptions. In particular, he suggested that there were three prime areas where management must recognize considerable change of role.

> Technology has encouraged the pursuit of large-scale operations and brings with it new problems of integration.
> Labour needs are often substantially reduced but should be reinvested rather than discarded. In this way they become an asset in the same sense as capital.

The independence which can result from effective use of information technology no longer supports a need for hierarchical structures.

Specific examples of situations where these apply resulting from information technology are easy to find. The impact is not only the result of technology, however, but also specifically results from information systems. Many information systems could be seen to be effectively replacing the role of middle management and substantially reducing the supervisory roles required. The system may have such strategic implications for the firm that the complete structure could collapse without implementation of the system. A recent example concerns machine-tool manufacturers in the British Midlands where a concentration of six enjoyed a major share of the market. Five of the group decided to implement Electronic Data Interchange (EDI) which would allow customers to order through direct electronic access to the machine tool manufacturers' system. The one company who resisted this change believing that it would involve too much structural change lost 24% of sales orders over a 3-month period and was forced to adopt the new technology in order to survive as a company.

Technology and the attendant systems must therefore be seen as a major change agent and the organizational model must be able to respond to this challenge (Benjamin & Scott Morton, 1988; Nosek, 1989). In the design of the model it is imperative that we not only consider what is actually happening but also relate this to what may happen when the information system is in place. Basically, this can be achieved by building up a model of the decision-making process and designing a system to support this independent of the physical organization structure.

4.4 Decision-making models

One of the most common decision-making models of an organization, that of Anthony (1965), is shown in Fig. 4.14. This serves to highlight that different levels of management will have different information needs. The lower in the hierarchy one looks, the more routine, short-term and precise will be the decision-making. In contrast at the top of the hierarchy many more subjective decisions for long-term developments will have to be made often with only vague data available. Within this classification, there is still a need to explore in depth the way in which decisions are made. Simon's (1976) model of decision-making presents us with three basic types of decision: structured, unstructured, semi-structured.

Structured denotes that the process used to make the decision is known. In this sense it is programmable for instance if we decide to use the Dow Jones index level to monitor whether we should sell stocks we could set a minimum level where the decision would be automatically made. Unstructured decisions

Fig. 4.14 A simple decision-making model for an organization.

are ones where you do not know how you processed the data, they are
frequently referred to as inspired or foolhardy depending on your intuition or
luck. Semi-structured situations are those where part of the process is
understood but where the ultimate decision is a matter of choice. An
alternative way to describe these indicates the amount of risk involved:
decision-making under certainty, decision-making under risk and decision-
making under uncertainty.

As information systems are developed along this scale it is obvious that they
become support tools rather than replacement systems and so, at strategic
levels, they should be enhancing the quality of decision making. Such Decision
Support Systems (DSS) utilize models of the decision process such as Simon's
three-stage continuous process (fig. 4.15). The DSS does not make the decision
but will both help in providing choices and also by clarifying the actual
decision process.

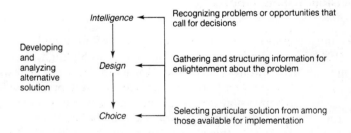

Fig. 4.15 Model of the decision-making process: the three stage continuous process.

The nature of information required will vary depending on whether we wish
to identify which actions can be performed, and in what sequence, or whether
we wish to select a course of action.

In the development of the decision-making model we must identify a variety
of different information:

    Descriptive: what operations to perform
    Programmed: how to perform specific operations
    Structural: model of the real world to use
    Statistical: estimated value
    Actual state: standards to be used

Their use in DSS will be explored further in Part III of this book.

From fig 4.14 we should see that it is not enough merely to identify the information requirement at each level in terms of type (planning, tactical, control). It is necessary to identify it in terms of the specific decision process for which it will be used. This is quite likely to mean that we will adopt completely different approaches to the development of the information systems contingent with the particular systems model. It is this issue which we continue to explore in chapter 5.

4.5 Summary

This chapter has introduced various views of organizations and tried to show that there is no single approach ideally suited for all organizations. Organizations represent continual processes of change. It is this contingent nature, the notion that the form of an organization is related to what it does, the environment in which it operates and the people who make it function, which suggests that the specifics of the situation will determine the most critical organizational variables to be considered when designing an effective decision-making model. A bank, for example, with a very rule-based structure at most levels of decision-making would require a completely different information system to support the decision-making compared to an entrepreneurial stockbroking investment adviser. Yet both are very much in the same business, that of using other people's money to make money.

The development of the information system model must necessarily adopt a similar contingent approach. We can describe an organization as a single information processor. In it organizational performance is a function of the match between the structural capacity to process information and the real information needs of the organization.

A system which fails to produce this match, no matter how technically brilliant a design, will directly impede organizational performance.

5 Models of information systems

5.1 Introduction

An academic institute in Hong Kong asked us to perform a systems-planning exercise for a large-scale information resource management problem. The institute proposed to establish the Asian Research Centre for Information Systems and Technology (ARC) and we were asked to develop the full proposals for the information systems and technology to launch (and support) the ARC.

The overall aims of ARC were to act as coordinator and stimulator for persons/organizations with interests in research using IT. This usage could be simply at the application level such as the use of IT in medicine, accounting, building and surveying. Or it could be at a level of research into information technology and systems such as development of parallel processors, artificial intelligence or the impact of IT on organizations.

The centre would have to provide an extensive information service and utilize the latest technology and bibliographic searching techniques to match research requirements against available resources.

5.1.1 Information modelling

This particular problem was very much in the area of information science; it was concerned with the development of an information retrieval system which needs to be highly responsive to user's perceptions of information needs. The interaction of information needs with information resources is the essence of a library's existence. Figure 5.1 illustrates this point.

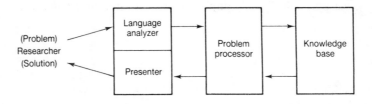

Fig. 5.1 Model of information flow during research.

The researcher can present his problem in a variety of ways — free form speech, pre-set codes, key words. He may use a number of languages to ask questions at a very global level down to a very specific level of detail.

Obviously, the system must be capable of dealing with the input in whatever form it is given. Similarly, the output could range from complete document transmission to a simple indexing summary depending on the value added measurements which apply in this system. It is therefore essential to acquire a global understanding of the information problem by detailed background research into information science and specifically into bibliographic retrieval systems. It is also essential to relate this to the environmental context — what expectation of information would a user have in a multi-cultural, multi-institutional system?

5.1.2   The organizational model

The ARC is meant to operate within an academic environment and an existing organizational model. This model can be described, using the configurations of Handy (1985) and Mintzberg (1979), as a bureaucracy. More specifically it is a professional bureaucracy with the following characteristics:

Democratic with power disseminated to the professionals
Extensive autonomy given to the professional
Little or no control of work outside the profession
Major problems of coordination and innovation
More loyalty to the profession than to the organization

Put simply, academics are egocentric individuals who do not believe in conforming to organizational norms and who very much value independence to the point where interdepartmental communication may be non-existent, and even interpersonal communication may be extremely limited. An information system which is going to provide information across these boundaries will have problems from the start.

Two models for the ARC are illustrated in fig. 5.2 where model 1 allows operational autonomy to the Research Centre with strategic interface to the parent organization and possible communication interaction problems, whilst model 2 subsumes the Research Centre into the superstructure of the professional bureaucracy with its contingent decision-making model and regulated information flows.

The two models must also reflect the open systems environment in which the centre will operate and which may have interaction involving a number of political, technical, social and cultural factors. The purpose, tasks and people related to ARC very much favoured the adoption of model 1 and it was this which was applied throughout the information system planning study.

This brings us to the stage of developing an appropriate information system model and an explanation of the specific steps involved. In order to produce a

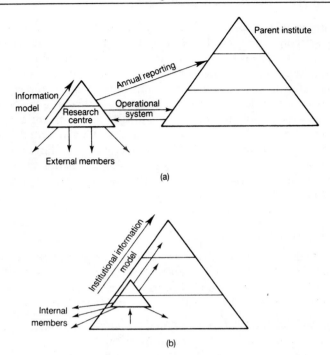

Fig. 5.2 *Information flow in organizations: (a) model 1 allows operational autonomy to the Research Centre; (b) model 2 subsumes the Research Centre into its parent organization.*

model of an information system you have to examine: the specific attributes of the information required; the levels of decision-making systems appropriate to the organizational model; the technological nature of the system related to the stages of system growth prevalent in the organization and relevant to the information system; and the impact and change which may result from the system on the current organizational model. These issues will be examined in the following sections of this chapter.

5.2 Information attributes

In fig. 5.2 we provided a simplified model of the organization and its operating environment. Model 2 effectively frees the ARC from the constraints of working within the information flow of the parent institute. This is important because the complex management reporting structure of the parent could stifle development and creativity in the new organization where information will flow in a much less formal manner. Nevertheless, there will still be a defined information flow which relates to the three levels of management function as shown in fig. 5.2 and at each level information will have its own set of attributes (fig. 5.3).

Attributes	Management functions		
	Strategic planning	Management control	Operational control
source	external	←——————————→	internal
scope	summary		details
facts	soft		hard
accuracy	approximate		exact
redundancy	some		none
horizon	future		past
frequency	occasional		regular/often
timeliness	delayed		current

Fig. 5.3 Different levels of management function have different information attributes.

At operational level in the ARC we are providing a user information service but we must also identify the costs of offering and using the service. This will require regular accounting information detailing the precise usage of services against the cost of services on a regular monthly basis. At strategic level we will be far more concerned with patterns of usage, projected requirements and indicated costs and benefits. This will include data external to the system itself such as major research trends worldwide or economic forces in Asia. An analysis of these factors and an identification of the range and content of information requirements appropriate to specific management levels does not alone guarantee quality, however. It may merely imply quantity. Quality is a highly subjective measure and may be eroded by many factors including errors, bias, age, and redundancy of information.

Sometimes poor quality is a direct result of attempts to eliminate the major bug bears, such as when redundancy is introduced to minimize errors in a system. This can lead to a state (well known by management) of information overload. Work by Miller (1960) shows that an increased number of variables helps distinguish information but that there comes a point when one more variable becomes too many. The magic number is 7 ± 2. Any number less than this provides too little information. Any number greater than this results in a marked decrease in response rate.

This reaction can be manifested in a number of ways by the individual:

message not received, error rates increase, queuing applied, priority splitting and detail suppression.

Within the organization as a whole it may result in

delegation, avoidance.

In order to compensate, data-reduction techniques can be applied but these too can be highly subjective. March & Simon (1958) use the term 'uncertainty absorption' when inferences are used instead of the data itself. The exact question, therefore of 'what information is required?' can only be answered at the detailed systems requirement stage discussed in Part II of this book. At this stage we should be able to identify the information requirements at different levels of decision-making within the organization and the appropriate information attributes to support these levels.

5.3   System taxonomies

The most commonly used taxonomy in system modelling is based on Anthony's (1965) three-layer model of the organization which provides us with four categories of information systems models as shown in fig. 5.4. This broad division can be classified as follows:

Fig. 5.4   There are often four layers of information system within an organization.

Transaction processing systems: Their main characteristics are that they process the relatively high volume of routine business events of the organization. They tend to be predefined and relatively simple in nature and tend to access structured files or databases. Typical examples would be accounting and administrative systems. Such systems are generally aimed at reducing general and administrative expenses.

Routine operational control systems: They tend to carry out monitoring and exception processes resulting from the transaction processing systems. These will generally result in a reduction in the costs of manufacturing or selling goods or services. In particular, production systems are highly susceptible to automation having:

Many interacting variables

A need for a high degree of accuracy, yet where speed in processing data is essential

Many repetitive operations and large amounts of data

Examples are marketing (order entry and processing), distribution (route optimization and carrier selection) and inventory control.

Planning and analysis applications: Here there is a high degree of volatility. It is likely that further *ad hoc* processes will be generated, resulting from the recipient's reaction to the answer to the previous query. These applications tend to have lower processing volumes, with greater volatility of requirements. However, they are heavily dependent upon good presentational interfaces and require heavy computing power per request to support them. These applications themselves split broadly into:

Numerically-based modelling processes such as economic forecasting systems, operating budget simulations

Text-based intelligence processes such as office support systems, management support systems

Tozer (1986) suggests that it is really more accurate to envisage a whole parallel 'information triangle' of support systems against the main information systems and offers a view of the current information system coverage against the potential (fig. 5.5).

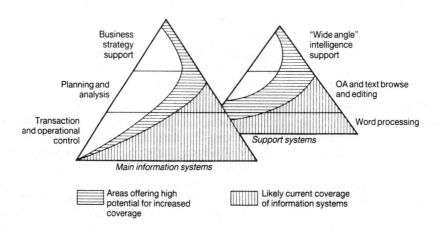

Fig. 5.5 The information triangle: the main information systems are backed by a parallel triangle of support systems.

This is where it becomes much more difficult to quantify the cost benefits since these are generally indirect. We may provide an improved customer service but how do we identify the increase in revenue resulting from this, given all the other interacting variables?

Strategic applications: These may be of almost any type, with any mixture or combination of charcteristics. Their inherent characteristics are that they are mostly concerned with external information. The user-interface is highly critical to their success, to the extent where considerable intervention is required in most cases. The requirements for them are almost entirely unpredictable and extremely volatile.

These systems are concerned with developing a competitive edge. For example, Parsons (1983), having shown how IT can change an industry's products and services, markets and production economics, goes on to show how competitive advantage can be gained by the use of the technology in a range of market forces, in relation to buyers, suppliers, product substitution, new entrants and intra-industry rivalry. He suggests that the three major areas where IT can have an impact on corporate strategy are in:

cost reduction, product differentiation and creating a particular niche or market.

Research matching the competitive forces against the opportunities presented would indicate eight major competitive strategies that can be assisted by the use of information systems and technology:

Establishing entry barriers
Introducing or raising switching costs
Differentiating products/services or company as a whole
Limiting access to distribution channels
Ensuring competitive pricing
Reducing supply costs and easing supply
Increasing cost efficiency/effectiveness
Using the information resource as a product in itself

Relating this to the concepts of value-added service (Strassman, 1985), as discussed in chapter 2, we can suggest that companies with high value-adding potential, but poor resources in terms of their information systems are extremely vulnerable to competitors with better information systems resources and propose a framework for systems strategies (fig. 5.6).

This classification of systems as one of four basic models highlights the idea that, within an organization, different types of business roles need different types of information, varying in degrees of detail, timeliness, completeness and precision, and emanating from different sources at different frequencies. It is not intended to suggest that these are distinct stand-alone implementations: quite the reverse. Given that all four systems models are an inherent part of the organization's effective functioning, the system designer must be able to integrate a specific model into the global model of the

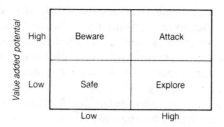

Fig. 5.6 *Systems strategies for organizations with high and low value added potential and high and low quality information systems.*

organization's information model. Before we examine that in the next section, we will consider how these classifications could relate to ARC.

At the transactional level, the basic administrative and accounting procedures will be to maintain memberships, invoice and billing procedures, receipt of papers, inventory control, recording of specific research contracts etc. Initially, these could be performed manually and systems could be developed over time to accommodate these functions.

At the operational level the actual service provided by the ARC will be automated. The extent to which the information service is fully automated will relate to the anticipated user needs and the related technology costs. For instance, unless all the receiving institutes had electronic mail systems the ARC would have to provide hard copy. Similarly, the cost of a full electronic document search might greatly exceed the value of the service, the requirement could possibly be met with a key word search on title and hard copy or microfiche transmission of the full text.

At the planning level, the ARC will be concerned with the overall economic feasibility of the operation and an improvement in service. It will have to justify its existence and show that the original 'key results' are being achieved. The ARC will also have to estimate budgets on the basis of projected income and anticipated expenditure. At the very least, it will have to justify the cost of the resources used — staff, technology, accommodation etc. The systems required to support this must analyze current use, project future use and forecast budgets. These will have to be related to the organizational strategic plan and the IT plan over a number of years.

Finally, we come to the strategic level. It is here that many organizations make a classic mistake. They assume that they do not live in a standard competitive environment. Are education, government, public services, social clubs in a competitive environment? Indeed they are. To some extent any organization competes for a share of limited resources. In this case, the ARC is being set up to attract research funding which will filter through the host

institution and therefore be under its overall control. The ARC needs to ensure
that it accumulates a supply of top quality researchers in order to persuade
organizations to pay for their services either by direct negotiation of research
contracts or by stimulating research projects which will attract government
funding. To some extent, therefore, it must corner the market and deter
competing services from entering the field.

Typical examples of such systems are the development of on-line order entry
systems provided to customers by the suppliers (as in the case of the machine
tool manufacturers – chapter 3) or (as in this case) on-line searching techniques
to users external to the host institute. Another strategic requirement could be
the development of an open network system such that users in the system could
go directly to each other rather than through the ARC. The strategic
disadvantage here could be the loss of central control.

All four system models form a part of the information system model for the
ARC but before we can fit this into a framework for development we need to
look at the overall portfolio of applications required and the stages of
information systems and technology growth within the organization.

5.4   Stages of systems growth

One perspective for analyzing the overall information model can come from
the historical view. Here the various phases of computing developments in an
organization are analyzed and a normative model is developed.

A widely expounded theory of this nature is the Nolan Stage Model. This
model, which is empirically based, has undergone continuous refinement since
first being put forward in 1973. The ideas were formulated as a result of some
analysis of North American companies. In these studies Nolan (1974) used the
computing budget as a measure of change. He was able, as a result, to isolate a
number of turning points in the plot of budget against time. These could then
be identified, by examining technical and organizational factors, as marking
the end-points of identifiable stages.

His hypothesis was that organizations pass through six stages in their
progression from initial involvement with computers to a mature information
systems environment.

Initiation
A period during which the first computers are acquired and early attempts to
develop applications are made. The projects are not necessarily the most cost
effective, but are more likely to be those close to the hearts of the people who
originally proposed the computer acquisition. This is a period when the
technicians tend to dominate decision-making on project control and
hardware/software configuration. The rate of expenditure growth is relatively
slow.

Contagion

At some point the potential of computer-based systems becomes apparent and systems development commences on many applications perceived as contributing to the organization's performance. The growth in expenditure on staff and equipment accelerates sharply as enthusiasm develops. While the technical specialists still dominate project decisions, the role of the users starts to develop, initially among the less conservative executives and supervisors.

Control

Expenditure levels rise. Problems surface concerning underestimation of project resources, user dissatisfaction with systems, and disagreement over priorities. It becomes clear that a greater degree of control is necessary. Information systems are no longer perceived as being automatically profitable ventures and the situation is often regarded by senior executives as being out of control. As a result, a number of constraints are rapidly imposed, such as introduction of a steering committee for policy formulation and project selection, stringent budgetary controls, and effectiveness audits and management standards.

Integration

It takes some time for an organization to modify control measures to the point at which an effective environment is created. Steering committees take time to find their true role while they come to grips with the major issues and the information systems function needs to adjust to a relatively austere and stable environment. User involvement in policy gradually increases as experience is gained.

Data administration

The concept of the set of data being a major corporate resource becomes well accepted as experience with the sharing of data across applications increases. This increased ability to store and control data resources forces the focus on data management. Data becomes a key factor in planning and administration is standardized. This often results in additional controls being placed on designers and users which may result in problems similar to those experienced in the third stage, control.

Maturity

The implication is that this is never reached. Users adopt a dominant role; data resources are controlled but flexible; the flow of information within computer systems reflect the 'real world' application. The planning goal is to reach a condition where the best possible use for overall effectiveness is made of the data resources.

Nolan (1981) has since revised this model to take account of the micro revolution in business and has replaced the former stages 5 and 6 with *architecture* and *demassing*, reflecting the current concerns of responsiveness and adaptibility. He sees the major problem as one of integration and suggests that this is the most critical and complex area of an organization's concern.

One of the major problems with this theory and, indeed with any historically based theory, concerns its predictive value. Can it be said to apply to organizations in the future, especially given the rapidly changing rate of information technology? Can it be applied to all organizations — small or large?

The importance of examining Nolan's theory here is not to suggest that it is an accurate predictive model (although there is considerable support for this). Rather it is to point out that an organizational systems environment will exist and needs to be analyzed to identify whether certain approaches have much chance of success. There is little point in developing a user-oriented multiple access system in an environment where the major emphasis is one of centralized control with formalized standards. Indeed, Nolan *et al.* (1986) point out that the most important factor in competitive success with information systems lies in 'creating the culture to make it happen'. The enterprise must learn how to select and develop the technologies critical to their success and ensure that it is all hooked together effectively.

The question remains: how does the organization select applications for information systems development? This can be separated into two levels of decision. The first concerns the total portfolio in which an organization might wish to invest. The second relates to the specific systems which will give maximum return or value to the organization. Both of these issues are addressed in detail in chapter 7.

5.5 Technological classifications

The classification of systems models so far proposed are not necessarily those which would be used by professionals in the information systems field. It is far more likely that they would classify systems using terms such as batch, on-line, real-time, distributed, networked, where it is the technological nature of the system which defines the class. Those familiar with systems technology will realise that this is to some extent historically based since it is only in the last 20 years that the technology has become widely available to take us out of batch-processing mode.

It is not solely the technology but a combination of the technology and software system which defines the character. To some extent, all systems are data based, whether the data be relational, networked, hierarchical or simple stand-alone files. Nevertheless it is likely that the system description will reflect the specific software supporting the organization of the data. An organization may wish to have a management information system (MIS), global office automation (OA), and electronic data interchange (EDI). What they may get is an on-line distributed relational database with downloading of selected systems to office communications through a local area network and gateways interfacing to a wide area network for electronic data transfer.

Does this mean that there is a radical difference in perspective between the information systems specialist view of a system and the organizational view? The answer is that this should not happen.

Just as there are different information requirements for different decision-making levels in an organization and different communication channels, so there are different technological configurations which may be appropriate for each. It may not be a sensible move to provide an on-line desktop system for a managing director to obtain his monthly breakdown of budgetary analysis, but look at the difference it can make to order entry if the clerk has a direct input system available requiring the minimum of transcription and providing immediate feedback on item availability.

System models must consider the most appropriate information interaction modes and relate the basic system requirements to the information requirements level. Figure 5.7 shows the impact of using this model.

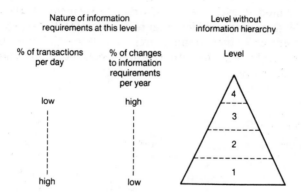

Fig. 5.7 *The nature of information requirements is affected by basic system requirements.*

At level 1 there are many employees requiring a highly structured work environment, and generating a high volume of transactions. Hence, the systems and architectures to support this level of system should be designed to optimize for these aspects. They should be highly structured, easy to monitor, difficult to tamper with and they should perform a high volume of transactions at a low cost.

At level 4 there are very few individuals generating a low volume of transactions, but needing various kinds of information at different times.

There is a continuum of the two aspects of information requirements from the top to the bottom of the hierarchy. At the lowest level, there is a high transaction rate but a low need to reconfigure data and vice versa at the highest level.

If the system and architecture requirements vary at each level this implies that they should be implemented separately. This presents a major obstruction to the development of integrated information systems. Traditionally, management information systems have not been designed at all. They have been spun off as by-products while improving existing systems within the company. No tool has been so disappointing in use.

What has happened over the last 20 years is not the top-down development of an MIS but the development of subsystems which try to act as mini-MIS in a specific functional area. Instead of one global system we have a myriad of systems spanning the vertical hierarchy without horizontal integration.

Mattison (1987) proposes a solution. It is time to consider subsystems based, not upon the need to service all levels of the information hirarchy, but upon their ability to meet the needs of a particular level as efficiently as possible. This means the development of systems at levels 1 and 2 of fig. 5.7 where control, high volume and efficiency are the key and they can be unencumbered with their own management reporting systems. A global information system must be implemented at levels 3 and 4, giving management a truly overall view, unprejudiced by departmental bias. Figure 5.8 illustrates how, by capitalizing upon the different computer architectures, and using the one best suited to meet a certain level's information requirements, both informational and operational efficiency be served.

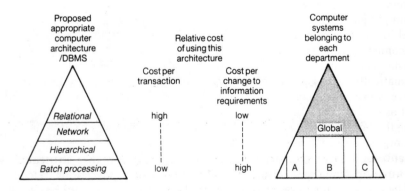

Fig. 5.8 *Informational and operational efficiency can be served by chosing the right computer architecture.*

The people at the top levels of management are the only ones requiring a truly global view of what is going on. The employees at the lower end of the pyramid may work more effectively with a limited view of the corporation. A major advantage of the approach is the recognition of the fundamental impossibility for most organizations of designing a single megacomputer system which would encompass all of the organization's information requirements. Instead this approach concentrates on providing the right level of information needed at each level of decision-making. In so doing, it effectively insulates the lower level of systems from the impacts of organizational change and can build the global system to optimize on this requirement. This brings us to our final discussion topic in this chapter — systems and change.

5.6   Systems and change

Throughout this book continual emphasis is placed on the need to built adaptive systems which can respond to the constant changes which impact on every organization. At this point, however, we must also accept that an agent for major change is the information system itself. While we have stressed the need to design models of the organization, information and systems we must accept that that is exactly what they are — models. No matter how hard we try to approach reality we will still end up with an approximate model. It is therefore inevitable that the system will provide for a different 'reality' and as a result of using this system reality will change. This can take various forms.

Job roles may change quite radically. Office automation often results in the demise of the personal secretary as much of her basic job disappears leaving the need for an administrator over a wider area of responsibility. Planning systems often leave middle management redundant.

Simply having better quality of information must change job roles at every level in an organization and some of these changes may not be anticipated or welcomed by the job holders.

The shape of the organization may alter. Distributed systems may dramatically reduce the need for central offices and central control functions. There is even the suggestion that the office itself may become a thing of the past as communication can take place just as easily from home. Systems may have the opposite effect and impose controls and additional hierarchies within the organization. Change at this level is inevitable since the structure of the organization represents the information flow and hence changes to the information model impact directly on the organizational model.

The nature of the organization may be changed. The essence of information systems is to improve the effectiveness of the organization and so the organization may be given the opportunity to grow, diversify or redirect its focus. The development of strategic systems will very much impact on this area although as yet, few companies have realized the full extent of the opportunities possible, as we will discuss in Part III.

Information systems mean change. As such the design of the information systems model must identify both the opportunities for change and the constraints. The system must offer opportunities which the organization can cope with — not ones which they cannot exploit or even survive.

5.7 Summary

This chapter has tried to identify the many faces of a system model. It relates to the organizational model, the information model and to the global systems model already existing within the organization. Just as there are contingency models of organizations, so there are contingency models of systems and these may require totally different technologies and architectural approaches for implementation. The next chapter looks at the range of information technology and the various applications and environments for which it can prove suitable and will return to the ARC model for a brief review of the technological implications involved.

6 Information technology: computer and communication systems

6.1 Information technology — what is important and why?

Throughout the preceding chapters we have been examining the symbiotic relationships between different models of information systems and the organization models in which they are found. Assuming you are convinced of the importance of strategic planning for any successful information system then the next step is to look at some of the tools which may be chosen to support and implement a management information system (MIS).

Let us start by asking what we mean by 'information technology'. Technology means the application of science. We have already discussed what information means. But this does not mean that the definition of IT is self evident. The term IT is one which, in present colloquial usage, means different things to different users. The reasons for this are historical. The concept of IT is a recent one and since it is closely related to the fast-changing world of microprocessors, the language used to describe the coming together of telecommunications and computers is itself evolving.

It is sensible to take a very broad view of the meaning of IT and its application in information systems. A good basic definition used by the British government says that IT is the acquisition, processing, storage and dissemination of information by a microelectronics-based combination of computing and telecommunications. The key to success in using IT must be pragmatism founded on a thorough understanding of the most important considerations when selecting the best way to implement the information systems model to ensure its long-term usefulness and adaptability. If a device is useful in helping to implement strategic plans and build a robust, adaptable information system then use it and argue later about the semantics of what is included in, or excluded from, IT.

6.1.1 Why is IT important in strategic planning?

As technology becomes more important to the success of an enterprise it becomes increasingly important that senior management takes responsibility for it, enabling the resources required to implement it to be found. Without implementation which realizes corporate-wide opportunities there may well be no motivation to plan at all. As planning is critical to the management of change and the diffusion of technological innovation throughout an organization, those involved in strategic planning are necessarily also involved in the formation of technology policy which can give direction and leadership in the use of IT.

In a recent survey conducted by the Center for the Study of Data Processing of Washington University (Herber & Hartog, 1986) on the key issues facing MIS managers, the issue rated most important was *the alignment of the MIS with the goals of the business*. To ensure that the business objectives of the corporate leadership are met, the key decisions about information technology must be linked with corporate strategic and tactical objectives. This makes obvious economic sense at a time when competitive presures are impinging on many organizations.

Ranked as the second most important issue in the survey was *data utilization*. These two major issues underline the importance of providing the right information to the right person in the right form at the right time. The realization of this is achieved by implementing the various parts of the system in the most appropriate way — sometimes by using IT devices and sometimes by more traditional methods. Human clerks have a wonderful capacity for 'real' (as opposed to 'artificial') intelligence which is often vastly superior in coping with situations which do not arise very often but require initiative. The difficulty is in achieving exactly the right mix between men and machines.

The third issue from the survey picked out an often overlooked area of successful adoption of IT: *the education of senior personnel*. We will cover this when we discuss implementation of IT in chapter 10. An important way in which the organization can meet its primary objective, to have the information system support the goals of the business, is through the education of its senior personnel.

Information can take many forms including: sound, text, diagrams and graphics, images, either still or moving pictures and a combination of these.

When we discuss the use of technology to handle information then we must address the various forms that information can take. We shall not list here all the equipment which might be useful in storing, processing or feeding data in or out of various devices. However, we will cover the aspects of information technology devices and services which are important to the strategic planner since a knowledge of their characteristics is essential to the 'survivability' of the system he is to create.

As an organization initiates integrated system planning and implementation, policymakers should provide end users with useful information on the acquisition and use of integrated IT systems. In addition to information, it is often appropriate to lay down more precise guidelines defining company policies and standards covering IT integration and acquisition. This is necessary to ensure a coherent corporate technology policy is being followed, one which is also aligned to the strategic plans of the organization. This can only be done if those responsible for the policy creation are informed about the range of IT devices available, and the ways in which these may be utilized (fig 6.1).

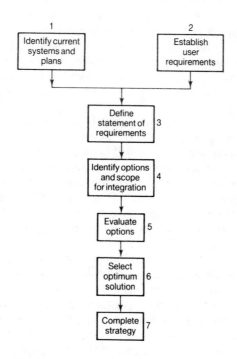

Fig. 6.1   Formulating an IT strategy.

A wide variety of devices are available which can be linked together to handle information. As well as looking at computer systems in general we will also discuss how different types of information are handled when they go into and out of a computer and how they can be stored and transferred between computer systems.

A few words will put the selection and acquisition of IT devices into perspective. A computer system is usually purchased as a set of items which are selected according to the needs of the purchaser. The way these work may be interesting to electronic engineers but is not relevant to this book. To get the best from your television you do not need to know how it works. The same is true about IT devices. What is important is:

Knowing what you want to use it for
Knowing what various optional extras are available

Deciding which of these are essential because of the needs

Deciding which are sufficiently desirable that the price justifies the additional expense

Take the analogy of buying a car. Say you want a family car to transport children to school. Cars are available in a range of models, with various extras. For your task two-seater models are obviously not suitable. You would probably decide that a four- or five-seater model would be right for the size of your task, and would then consider further selection criteria like initial purchase price, depreciation, running costs, and maintenance. These kind of common sense factors apply in general to all purchases. Information systems are no exception.

Having identified your basic need from the system you also quantify it with some allowance for growth. You do not want to pay for many additional features you will never use and you will need reliable fast service on demand. Certain features (often classified as intangible benefits) are going to be desirable and you will buy them if you feel they are worth their cost in terms of what you receive back. Decisions of this sort are highly subjective. Intuition and experience in making difficult business decisions will be called for when deciding on IT purchases as in any other area of the organization's endeavours.

The challenge facing the strategic planner when deciding on his information needs is in the analysis of present and future 'need' for information and in deciding about what information falls in that large gray area of 'desirable if it can be cost justified'. The power of available computer systems and related IT devices is not always fully appreciated by those who have not had the experience of using them.

Needs for information are often analyzed in terms of what has always been available through existing systems. It is only when additional IT products are being used on a daily basis that many users then begin to realize their full potential. At this stage they may regret not having bought more expensive devices with wider capabilities because they did not realise that these would be useful. This phenomenon of underestimating how useful IT really is, is based on ignorance through lack of experience. It is an important factor for the strategic planner to keep in mind. The power of IT may itself cause a realignment in the strategic plans of an organization as its adoption opens up new areas of opportunity.

6.2 Computer systems

The basic components of the computer system are similar to those traditionally needed by a person to process data. People store data in their heads or in files and reference books. Computers store and retrieve it using a variety of devices.

Both people and computers can output information by speaking, writing or drawing on different media. The amount of information a person can remember in his head is limited by the size of his memory which in turn dictates the speed at which he can do certain tasks. If he has to keep looking at a reference book he will work more slowly than if he has all necessary data in his head. This is also true for computers. A computer system should be big enough to provide the information needed in a timely and accurate fashion. Excess capacity is a waste of money.

For the most part, business systems designers should be able to take computer hardware for granted. There are some basic concepts of computer systems architecture which need to be understood. This is important because different basic designs are available to build computer systems which excel in the performance of different functions.

In any computer system the hardware consists of the physical components of the system, the devices used to put information in and take it out, to process it and store it. In its simplest form any computer system reduces to the boxes shown in fig. 6.2.

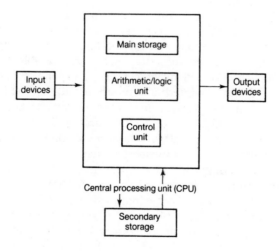

Fig. 6.2 A computer system reduced to its simplest form.

Fundamental differences in computer systems are difficult to define due to the dynamic nature of computing. It was not so long ago that the terms 'mainframe', 'mini' and 'microcomputer' were used as size classifications. With developments in recent years in miniaturization of electronic circuits these distinctions are now more a matter of marketing and price. New terms are always appearing, such as 'superminicomputers'. (Superminis are generally a company's top-of-the-line single processor computer and they are in competition with new multiuser computers built round Intel's 80386 microprocessor.)

An important aspect of computer systems is the speed with which they can process data. Low end minicomputers are capable of handling around 3 million instructions per second (they are known as 3 MIP machines). The most powerful superminis are at present rated at around 12 MIPs.

One of the most widely used terms to designate and measure the computing power of a processor is word size. Computers based on 8-bit-word, 16-bit-word, and 32-bit-word processors are common. The speed of one minisupercomputer is based on the central processing unit's 256-bit instruction words that each encompass seven separate instructions. The computer's heart is a compiler that analyzes the code beforehand, judging which groups of seven instructions can be linked to form each 256-bit very-long-instruction word. Other superminis used by top level research organizations achieve high instruction-execution rates by a method called vectorization in which the central processing unit (CPU) performs repetitive arithmetical operations simultaneously on a string of operands. However, most minisupercomputers use single instruction 64-bit words.

The continued recent development of the 32-bit microprocessor is by far the most important development for business information systems in the short term since this affects the small- and middle-range class of computers. New types of microprocessor-based computers are now available for applications which were previously handled by bigger, more expensive machines with a central processor built of hundreds or thousands of chips and other components. Single microprocessor computers processing between 5 and 10 MIPs now offer superminicomputer performance at a fraction of the cost of only a couple of years ago. As software becomes available for these machines they will increasingly be used for business systems.

The instructions the computer is following (the program) and the data it is processing is stored in Random Access Memory (RAM). To get to or from the processor and RAM, data goes along a pathway of a certain width known as a data bus. Some computers have 16-bit processors which transfer data along 8-bit pathways; others have 16-bit processors and 16-bit input/output buses and other combinations are also found. The ability to process more data than can be sent via the data bus to other components may slow the computer down; delays may occur when data is being sent because the CPU in a computer system operates at a much faster rate than lower level storage devices and peripherals. This discrepancy in speed is overcome by having buses composed of parallel channels thus allowing the processor to carry out interactions with many devices simultaneously. .

Generally the larger the word size the faster the computer works. The commonly used measure of a computers speed of processing, MIPs, is a useful absolute measure of capability of the processor. However, the type of instructions used in measuring this rate of performance may bear little resemblance to the normal mix of instructions found when a commercial system is working in a real-world environment.

Clock speeds are also used to measure the speed of a processor. A processor with a clock speed or megaHertz rate of 10MHz will complete a processing job more quickly than one rated at 6MHz.

Co-processors are sometimes used to relieve the computer's main processor of some of the burden of performing numerous functions. These co-processors may be dedicated to specific tasks. One of the most common is a maths co-processor which handles addition, subtraction, multiplication, division and trigonometric operations very quickly. The effect of having a maths co-processor for a job like hidden-line removal in computer-aided design can be quite significant in reducing processing time. Designed specifically for graphics applications and embedded in systems architectures, dedicated processors may give performance 10 to 100 times faster than that of standard co-processors. This has meant that workstations and PCs which rely more on mathematical operations are now economical to integrate into desktop computer systems. Rising computer capabilities and falling costs make it feasible to tackle jobs like three-dimensional images and solid modelling of complex shapes with desktop computers. Traditional data processing requires a different computer architecture from that needed to perform large quantities of mathematics. Maintaining a large database like a mailing list requires relatively few mathematical operations and the technique of virtual memory, which is efficient for machines which run many applications simultaneously, is not optimal for extensive 'number-crunching' applications.

In mainframe systems special function processors are strategically located throughout a computer system to increase efficiency and throughput, or the rate at which work can be performed by the computer system. These additional processors can handle tasks like data communications and data retrieval from secondary storage. Some large computers have more than 100 processors.

Different processors are built with different instruction sets: the instructions which are built in to the hardware can vary from one machine to another. One argument puts forward the case for the processor to have built in to it a set of instructions which closely resemble a high level language such as PASCAL. This is to allow inexpensive hardware to replace expensive software. On the other hand, proponents of the Reduced Instruction Set Computers (RISC) say that the majority of all instructions actually executed is accounted for by a very few of all the possible instructions. Therefore, designing a reduced instruction set processor speeds things up. Both sides have their supporters but these different ways of actually building systems also form the basis for comparing one system with another.

Computer systems come in sizes to suit every type of information system requirement. Microcomputer systems can serve as information processors for small firms or as intelligent terminals in a larger computer network. IBM announced their new line of personal computers known as the Personal System/2 in 1987. Versions of the PS/2 either from IBM or competitors are available with 16- and 20-MHz Intel 80386 processors, hard disk capacities from 44 to 628 megabytes and up to 2 Mbytes of RAM.

Until recently microcomputers were only designed for use by one person at a time. Technological improvements have been so rapid that sometimes it may be difficult for a single user to tap the full potential of state-of-the-art micros and to utilize the unused potential hardware. Software vendors are marketing products which permit several users to share one system at the same time. These multi-station micros have several monitors and keyboards attached to them which are called *workstations*. A convergence of PCs and workstations is becoming apparent, with less distinction between software for personal, mini and mainframe computers. Before the appearance of the 80386 chip, PCs were relatively cheap while workstations cost up to ten times as much. Workstations had 32-bit architectures while PCs were limited to 8-bit or 16-bit processing. Workstations offered very high resolution graphics while PCs were primarily text-oriented with graphics on low resolution accessory cards. Now almost every hardware maker is introducing 80386-based products which, with their built-in ability to run existing versions of MS DOS, make them ideal for businesses who need more power. Combined with the success of desktop publishing which has increased the demand for more power, this has placed considerable strain on a previously acceptable 8- and 16-bit architectures. The generic requirements for desktop publishing are now surprisingly close to those for an engineering workstation. As PS/2 clones become available PC standards are likely to blur further as options proliferate. Apple Macintosh and other personal computers based on the 68 000 chip are rapidly gaining in acceptance and increasing market penetration. Many believe this popularity is because of the very user-friendly interface probided by much of their software which makes it quick and easy for very inexperienced users to benefit from the power of the computer particularly in the area of page-composition software and through the use of mouse-driven icons to communicate user instructions to the program.

To confuse the terminology a step further, micros themselves can also be used as workstations to link users together to a mainframe computer. With the installation of a data communications adapter a micro can act as a stand-alone computer or as an intelligent terminal to a mainframe computer. An intelligent terminal can do some jobs by itself; for example word processing can be done on a microcomputer standing alone, then the processed document can be sent to a mainframe computer when the micro goes on-line and is used as a terminal. Dumb terminals act solely as input and output devices linked to a remote computer and cannot do any processing by themselves. Intelligent terminals can have various amounts of intelligence and the terminal selected will be chosen on the basis of the need of the user within the overall system configuration.

The difference between mini and mainframe computers is not really clear, nor does it really matter very much — the different names are sometimes applied merely in the size of the processing job which is being handled. Both minis and mainframes can support multiple users, a range of programming languages, and a variety of different storage and input and output devices. Perhaps it is still safe to say that minicomputers are found in small-to-medium sized companies and will probably consist of a large processor shared by a variety of users through terminals and usually running several different types of program at the same time. This is called *multiprogramming*. By allowing the concurrent execution of two or more jobs at the same time computer resources are more efficiently used and jobs are completed more quickly. Minicomputers usually serve as stand-alone computer systems for businesses of about 10 to 400 employees. They have the capabilities of mainframe systems which could be a thousand times faster. Minicomputers are likely to have about ten times the processing capability of a state-of-the-art single user micro.

Trends in distributed processing are likely to continue due to rapid advances in technology leading to cost reductions which now allow those implementing information systems to justify IT systems which would have been out of the question only a year or two ago and at the same time making the task of a strategic planner even more dynamic. Distributed processing means that logically related information processing functions are spread over multiple, geographically separated, computer systems. It is also used to describe the distribution of computing resources to diverse organizational units. The underlying assumption is that there is some hardware, software and or managerial connection or coordination between systems. Data can be processed logically with only that needed by other departments sent onward. Information needed for corporate management such as sales statistics and so on can be forwarded through networks to the corporate system. Similarly, information needed locally, such as price changes, may be sent back from the corporate system.

But *caveat emptor*! Let the IT buyer beware! As with many new developments, organizations which are, for example, accountable to share-holders, will often adopt newer IT ideas only after they have been thoroughly tested in the market place for a period of time. This allows time for problems to appear when new ideas are implemented on production systems. There are many examples of IT products which have evolved through versions 2, 3, 4, . . . to be vastly more reliable than the original mark 1 version although the underlying function of the product has remained unchanged. Research and development costs in IT are often enormous and occasionally products are put on to the market without having been thoroughly tested. This allows the developer to cut his costs: he starts getting sales income sooner and his testing is done for him by his customers. Faults are reported back to the supplier who then patches these up and issues an updated version — sometimes free to registered users and sometimes at a small charge. The lesson to be learned by strategic planners is to resist the blandishments of salespeople with fabulous new IT products which appear to be leading edge technology unless these are also backed up by solid users' reports in similar applications. Successful IT planning requires reliability and robustness which very often are not characteristics found in brand new IT products. IT product selection criteria will be discussed in chapter 9.

6.3   Data storage

Data storage technology (figs 6.3, 6.4) is a dynamic subject with costs having decreased by more than 90% in less than 10 years. Different memory technology is appropriate for achieving certain ranges of access times. The trade-off between storage performance and cost should shape the final form of any information system. Data to be stored should be categorized according to how often it needs to be accessed and how often it needs to be updated. The problem facing the strategic planner is still the same — how to estimate the value to the organization of providing certain information on demand which may be needed only occasionally but which, when it is needed, will impact on key business decisions. Conversely, what will be the cost to the organization in terms of realizing its corporate objectives if this information is not available or if it is out-of-date?

Primary storage is used for data and programs being temporarily stored during processing. With a large primary storage memory a computer can

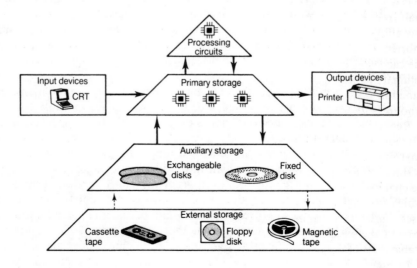

Fig. 6.3   The computer's storage hierarchy.

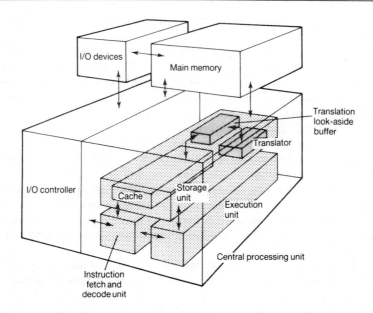

Fig. 6.4 The central processing unit (CPU) in a typical mainframe computer.

handle bigger programs, do more tasks simultaneously and so on. This type of memory can be accessed with no mechanical movement at around the speed of light. Cache memories — buffers that hold information from main memory so that a processor can reach it quickly — have long been an essential part of mainframes and many minicomputers. Now they are being incorporated into one-chip microcomputers as one-chip caches that make access time even shorter. Performance of most computers strongly depends on the quality of the cache design and the way it is implemented. Caches continually obtain and retain items which the processor is likely to need in its current operations. They function far faster than does main memory, which is designed to store large amounts of information economically rather than for speed of access.

Research work on non-volatile primary storage continues. Random Access Memory (RAM) is high speed memory which is termed volatile memory since anything in it is lost if the machine is switched off. Read Only Memory (ROM) is static, non-volatile memory which can be read by the computer but cannot be changed by the user. Turning the computer on or off does not affect ROM, which usually contains programs and instructions which the computer often uses. On some computers you can buy additional ROM chips if you want to expand the capability of your computer. It is a cost effective way to make stable data easily available.

In microcomputers the most commonly used chip is a metal-oxide-semiconductor (MOS) chip but CMOS (complementary-MOS) chips are frequently used in portable or lap-top computers because of their low power requirements.

Taking the example of microcomputers for office systems, the size of the memory required should be dictated by the application which will be run on that machine. Types and sizes of computer memories available need not pose many problems since it is much more important that the needs from the system are well thought out. Once strategic priorities are clear the problem of hardware selection is greatly simplified.

Secondary storage devices are used to store programs or data not currently needed in main memory and are normally on line to the computer and may be accessed by the computer with little or no operator intervention. In evaluating the correct mix of IT devices to support the information system it is important to understand the advantages offered by different types of secondary storage so that well-informed cost–benefit judgements may be made. Traditionally the two major forms of storage have been direct access and sequential access devices.

Serial access devices keep records stored from beginning to end and to get information it is necessary to read from beginning to end until the desired record is located. This type of storage is cheap and is excellent for jobs in which most records have to be processed, like monthly payroll records.

Direct access storage is required if records are to be updated on a more random basis, or for enquiry systems when information may be needed from records in any order. It is also essential if information must be kept up-to-date at all times — examples are bank account balances or seat reservations for airlines. Such systems would offer little valuable information unless the data was always correct.

Magnetic disks are commonly used for storing data which must be accessed directly and these can be fixed disks which stay permanently in place or exchangeable disk packs which like magnetic tapes can be mounted on the retrieval device (in this case a disk drive) as required. Disks come in various sizes — standard (14″), mini (8″) and micro (5¼″ and 3½″). According to their diameter they can of course hold a varying amount of information (figs 6.5, 6.6).

With the huge number of 5¼″ floppy diskettes already in use the adoption of the 3½″ microfloppy disk will meet some resistance. However the 3½″ floppy disk has more capacity and is more convenient and reliable since it overcomes any problems of exposure to smoke, dirt, dust and so on. It was originally pioneered in 1982 by Sony and it is generally accepted that its development was fuelled by the recognition that the 5¼″ floppy was rather bulky relative to the amount of information it stored as well as susceptible to damage. The 3½″ format requires less power (about ⅓) to run the disk drive than that needed for the 5¼″ disk. Also it stores 1 or 2 Mbytes of data compared to the 5¼″ diskettes which store about 360 kilobytes (Kbytes) of data.

Originally hard disks were found only on mini or mainframe systems.

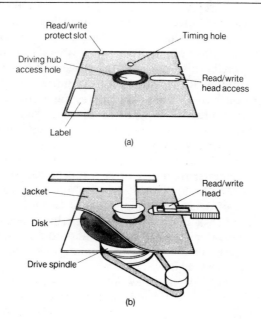

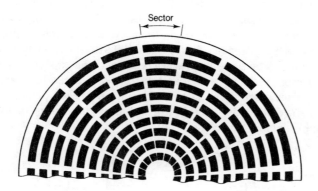

Fig. 6.5 Floppy disks: (a) exterior view; (b) a disk in action.

Fig. 6.6 Organization of a floppy disk: a track is one rotation; a sector is part of a track holding a certain number of bytes.

However over the last few years their cost has dropped dramatically and they are now common on microcomputer systems also, being available in an ever-increasing range of sizes. A 20 Mbyte hard disk on a microcomputer can hold the equivalent of 55 of the $5\frac{1}{4}$" floppy disks and data can be read from it at least 20 times faster. The rapid change in the cost of storing data on hard disks will affect the type and volume of information which can be now readily stored and quickly and cheaply accessed and this in turn will create new possibilities which will affect the scope of what can now be considered by those involved in strategic planning. Many techniques have been evolved to store data on disks in an efficient manner, both to save wasting space and to minimize the time taken to retrieve required information. Access times are often quoted for getting to a record on a disk. These are interesting statistics for the system designer. However, in practice it is often the case that because of poor program design, the mixture of jobs being run concurrently on the same system or simply lack of expertise on the part of the system manager that computer systems do not achieve manufacturer's published response times.

When the first Winchester rigid disk drive was produced in 1980 its capacity was 5 Mbytes (figs 6.7 and 6.8). Today, drives of the same size, store as much as a gigabyte (Gbyte) of data and within a year or two it is expected that they will hold even more. Disk drive capacity is a critical technology in small computer design. The $5\frac{1}{4}$" disk drive is now standard for most hard drives in personal computers although $3\frac{1}{2}$" hard drives are also available. The $5\frac{1}{4}$" disk drive works with stationary read–write heads which fly over the surfaces of the rotating platters on a layer of air a few millionths of an inch thick. The arms containing the read–write heads move from track to track but the heads never touch the moving disk surface. Most hard disk drives look the same. The majority have black plastic front panels with a small light in the lower left-hand corner which flicks on when the drive is reading or writing data. However, the technology differs from one hard disk drive to another depending on its capacity. Low end drives of 10 to 40 Mbytes of data use designs and materials which lend themselves to high-volume low-cost production while high capacity drives from 100 Mbytes to a Gbyte adopt more costly approaches. There are several ways to raise the capacity of drives. One way is to put more platters in the case; current drives can have as many as 8. Capacity also rises when more data can be put on to each platter. The highest density magnetic disk media are thin films of alloys of various metals — cobalt or chromium — plated on to the disk.

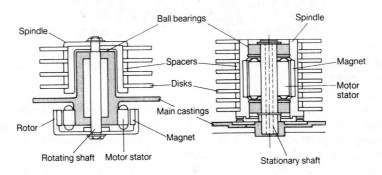

Fig. 6.7 A Winchester disk.

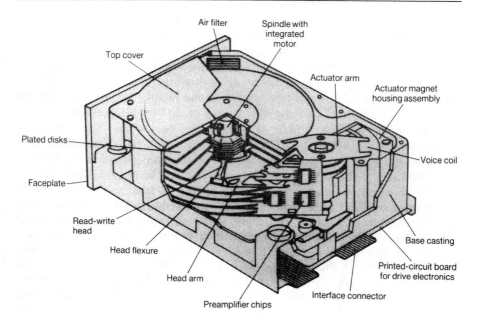

Fig. 6.8 A cut away diagram of a typical high capacity 5¼ " Winchester disk drive.

Distributed processing and likely trends in how we use computers in building information systems are likely to be greatly influenced by the technology of compact data. Compact Disc Read Only Memory (CD-ROM) is a compact disk which can store digital data which can be read by a computer. Each 12cm disk can hold the equivalent of 270 000 pages of A4 text, 5 000 images, 16 hours of sound or 1 500 standard 5¼" single-sided floppy disks. The importance of CD-ROMs to the strategic planner is the type of information they can contain and how it can be manipulated, since they offer a cheap way to mass produce large amounts of data which can be easily distributed. This could easily become the cheapest way to distribute massive amounts of computer-readable data.

Thirteen of the companies involved in development of this technology got together to form the High Sierra Group (HSG) which has agreed on a standard format, called HSG, which will allow CD-ROM disks to be created in a single format and read by different computers using different operating systems. Associated with this is Microsoft's development of an extension to its vastly popular MS-DOS microcomputer operating system which enables any computer running MS-DOS 3.1, or a higher version to read data from any HSG formatted CD-ROM disc. For those interested in strategic planning the importance of this is the accessibility it offers in vastly expanding the potential of the existing microcomputer-based systems which are already in place on so many desks. Users are already familiar with MS-DOS so can now use the CD-ROM technology without learning any new operating system. This offers true added value easily and quickly.

A CD-ROM player like any other mass storage device sends digital signals straight to the computer. However the signal delivering data to a computer has to be much more reliable and error free than can be tolerated by say someone listening to a recording of a symphony orchestra. CD-ROMS presently can not be created by the user: they are read-only devices — although CD-Programmable ROMs (CD-PROMs) are being developed. Erasable optical recording has been introduced in complete commercial data storage systems including some for desktop computers and workstations in 1988. Data storage will face an enormous change when this technology is tried and tested. Storing 600 Mbytes of information on magnetic tape requires 31 reels and takes roughly 16 hours of loading, recording, verifying, and unloading. The same amount of data can be stored on a single magneto-optic disk $5\frac{1}{4}''$ in diameter, the size of an ordinary compact disk — this is up to 1000 times more information than a floppy disk of the same size. The most advanced Winchester disks carry 43 megabits in a single square inch while the magneto-optical disks are just as portable as floppies but carry 300 megabits per square inch, provide random access to information in a fraction of a second and have a much longer life than tapes or floppy disks since they are immune to wear and damage caused by head crashes when the mechanical head accidentally touches the disk surface. They are almost impossible to erase accidentally. The unique combination of erasability, high capacity, fast access, portability and reliability will open up many new applications such as high resolution colour image processing, storage and retrieval, desktop publishing for colour brochures, medical imaging and image construction and editing. Furthermore the data will be erasable so that the same disk can be used many times. Before such systems are in wide use though, drives must be developed and manufactured and standard interfaces established so that the drives can be integrated into complete data storage systems.

For a read-only medium, encoding need only be done once for tens or even hundreds of thousands of disks while decoding is done in real time for each disk by the player. Therefore, while decoding must be done cheaply, encoding can cost much more. A new consumer product called compact disk interactive, CD-I, promises exciting possibilities. It aims to meet the needs of users and to fit in to existing consumer electronic hardware as a real-time audio–video disk and player which can be coupled to existing products like televisions and stereo systems, while paying attention to maintaining the high quality synonymous with CD audio. A read-only medium like this becomes interactive through software. Instructions are coded on the disk to tell the system where to seek the next piece of audio or video information to be played or displayed in response to actions by the consumer. The user communicates with the system by using a pointing device like a joystick or a mouse to move an indicator on the screen.

Developers of CD-ROM software have also become interested in hypertext and hypermedia. Hypertext is not only possible on CD ROMs but essential because the volume of information located in one place makes traditional indexing methods unworkable. A similar development which may attract more users is the WORM, a write-only, read-many-times disk, which, as its name implies, can be created by the user then read many times. Unlike magnetic disks, WORMs cannot be overwritten and they hold slightly less information than a CD-ROM disk. To encourage the adoption of CD-ROM technology some companies are including the loan of a CD-ROM in the licence fee for supplying information in this format. Types of databases available already include 23.5 million addresses and postcodes of the UK Post Office address file on a single disk, financial databases, Sweet and Maxwell's Common Law Year Book, encyclopaedias and so on. Optical storage, digital audio, and compressed digital video accessed through a computer make hypermedia possible. Work remains to be done on developing and producing programs that exploit and coordinate information from all the media. Probably the most significant hypermedia product so far is currently the Hypercard from Apple Computer Corporation of California. This is now included with every Macintosh computer and is an operating system for hypermedia applications which includes drivers for CD-ROM and analog laser videodisk players. The most obvious use of a system like this is as a database manager but developers expect applications to evolve in entertainment, continuing education, service manuals and information systems.

The prediction for the next 5 years is for the appearance of even smaller, higher capacity storage medium such as integrated circuit (IC) memory cards. Two Mbyte memory cards should be available soon and may radically alter the way we store data.

As industry standards appear, new developments will increase and this technology is certainly one to watch in the information systems development field in the next year or two especially if we also get a single standard for graphics displays in personal computers which allow high resolution display of text and graphics. The developments heralded by the IBM PS/2 together with greater demand for screens which can support desktop publishing are likely to encourage the appearance in the market of economically attractive products sooner rather than later. Strategic planners must keep abreast of the latest developments and be ready to include them in their corporate technology planning when they judge the time to be right.

6.4 Input and output alternatives

Having briefly looked at computers and primary and secondary storage we should now turn to look at the ways that information gets into and out of the computer. Determining the output we want from an information system means that we need to understand the information needs of the users. Once the necessary output is known then we have to select the appropriate device to communicate the information to the user. We have to decide between hard and soft copy devices. Soft copy output gives us what we want in temporary form usually on a screen. Sometimes it is easy to determine whether hard or soft copy is preferable. Generally speaking soft copy is useful for rapidly changing information while hard copy is better for less rapidly changing information since it is up to date only when it is produced but may become out of date when referred to later.

Printers are an essential part of any computer system whether it be for a single user or for a multinational corporation. Many different types of printer are available which are suitable for different uses and can cost vastly different amounts. The values by which we judge printers are

Speed — usually measured either in characters per second or pages per minute

Quality — usually described as draft, near letter quality and letter quality cost

Even comparing different alternatives on the basis of cost is not straightforward since users can select from optional font cards, additional system memory and other options which make cost comparisons difficult to draw.

In selecting printers users will also consider reliability, noise, size, and methods of feeding in paper. Each type of printer has certain unique qualities and advantages that meet different application needs. Understanding what each printer can do will help to make better decisions in what to acquire. A more detailed description of the differences between various types of printers with recommendations on when they should be used is contained in chapter 14.

Computers can output microfilm or microfiche which can be read on special viewers. The computer miniaturizes images on to a small video display which are then recorded on to microfilm by a camera. This form of output is a useful alternative to on-line computer based systems when up to date information is not critical (as in a library catalogue) and is used extensively for archival purposes. However as the costs of on-line information systems with their advantages of direct access and immediate updating continue to fall these types of output devices will become less attractive.

Camera systems are gaining popularity with the increased use of colour in graphics. They provide the user with the in-house capability to produce 35mm slides. Effectively the user photographs the screen so the quality of the result is dependent on the resolution of the screen display.

Output generated as soft copy is what you see on a display monitor, or what you hear from your computer's speaker. The video display gives immediate feedback and can display both text and graphics. This type of device is sufficiently common that it requires no detailed description here. The main considerations applying to video displays for an information system are whether there is a need to display high quality graphics and whether there is a need to use colour displays. Display quality is affected by *resolution* which refers to the number of points per unit of area that are used to convey information. A display with 512 points per horizontal line and 512 horizontal lines on the screen has a total of over 262 000 individual points. This figure affects how much memory will be needed to support that display in interactive mode so it follows that the prime limiting factor for resolution is the memory size of the computer system. There are no fixed rules about what would be called high, medium or low resolution quality. Displays with a resolution of up to about 1000 by 1000 probably constitute medium resolution and these will be advisable for displaying good quality business graphics. Higher resolution screens will be needed for specialist applications like computer-aided design.

Colour requires much memory since each point on the screen will need to be described in terms of hue, intensity and saturation. The issue of whether or not to use colour is largely subjective. In business, attention can be drawn to specific data through the use of colour, and by adding colour more information can be imparted to the viewer. Also, most people prefer to look at coloured displays rather than monochrome ones. However, too much use of colour can create confusion. And monochrome monitors are much cheaper to buy. Without a colour hard copy device there is not much point in displaying results on the screen in colour if they are subsequently going to be reproduced in black and white. Some work has been done which has shown that monochrome displays are more restful for long-term use and amber screens are recommended in this respect.

An interesting combination of input and output technology is available in the touch screen devices. A series of beams which criss-cross the screen are emitted from the frame surrounding the screen. Whenever the beams are broken by a finger touching the screen the intersection of the blockage is calculated by the computer and the point on the screen selected by the user is communicated to the system. This is good for public enquiry systems but the screen does get quickly covered in finger marks which can then make the display difficult to read.

Keyboards are the most common of all input devices to computer systems and some interesting work has been done to experiment with alternative layouts to the QWERTY keyboard. However other input devices such as mice, joysticks, and scanners are rapidly gaining acceptance. These devices all share the characteristic of being easy to use and requiring very little training in achieving maximum level of skill in using them.

The ultimate input device for user friendliness will be voice input. This technology is already economically available even for microcomputers but is speaker-dependent. This means that to communicate your commands successfully to the computer you have to train it first to recognize your voice speaking certain words. This has tremendous potential in increasing efficiency in using information systems and we can look forward to useful progress in this area in the next few years.

Present speaker-independent systems are very limited in their practical application since they require such a very large database to accommodate anyone's voice pattern. The best any company says it has done is a system that recognizes large vocabularies spoken with pauses and by a particular speaker. Other companies have speaker-independent systems with limited vocabularies. Most speech recognition systems now in use can handle only isolated words from a small vocabulary and are found in a variety of inspection and inventory applications. The units are trained to know only one speaker at a time and typically know no more than 50 to 100 words, though sometimes the user can load different vocabularies for different tasks. Most isolated word or connected speech recognizers rely on a pause to let them know when a word or phrase is finished. However many utterances can be interpreted in more than one way depending on the word boundaries and with continuous speech the task becomes much more difficult. The voice operated typewriter would be a useful office tool and several organizations have put a great deal of effort into developing one. While the ideal dictating system would be speaker independent, current efforts are aimed at producing speaker dependent models first. The feeling is that 5000 words of continuous speech are needed to make an automated dictation system workable but even a few hundred words could be useful in some applications. Structured text such as accident reports have limited vocabularies and for the most part a rigid syntax makes recognition easier.

Voice response units can output information in two ways, either as prerecorded messages or by means of a speech synthesizer. In recorded voice response units the actual analog recordings of sounds are digitized and sorted on a memory chip. These chips are used in specific applications where the correct message can be selected by the controlling computer program and played back to the user. Lifts, automatic teller machines and many other machines use this system of voice output.

Speech synthesizers are capable of producing at least 64 different sounds and these can be combined to resemble the phonemes that make up normal speech. Virtually any string of words can therefore be read out by the computer to the user. Although the resulting voice may sound a little artificial, nevertheless this form of output can form a significant part of many information systems.

In the mean time, before we can dictate our letters to our computer system we can already use scanners to read printed information directly into information processors, databases and spreadsheets. Small hand-held scanners are available as well as large desktop models. Inexpensive document scanning is a useful IT application for many businesses. Hand held models are inexpensive in comparison to any other optical character reading device.

6.5   Rating computer performance

The value of a computer system depends on it doing the job for which it was purchased and this means that it must be right for the application and the workload and must do the work in an acceptable time. An evaluation that is valid for one organization may not be at all relevant to another, just as an evaluation done by one organization may no longer be correct for the same organization a year later. Evaluating a computer system should include both qualitative and quantitive measures. Compatibility is very important. The scope of compatibility can determine what software and peripherals are available as well as the ease of sharing programs and data within an organization. While compatibility is desirable to ease the transition to new hardware it can also inhibit desirable innovation. Companies can be reluctant to adopt new technology or software even if it appears very useful, if it also means writing off a sizeable investment in terms of existing developed programs or involves the conversion of a lot of data. Quantitative issues include costs of acquisition, installation, operation, training, application development, and maintenance.

The productivity of a system can be measured in terms of cost performance ratios but should also include ease of interactive access, availability of high speed graphics, powerful editors and debuggers, and good documentation. Without these additional features it may be impossible to exploit the power of the computer fully. Computing speed is often important too. It helps system designers to estimate what the likely performance will be when the system goes live and aids in development of software which will effectively utilize the computer's architecture. Measuring the power of any computer is fairly difficult. The performance of a computer is a function of many related considerations including:

> The current application
> The size of the job
> The algorithms being run
> The level of human effort and expertise which has been expended to optimize the program
> The age of the compiler (new ones often have bugs in them which are only discovered over time)
> The architecture of the computer

No single approach to evaluation addresses the requirements of everyone who needs to measure the performance of a system. One of the most popular techniques used is called *benchmarking*. This is when a set of well known programs is run on a machine to compare its performance with others. It is rather like the road test reports on new cars. Benchmarking can be used to measure system performance simply — in terms of whether it can do the job, or relatively — to help select the best system from various alternatives. Users of systems can also apply the results of benchmark tests to advise them which coding styles will get the best from particular machines. Performance evaluation must include accurate characterization of the workload done by performing initial tests using simple programs followed by further tests that gradually increasingly approximate to the real load likely to be put on the system. Good performance evaluation is very important when acquiring expensive large systems and obviously will justify a great deal of effort being spent on such benchmark tests before a purchase decision is made. For simpler systems the performance will not generally vary very much from application to application.

The point of constructing a benchmark is not to produce a single number representing a computer's performance. That would be as silly as trying to describe a car's total performance solely in terms of its top speed on a flat road. Many other factors like its performance under load, how often it needs servicing, the cost of spares and average miles to the gallon under normal running conditions are far more useful information to the prospective car buyer.

For the person evaluating a computer system the aim should be to understand how the overall performance is affected by system components like architecture, compiler, operating system and peripherals and to create a set of realistic expectations for the users. Meaningless results will be inevitable if evaluation:

Neglects to characterize the workload
Uses programs adapted to a special computer system (unless the same configuration exactly is proposed)
Selects inappropriate workload measures
Ignores the difference between frequency and duration of execution

6.6   Communications systems

This chapter has discussed the building blocks of information systems by describing the various alternatives which are available in constructing the hardware for the system. Now we have to look at how we can share data and information between people and between computer systems. There will be further discussions of aspects of office automation which rely on data communications like electronic mail in chapter 14. This selection will address the issues important in developing a strategy which can assist in allowing the various tools and devices to communicate with each other and with the outside world.

The first applications implemented in communications environments were simply the extensions of existing centralized applications. However, whole new types of applications are becoming available with communications-based systems. Once bank branches were linked to their central bank for the purpose of expediting cheque cashing, the possibilities of offering automatic teller machines also using the same communication devices became much easier to justify. As more and more applications are added to communications networks dependency on the organization's computer system becomes more critical with the concomitant requirement for high reliability, and recovery from errors.

This shift brings also a need for greater generality. On-line systems provide access to a much wider variety of data by different parts of an organization and this in turn has meant that data needs to be stored in such a way that it can meet the demands of any particular application. What this means in practice is an increasing demand for terminals which can switch rapidly from one job to another and ultimately that all applications should be available at all times from one terminal. The underlying systems facilities to enable this assume common protocols, and as user interfaces require more and more access to more and more data the importance of commonality increases.

This is implemented at the user level through screen management systems with multiple overlapping windows, and non-keyboard control through devices like a mouse. These considerations actually affect the entire design of a computer-based system and are not just factors which affect communications. The introduction to the common business environment of intelligent workstations with communications facilities will in itself change the way the organization operates by offering new ways of working such as teleconferencing and electronic filing. The tools of the electronic office (fig. 6.9) are discussed in chapter 14. What is important to understand at this point is how much the changing technology is itself a driving force for change in an organization, and not merely a passive tool which can be used or left alone. The pace of development in computer communications technology is primarily driven by the development of integrated circuits and the rapidly falling cost. What seems to be true is that we are now close to the ultimate physical limitations of today's materials and organization so progress will become increasingly difficult.

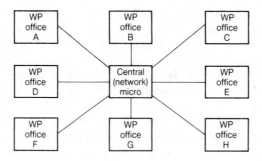

Fig. 6.9 A simple schematic of an integrated office system.

The future will bring new two-way communication networks for written messages with the same degree of pervasiveness as today's telephones. Examples of today's electronic mail networks such as ARPANET, CSNET, and BITNET still appeal to rather special, highly skilled and rather small user classes. Once there are enough subscribers, electronic messaging will spread rapidly. An example is the use of Teletel, the French videotex system, for electronic mail. Originally Minitel terminals provided for French users were intended to replace the printed telephone directory but their use for electronic messaging has grown rapidly. The TAT-8 transatlantic fibre-optic transmission (to be followed by TAT-9 by 1991) will soon dominate intercontinental communications. Satellite links will certainly continue to play a key role in cases where mobility, remoteness and very low traffic densities are factors where the broadcasting capability of satellites has a commanding advantage.

6.7 Communications hardware and distributed processing

To allow data communications between different workstations and computers, telephone lines are often used for data transmission. Since they were designed for voice transmission a device called a *modem* (MOdulator and DEModulator) is used to convert digital computer signals to analog signals so that they can be carried along phone lines and re-digitized for processing by the receiving computer. Modems are intelligent devices which do some processing on their own such as automatically dialing up the telephone number for another computer and answering incoming calls.

Multiplexors (the use of a common communications channel to send two or more signals) are used to combine data streams from independent lines along a specially leased or installed high speed line. Private links can be leased from the local telephone or communications company which will allow the establishment of 'closed user groups' on public networks, providing the utility and convenience of a dedicated network. As data communications grow and the cost of low speed lines and other hardware escalates, multiplexing can provide a cost saving solution. One high speed line linking several terminals from say an airport reservations counter might be much cheaper than having several low speed lines connecting each workstation to the host computer.

With the trend towards distributed processing it is becoming more common for organizations to have more than one computer system. New devices for electronically connecting computers and workstations in the same way as telephone operators manually connect callers are available for data PBX (private branch exchange) switching. The transmission media used for data communications currently is mainly the telephone system. The organization's existing PBX provides a natural, low risk way to gain the benefits of networking. Although not completely without headaches, the multitude of telephones already installed and the underlying data communications network which connects them offer possibilities for enhanced telephones which include computer terminals, or microcomputers with additional features allowing them to replace the telephone on your desk. This would allow access to any user to any device which could be attached to the nearest telephone, enabling resource sharing across geographically separated locations as well as access to many publically available databases. The PBX must therefore take an important place in the development of communications strategies.

Optical fibre will eventually replace copper wire traditionally used in telephone systems. An interesting comparison between speeds is that in the time it would take to transmit a single page of the *Complete Oxford Dictionary* over the telephone line, the entire dictionary could have been transmitted over an optical fibre. The goal of a unified digital telecommunications network may be realized through integrated services digital network (ISDN) (fig. 6.10). Initially the network will combine in a single architecture various existing forms of communication (such as telephone service, telex, facsimile, and data retrieval) that are now the province of independent specialized networks. Ultimately ISDN is seen as the medium for communictions such as video conferencing. ISDN will evolve from the digital telephone networks of various countries and will eliminate the cost and inconvenience of separate networks by standardizing interfaces and protocols before the terminals themselves are developed and well before some of the potential applications are developed.

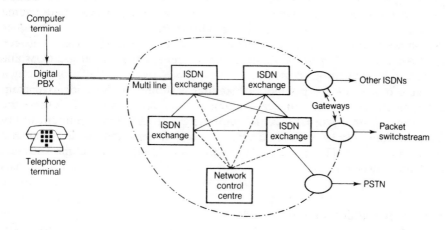

Fig. 6.10 British Telecom's ISDN network.

Most newly installed telephone switches now use digital technology to transmit information but transmission between the central office and the subscriber is still analog which necessitates the use of a modem for digital to analog (and vice versa) conversion when digital data is to be transmitted say from one personal computer to another. ISDN will extend digital technology over the entire system. The ISDN concept is being tested in field trials in many countries including Belgium, Canada, France, Great Britain, Italy, Japan, USA and West Germany with the aims of providing feedback for further development work, to develop practical applications, to ascertain the willingness of business and residential users to pay for the services and to stimulate the development of related technology. Those countries at present testing ISDN are expected to lead the world in implementing it. For most developing countries the high cost of ISDN will slow its introduction. Thus the interface between analog and digital services will be critical in maintaining a global network.

Of course data communications and some media integration are possible without ISDN. The logical integration of a PBX providing voice channels with a local area network carrying data can provide such capabilities. Network planning is becoming increasingly important as we see how it is increasingly difficult to separate any aspect of IT systems from any other part of the organization's systems. The implication is of a fully digital network leading naturally to the next stage where data, voice, text and images can be stored and transmitted throughout an organization. It is essential to adopt a communications strategy which takes advantage of the new services constantly becoming available via public networks and which meets the requirements of the organization for communication both between different members of the same organization and between organizations. For a cluster of business users a local area network (LAN) would not only provide communication between the various users but also gather traffic and other destinations. A PABX would do the same for voice traffic. A gateway could then serve as the bridge between the LAN and PABX and the ISDN network connecting to other locations and remote communications partners.

The problems of compatibility of standards should not be underestimated. Equipment at either end of the communications line must 'follow the same protocol' in other words, talk the same language. All data communications can therefore only be achieved after an agreement on standards is established between the users. This is not difficult within an organization but may be more difficult between organizations.

6.8 Value added network services

Value added network services (VAN) are available commercially providing telecommunications value added network services. They do more than just transmit information; they manipulate, store, translate and re-order information. VAN services are run by organizations who use the basic data carrying facilities of the telephone and data transmission companies and offer additional facilities. They offer an easy way to establish a network and also allow dissimilar terminal equipment to communicate with each other through the provision of speed, code format, data structure and protocol conversion. This service allows users to avoid being locked into a particular manufacturer and to utilize a wide range of terminals in their systems. Support services from the VAN operator help users to operate their communication networks and provide high reliability, economy and compatibility. The range of services includes personal answering services, viewdata, automatic ticket reservation, facsimile transmission services, database and information base access, computer conferencing and so on. Just as computer systems can buy applications software from a number of competing makers so operators of networks might include a multiparty conferencing package from one manufacturer, a package from another that defines a dialing-from-terminal service and software from a third that provides for data communications in a hybrid cable television system. Store-and-forward and real time communications complement each other and allow calls to be completed that could not go through with real time communications alone. Messaging is also important as a record communications medium. High speed communicating copiers, information services and colour will become part of standard facsimile service.

6.9 ATMs and POS

Automatic teller machines (ATM) represent another application of computer communications technology which have been very successful in duplicating the work of bank tellers at approximately half the cost. Because the procedures of the teller have been duplicated by the ATM the device is not considered revolutionary although many customers have changed their banking habits preferring to use a machine rather than wait in line for personal human service. In the USA almost 60% of the population are active card holders in that they use a card at least once every 2 weeks. There is little doubt that bank automation including ATMs is used to develop an organizational competitive edge.

ATMs may be becoming increasingly difficult to justify since as the number of tellers is reduced technicians and programmers are added to support and service ATMs. In spite of this recent studies have shown that many bank executives believe that ATMs should be a part of their strategic plan. The personnel of Dallas Federal Savings, a US$2.2 billion stock company, wanted to know how successful their ATM network had been. After a comprehensive cost–benefit analysis they determined that the ATM was essential to competing in the market and as a result were able to reaffirm the initial strategic decision. In most countries ATM is no longer used for the single purpose of replacing tellers. Most banks agree that the number of customers using ATM needs to be greater than 50% to break even. This can be typically translated to 10 000 transactions per month per ATM. This leads to the conclusion that if the install base for ATM is to increase significantly there must be renewed emphasis on marketing and education. The marketing plan has to be part of a retail bank strategic plan designed to meet predetermined objectives. The consumer will continue to embrace ATM as the number of services it offers grows. Some of these include trading stock, stock portfolio analysis, market quotes, catalogue shopping, paying bills and personal financial files. Many of these applications require the use of a personal computer in an office or home environment.

Point of sale (POS) devices connected to computerized banking are now beginning to proliferate. POS networks are well established in California where 8000 terminals process 3 million transactions a month on the Interlink network.

Some petrol stations in Europe and Japan have on-line POS systems but in most places outside the USA smart cards are becoming the preferred replacement for cash. Such smart cards can authorize transactions on their own through an embedded memory chip and therefore do not need to rely on telephone links between the retailers POS terminal and the company's central computers. Where such communication is expensive a telephone-based electronic banking system would be prohibitively expensive and in such countries smart cards would seem a better choice than POS. A number of experiments have taken place in the USA but the future of smart cards or POS there will depend probably on Visa and Mastercard's assessment of the relative economics of both systems. For retailers and customers the transition to a bank card based POS system would require no new cards and stores with electronic cash registers would only need to attach a card reader and a numeric key pad for the customer to type in his personal identification number (PIN).

Even the PIN may soon become obsolete for system entry to ATMs. It can be replaced by many identifiers including fingerprints, retinas, hand geometry, wrist veins, voice analysis and signature dynamics. With distributed networking of ATMs and with large communications networks such as Plus, Cirrus, and Nyce, availability to the consumer is becoming world-wide.

A recent study by the Bank Administration Institute and Boston University found that investment in retail delivery systems would continue and the sale of ATMs grow rapidly. This is due partly to the very high reliability of ATMs making users more trustful of their bank cards. This reliability also encourages the spread of POS which is attractive to the retailer in cutting out risks of bad cheques.

6.10   Topologies

When describing network topologies we are considering the physical and logical configuration of the network (figs 6.11, 6.12). Local area networks

(LAN) fall into two categories, broadband and baseband. Most networks are baseband which means that at any one time only one signal can be carried. To allow more than one computer to use the network at once, time division multiplexing is generally necessary. Broadband transmission allows several signals to travel simultaneously which enables fast data transmission but costs more.

There is no ideal topology since the topology adopted should be shaped largely by the organization's requirements and its current technological base. The main topologies include star, ring and bus configurations.

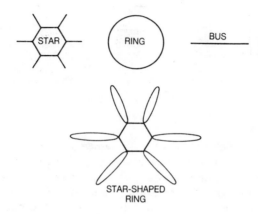

Fig. 6.11   Examples of local area network (LAN) topologies.

The public telephone system is the world's biggest computer network and telephone is a *node* in the system — every telephone can connect with every other telephone. Nodes in computer systems are usually terminals or computers.

The star configuration involves a host computer which is connected to a number of other computers. For one computer to communicate with another it must go through the host computer in the centre of the star. Most of the data is held in a central system and the nodes perform functions like data acquisition or distributed processing. The essential element in this topology is the control over the communications system exercized by the central installation. This is the most common growth pattern from a centralized system and IBM's System Network Architecture (SNA) is a good example of a system which enables the implementation of the central host approach. The central switching device can also be a PABX which is an attractive solution as it points naturally to integrated voice and data communications with the use of combined speech and data terminals.

The ring (or data highway) topology (fig. 6.12) is appropriate for linking

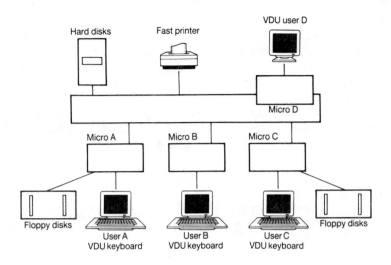

Fig. 6.12 A local area network arranged as a ring.

computer systems which are roughly the same size. No single computer is the focal point of a ring network and features common to this type of system are multiple processors and operating systems, databases and database software. A ring network can enable the creation of a unified network without the need to rewrite applications since the unifying aspect is the data highway which connects the computers. This assumes that all the machines on the system are compatible with the 'highway logic' which is an enormous simplification of what can often be a technically very demanding problem. The best known ring system is the Cambridge Ring. Ring systems are vulnerable; if one station goes wrong then the entire network may stop. This may be one reason why ring networks, despite their appealing simplicity, have not caught on.

Bus configurations permit the connection of computers and peripherals through a central cable and allow sharing of peripherals and data. These are commonly used in local area networks. Local area networks provide a way for microcomputers to communicate with each other and share other intelligent devices such as printers and file savers without sending signals through an expensive mainframe computer. Most LANs are application-oriented in that they are set up to meet the needs of the users and so are specific to the work environment in which they exist. LAN technology is therefore used in different and sometimes unique ways. They can transfer files between microcomputers of quite different architectures, they can connect workstations to a large central hard disk store or they can provide a gateway into a mainframe computer and through to the whole world of data communications. The distance separating devices on a LAN can be a few feet or a few miles. LANs based on industry-wide standards can enable office integration through

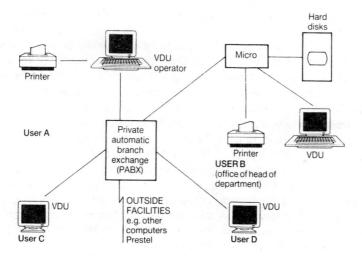

Fig. 6.13   An integrated office system controlled through PABX.

interconnecting terminals and permit orderly incremental growth and evolution of systems as well as saving money. However all is not plain sailing in using or implementing a LAN. A network's medium, access method, and data transfer rate can help or hinder the work done on the system and again it is appropriate to reiterate that the topology adopted should be shaped by the organizational requirements with a network strategy which is part of the overall process of strategic planning for integrated systems. As has been mentioned, LANs are based on two types of coaxial cable — baseband or broad band. The Ethernet LAN uses baseband carrying one data channel at fairly high speeds. However transmission rate does not equate to throughput rate. In all networks data must travel through several levels of software and through the physical transmission cable so the effective rate is not at all the same as the medium's maximum transmission rate. Most LANs operate on the basis that each computer linked in to the system is equally important. This is called a peer-to-peer configuration, in which no single station controls the entire network.

The access methods commonly used are the contention method and the token passing method. In the *contention* method each station contends for the right to control the network for data transmission. A station listens to the communications line and sends its message when the line is free. Through a system called collision detection the situation of two stations simultaneously sending messages which collide with each other is dealt with by the transmitting stations re-transmitting their messages after a random amount of time has passed since the detected collision.

In the *token passing* method, an empty token passes continuously round the network. If a station wants to transmit a message it fills the empty token with data which then continues round the system to its destination. This method is deterministic since every station is guaranteed regular access to the network.

Since the needs of a network will vary so widely from user to user it is perhaps unlikely that any one system will become the *de facto* industry standard. As usual cost will vary with standard of performance and there will always be different priorities among prospective customers.

The communications need of an organization can usually only be satisfied by the use of a combination of technologies. Many organizations will need to combine and integrate several local area networks and a wide area network. Organizations will keep a telephone service and carefully organize its interaction with other local area networks. The installation of a LAN should only be undertaken in the context of an overall communications strategy. The time frame of such a strategy usually covers many years: most organizations want their communications equipment to be written off over about 10 years.

A strategy study for LAN requirements should cover:

Development of overall plans for communication services
Translation of functional needs into technical specifications
Definition of the communications link demands dictated by a given programme of office automation
Development of structure plans for proposed LANs
Definition of the interface between elements of the overall communications strategy

Most organizations introduce their first LAN on an experimental basis with the aim of building up experience in using it. Careful analysis of the various technologies and their appropriateness for an organization's needs can be a demanding task.

6.11   Network protocols

The discussion on network protocols will be kept as non-technical as possible. The strategic planner must know enough detail to enable him to formulate a high level plan for compatibility and evolution. A protocol is a set of rules and procedures which define how two or more devices interact to transfer information; for example how data on the network should be formatted and how messages are sent and received. There are two general classifications of protocols, asynchronous and synchronous. In asynchronous data transmission, data is transferred on an as-needed basis and includes messages to show the beginning and end of the message. It is best suited to data communication involving low speed input/output devices such as video displays and printers. Synchronous communication enables high speed communication usually between computers and has no start and stop messages included.

Network architecture must enable devices to link together *and* to communicate meaningful information. Being able to dial direct to Japan is a good example of linking but unless you speak Japanese you won't be able to communicate meaningfully. The most important effort from the point of view of the strategic planner is the International Standards Organization Open Systems Interconnection model. This lays down a seven-layer architecture for the exchange of information among equipment from different vendors for connecting and communicating through telecommunications media (fig. 6.14).

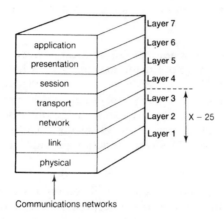

Fig. 6.14   The ISO Open Systems Interconnection (OSI) layered model.

The model describes the communication process as a hierarchy of layers each of which has a defined interface with the layer above and the layer below. This interface is made flexible so that designers can implement various communications protocols and still follow the standard.

Layer 1: Physical
This layer defines the physical connections between the computer and the network, including the mechanical and electrical aspects of the connection and defines the network's topology. This layer has been likened to the physical equipment which needs to be in place in order to make a telephone call.

Layer 2: Data link
This layer defines the protocol that computers must follow to access the network for transmitting and receiving messages. In speech conversations there will be occasions when you do not clearly hear the caller and you have to

ask him to repeat his message. The data link acts to ensure that messages transmitted are properly sent and received. The first two layers together are called the Hardware layer.

Layer 3: Network control
This layer defines how packets (bits of information) are routed and relayed between networks. It also regulates packet flow and defines how status messages are sent to computers on the network. In the telephone call analogy the telephone company takes the number you dial and routes the call through the public switched telephone network and sends a signal to the telephone of the person you are calling which makes the telephone ring. Thus a communication channel can be opened up on demand through the network.

Layer 4: Transport
This layer defines how you address the physical devices on the network, how connections between nodes are made and unmade, what the protocol is for, guaranteed message delivery and how to handle inter-network routeing of messages. In calling another party we usually greet him and check we are speaking to the right person before commencing our discussion. We also go through a fairly standard procedure in saying goodbye when we wish to terminate our connection. This is the function provided at the transport layer.

Layer 5: Session
This layer lets you write software that will run on any installation of a given kind of network. It functions as the conceptual interface to the transport layer for applications. In a telephone conversation we speak and when we pause the other party then speaks. We prompt with questions and confirm replies with comments like 'OK'. This form of spoken communication between two people applies to all conversations irrespective of what the subject of the conversation is.

Layer 6: Presentation
This layer defines how applications enter the network. In the phone call example both parties use a common language. If you make an international call and the recipient answers in a language you do not understand then you have made a connection up to level 5. The standard has broken down at the Presentation level unless the message can be passed between both parties in a form acceptable and comprehensible to both.

Layer 7: Application
This layer simply defines the network applications that support file serving. Conceptually this is where electronic mail and other network utility software exists. In a phone call this layer represents the actual message we want to communicate.

Even if devices are using the same protocols at the highest layer this does not mean you will receive exactly what was sent. If a coloured image was sent and you only have a monochrome display you will obviously not receive exactly what was sent. However, the purpose of the ISO/OSI model is to illuminate the various network standards which co-exist and to provide a basis for developing an overall network strategy. To date the only other standard which allows for a data communication user to progress up the ISO levels is to adopt packet switching as standardized under recommendation X-25 but even here we can only go up to level 3 in the ISO model. There is still a long way to go before the user can undertake the application. Any corporate strategy should aim to utilize standards conforming to the ISO/OSI model and address the task of migrating existing nonconforming networks towards the overall network strategy.

6.12 Summary

This chapter has emphasized the importance of IT in the implementation of successful information systems. For the strategic planner a thorough understanding of available IT devices, and their advantages and disadvantages is absolutely essential in the achievement of alignment of his strategic plans with the overall aims of the organization.

To round off this section let us briefly return to the needs of the ARC described in chapter 5. To recap, the ARC is basically a user information service which requires careful accounting control to monitor precise usage of its services not only for billing users but also for planning purposes. Assuming that such a centre will have to start small and aim to grow as its customer-needs expand then the approach to selecting the necessary technology will be very similar to the selection process adopted by any organization. In chapter 10 the problem of planning for change is discussed in some detail. However at this stage it is also worth emphasizing how important the changing needs of an organization are in affecting the choice of technology to support the business's activities.

While starting off in a small way which will still be efficient the ARC should probably buy a personal computer with a 30 Mbyte hard disk which initially will be able to store all its records and programs. Personal computer systems are generally easy for clerical staff to use and there is a wealth of available software which can be bought. While the ARC may think that some customization of software packages would be desirable, this type of modification is expensive and will not be justifiable to start with. Certain compromises will have to be made between what may be desirable and what is affordable while still being robust and reliable. An accounting package which can read the same files as the database software would be essential — reinforcing the theme of standards which was discussed earlier in this chapter.

Statistics on patterns of usage and projection will also be readily generated from standard data files through proprietary software or the purchase of an accounting package with additional statistical analysis facilities. ARC should also carefully evaluate public brand software. This is readily available at very small cost and there are no problems with making copies or inadvertently infringing copyright legislation.

By selecting a personal computer which is popular in the local market and proprietary software the ARC administration should be virtually guaranteed a trouble free system. Even if things go wrong there will be service support readily available to get things moving again quickly. A high quality printer will probably be desirable. The final appearance of correspondence (assuming that not all our correspondents will be able to receive electronic mail) gives a good impression of the ARC's professional approach to its operations. The purchase of a medium speed (say 1200 baud) modem will ensure that the ARC office can communicate with the outside world and, through the various network services, gain access to information stored on computers throughout the world through networks like ARPANET and BITNET. Again public brand software for data communications will be perfectly adequate. The integration of a facsimile (fax) machine with the basic computer system will probably be the next purchase, followed by perhaps additional personal computers and a central hard disk server to expand record storage capacity and enable data-sharing through a local area network, the LAN will in turn be linked through a gateway device to the organization's central mainframe computer to provide massive data storage facilities.

This is a brief description of how the ARC organizers should see the available technology aiding them to implement their plans and how they should allow their IT purchases to grow with them as their business grows and their needs change. Changing technology means that IT users can never guarantee that their purchases will always turn out to have been the right choice. However, an understanding of the capabilities of available technology added to awareness of the information systems needs of the organization will enable IT users to be right most of the time.

Part I   Summary

This section of the book has been concerned with strategic modelling. It has tried to show that before you can begin to develop a system, or indeed use an information system effectively, you must have an understanding of the conceptual models of information and organizations, and you also must be able to relate this to models of information systems and the technology which can support them.

The examples which have been used throughout this section show a variety of different information needs related to different organizations. We have tried to stress that within a single organization many changes may occur and so information needs will also change over time. This is extremely important to recognize when you are developing an information systems and technology strategy. It is essential to incorporate the ability to react to change in the organizational environment.

Case study: The New Enterprise Administration

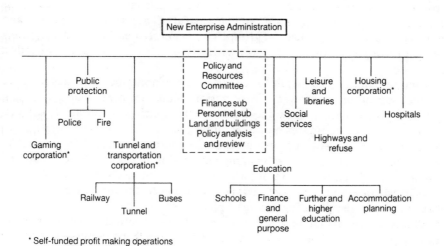

* Self-funded profit making operations

Organization chart for a New Enterprise Administration (NEA) showing major areas of responsibility.

In order to illustrate this we are going to look at a type of organizational structure which can be found anywhere in the world. We call it here a New

Enterprise Administration (NEA) unit. The NEA is operated separately from central government but nevertheless, has to conform with certain government regulations and procedures. The organizations chart which follows shows the major areas of responsibility.

A special feature of the NEA is the new enterprise operations which are self-funded and profit making. The operations and their contribution to the NEA's funds are listed below.

Tunnel and transportation corporation	18.3%
Gaming corporation	30%
Housing corporation	11%

The three operations constitute a total of 59.3% of the NEA's funds. The remaining 40.7% comes from central government funding through direct taxation.

Consider briefly the very different models of organizations and decision making models.

There is an aggressive management structure in the tunnel and transportation corporation operating as a bureaucratic model with a strong profit motive. In contrast there is a social services unit with a people culture and no sense of financial values. The housing corporation is largely task centre oriented due to the variety of work skills required and the distributed nature of the working locations. The education division is made up of autonomous groups encompassing a variety of disparate organizational structures. The gaming corporation is intent on (and successful at) securing large profits and run by a small but very powerful group. This is not to mention the many others who all form part of one single administrative unit for overall policy direction and control.

It should not be too difficult to see that the regular annual statistics required by the education division as information input to next year's planning exercises would hardly meet the needs of the gaming corporation for fast precise and accurate figures on the gambling stakes. The gaming corporation needs an on-line system with instant response and regular weekly management summaries and forecasts. The housing corporation needs to develop planning systems for a 5-year period in order to secure the finance for capital building costs in advance and this must be linked through to the highways and refuse division so parallel planning can take place.

All of these systems have to somehow be integrated into the overall decision-making process at NEA policy level since it is here that the purse strings are controlled. There would therefore be a great problem if the information systems and supporting technology were totally incompatible.

The most important issue is whether the systems support the strategic policies of the administration. It could well be a mistake to try to develop an integrated management information system for such an organization. Instead, the information systems at divisional level should more accurately mirror the organizational structure which they support but match the information needs to the strategic needs of the group as a whole. This is similar to the Mattison (1987) model described in chapter 5 where information systems are built to serve the needs of a particular level as effectively as possible with a global information system at the higher levels. In such a case it is quite feasible for each division to operate different technological environments as long as compatibility can be achieved at the higher levels either through uploading datafiles on to a separate system or by direct communication. The important common factor here is data and this as we shall see in chapters 7 and 8 is where the major concentration should be for standardization.

This scenario shows how one organization can consist of many different styles and structures, all of which require different levels and styles of information support. Although a government-based model is not atypical of many large corporations and, indeed, many smaller organizations operate quite different management styles and decision-making processes within different functional groups. There is a need, therefore to look at the organization as a strategic whole but also to design information systems at operational and control level which efficiently match those needs. The next section of the book goes on to examine how this can be done and the various methods which can be used to design and implement information systems to make them effective information solutions.

Part II   Strategies for information systems development

This section of the book is concerned with the development of a system and looks first at the identification of specific systems requirements and the specific development tools which can be used to build it. Again, the emphasis is on the selection of a contingent approach. In a sense, we are proposing the systems factory model where a variety of tools and techniques are available and the problem (or solution) is to determine the most appropriate for the situation. This applies also to the technology which will be used since a number of factors affect the choice over and above the 'best fit' model. Factors such as affordability, manageability and durability will all impact on this decision.

Perhaps, most importantly of all, we emphasize survivability. The system must be built to survive change as far as possible. This means that it should be capable of modification and upgrading without necessitating a completely new development.

What we try to present is an overview of the many approaches which could be taken and the considerations to be made when trying to select the best fit to the information system model.

7 Information systems requirements planning

7.1 Introduction

This chapter addresses three major issues of requirements planning:

What systems are appropriate to the organization?
Which systems shall we develop over a period of time?
What are the detailed development requirements of a specific system?

In Part I of this book we looked at ways to identify models of information systems related to the organizational information needs and identified a wide variety. But to develop these takes money. Any organization will have only so many resources which can be used to develop information systems. This will be further complicated by the conflicting demands of systems for hardware and software facilities, the synergistic effect of one system on another and the current IT environment within the organization. When faced with a list of urgent demands and a large group of potentially irate or even violent would-be users how does the IT manager choose between them?

Noticing that your competitor has implemented an on-line ordering system is insufficient justification to demand a similar service, yet this is often a typical reason. While it may be part of the whole picture, it has to match with the overall corporate objectives of the firm. The first step, therefore, is to develop an IT strategy from the corporate plan through a requirements planning exercise.

While the majority of management personnel perceive the need for strategic planning, few are prepared to accept this as a reason for assigning their particular needs a lower priority than anyone else's. This is particularly true when it comes to computer systems when it sometimes seems that only vindictiveness on the part of the IT manager stands between the user department and their dream system. The most common and often disastrous solution has been the development of separate systems by the users themselves. Such systems are totally unrelated to the overall information needs of the organization. That is not to say that there is no part for user developed systems in an organization. Quite the contrary, but they must be part of an overall plan and, given the current state of technology, must also conform to certain standards permitting compatibility for data exchange.

The next aspect of systems requirements planning is to identify the portfolio of applications which will be developed over the longer term of the corporate strategic plan and the appropriate means by which they might be developed.

At the more detailed level, we are concerned to identify the overall information requirements of the end user and the best way to provide for these. We are all familiar with the image of an information system as presented in fig. 7.1 but there is hot dispute concerning the approach needed to solve this problem. Once again there is no one correct solution but there are a variety of approaches which must be evaluated against factors impacting on the application system environment. We will look first at the process involved in the three stages of requirements planning.

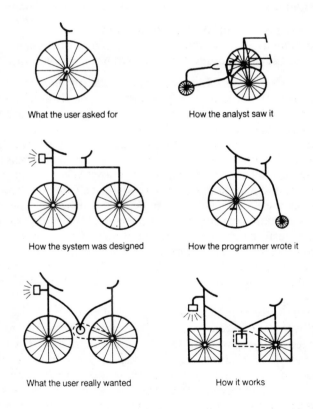

What the user asked for

How the analyst saw it

How the system was designed

How the programmer wrote it

What the user really wanted

How it works

Fig. 7.1 There is often a world of difference between what an end user wants and what he actually gets: but who is to blame?

7.2   Requirements planning and analysis

7.2.1   The process

Information systems are effective if they improve the overall use of resources in an organization. The requirements analysis process is used to identify whether an improvement will be the end result and, if so, whether it is the greatest improvement possible given the set of alternatives and the objectives of the organization. This brings us to the very thorny issue of how we can measure improvements.

In most organizations, the improvement is measured in terms of productivity related to profitability. This is still very vague. A few years ago a large New York bank concerned with its labour costs implemented a department-by-department system to measure productivity, defined as transactions per employee. The system was used to calculate a large portion of the bonuses paid to line management and strongly supported by senior management. The result was that line managers justified computerization of every possible system cutting direct labour costs radically in every department, except one, the data processing department. Increases here were not only in staff but on mass hardware and software acquisitions. There was no system to identify whether the trade-offs between the higher DP costs and the productivity of departments came to a plus or a minus for the bank overall.

The IT strategy has to be included as part of the corporate strategy of the organization, as we showed in Part I; it should typically follow a process as shown in fig. 7.2. (Try comparing this to the original strategic IT plan prepared by our government analyst in chapter 1: you will find this one much more simple to follow.)

The first step is to perform a requirements planning exercise which will identify those specific areas of critical importance to the firm and the information systems which might support them.

The next step is to evaluate these against the overall objectives of the organization and against the current and future IT developments and to select an appropriate portfolio of applications. This sounds simpler than it is, since neither proven techniques exist to perform this nor the value-free society to enable it to take place without the usual balance of bias, prejudice and pragmatism.

Finally a statement of requirements must be developed which allows us to match user needs to the appropriate development process and information technology.

Each of these stages require different people with different skills and techniques. Throughout each stage of the process, however, the users will have a role to play and perform an integral part of the decision-making process.

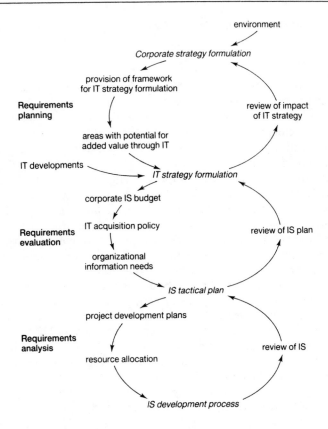

Fig. 7.2 The IT strategy must be incorporated into the corporate strategy.

7.2.2   Requirements planning

In requirements planning we ask what information systems we ought to consider as part of our overall IT strategy. This is a senior management brainstorming exercise where the strategic objectives of the organization are reviewed and the factors which are critical to achieving these identified. It is then necessary to examine these areas closely to see whether the potential exists for greater success through the use of IT. Boddy & Buchanan (1986) suggest that there are four main classifications of organizational objectives which can benefit from IT, labour control, information, operations, and strategy, and for each we should identify what specific objectives are being pursued and what the specific implications are. Typical questions would relate to job loss, improved decision making, and removal of operational inefficiencies. As we mentioned earlier, in striving to match organizational objectives, we may create new strategic directions. This innovational potential of IT is rarely realized unless the IT strategy is fully integrated with the corporate strategy. This is supported by Lucas & Turner (1981).

They identified three approaches, which depend on three different relationships, resulting in the information systems being developed:

>Independent of corporate strategy
>Supportive of corporate strategy
>Fully integrated with corporate strategy

Figure 7.3 shows that while strategic impact may result from all three methods it is as a secondary rather than primary effect.

Level of integration with corporate strategy	Primary objective	Secondary effect
Independent	Operational efficiency	Managerial information
Policy support	Aid repetitive decision making	Better understanding of problem dynamics
Fully integrated	Open new products markets direction	Change decision process

Fig. 7.3 Strategic impact of IT is a secondary rather than a primary effect of implementation of IT.

This is not the only way to identify which systems are required. Very few organizations have a well developed IT requirements planning strategy fully integrated with corporate policy and performed by senior management. A more common approach is to allow all and sundry to suggest their system requirements and to use an MIS steering committee to set priorities and/or allocate resources for IT developments.

One of the advantages of a steering committee can be to act as a liaison device that facilitates interunit coordination and conflict-reduction by giving reasonable representation to a cross-section of user management, IT management and other senior managers involved in financial decision making.

In summary, the identification of systems which are required should be tied closely to corporate strategy, but frequently also will be naturally generated from users suffering from ineffective information. The impetus may come from outside the organisation either from IT experts (particularly, the salesman type), or competitive awareness or breakthroughs in technology. Regardless of the source, the question to be addressed at the systems planning stage is 'What strategic objectives will be pursued through the introduction of IT in this area?'

7.2.3   Requirements evaluation

Most organizations would now find themselves at the stage where, far from looking for projects, they have to narrow down the field as to which of the many they should develop first. A study by McKeen & Guimaraes (1985) showed that where steering committees were involved in the MIS area they tended to favour:

Large projects
Projects with little vertical integration
Projects aimed mainly at clerical and supervisory levels
Projects with formal proposals and written cost/benefit analyses
Projects that could demonstrate both tangible and intangible benefits

These are not necessarily, a justifiable set of priorities.

Again, there are no standard rules, but there are some very sensible suggestions to be taken into account. One of these is to try to assess the return-on-investment which is likely to accrue from the particular IT investment. Methods such as that of Strassman, discussed in Part I, and more complex approaches to cost–benefit analysis techniques such as information economics are gaining favour as they prove their worth over a number of tested situations. A further consideration is the particular portfolio of applications which is required. As in any business or investment operation there will be some alternatives which offer high risk but a commensurately high gain and others which offer much lower financial returns but minimal resource demand.

Figure 7.4 illustrates this as a typical marketing analogy. In marketing terms, cash cows are products that generate large amounts of cash and as such they can help other products grow. Dogs neither generate nor require significant amounts of cash and are profit-poor although often a necessary support. Problem children are products with a low share of a fast growing

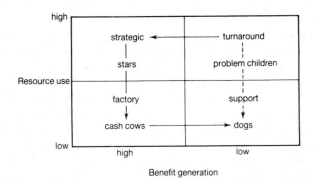

Benefit generation

Fig. 7.4   In any business different operations result in different levels of risk (resource use) and benefit (financial returns).

market and require large amounts of cash to maintain market. Stars are high growth, high share products with a modest positive or negative cash flow.

It may be appropriate for a particular organization to have investments in a full range of these, given their stage of IT development or to concentrate their efforts only in some.

A further area for consideration relates to the existing technology and expertise in the organization. (This is discussed in more detail in chapter 9.) It may be that the suggested use of IT rates highly on all these scales but its use will be inhibited by the existing environment. An example of this is highlighted in an independent survey performed on the productivity impact of using the MacIntosh computer in an IBM environment with separate system and operating standards. Despite the overhead of the two standards the survey concluded that the benefits obtained by introducing the MacIntosh greatly outweighed this disadvantage. Yet the single standard policy is still the most quoted reason for the single supplier policy adopted by many of the large US groups. As connectivity improvements accelerate, many of these problems will disappear.

Regardless of how limited a portfolio is developed it will undoubtedly offer a very wide range of development strategies and the selection of the most appropriate vehicle is the last question addressed in the requirements planning exercise.

7.2.4   Requirements analysis

One of the major problems affecting the traditional DP department is the adoption of a standard development approach to all projects. Such methods are often successful at building large, accurate, precise, custom systems but they work very slowly. Given the much wider range of applications required in a modern organizational environment there is also a need to develop systems rapidly, possibly by end users and frequently offering a choice between perfection and approximation (and information perfection may lie in the eye of the beholder). Different applications require different approaches to their definition and implementation and may also, depending on their strategic value, require very different management skills. The following issues will need to be addressed:

> What category of application is it (transaction, control, planning, strategic)?
> What type of management, planning and control will be required?
> What type of user will the system have?
> Who should design this application — DP, user, other?
> Who should develop it — DP, user, other?
> What level and type of support will be needed throughout?
> What design and development tools should be used?
> What implementation vehicle should be used?

In what technical environment should it be implemented?
How will it be maintained and by whom?

The answers to these questions will allow for the allocation of resources to the project to enable system development work to begin. It will also allow for a more accurate estimate of the costs of the system to be made prior to large-scale developmental work commencing.

This section has examined the overall process involved in requirements planning and we will now look at some of the techniques which can be applied throughout.

7.3   Requirements planning approaches

7.3.1   Critical success factors

The critical success factors (CSF) method was developed by Rockart (1979) and his colleagues at the Sloan School of Management. It focuses on the individual manager's perceptions of the few things which must go right in order to make the organization flourish and so can identify individual information needs. The method consists of three stages (fig. 7.5).

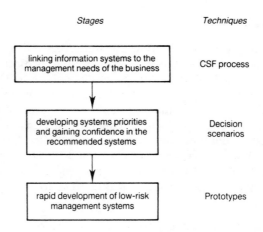

Fig. 7.5   The Critical Success Factors (CSF) method.

Definition of CSF factors can be very time consuming at first and, as they are very time dependent, need regular updating. The hardest part, however, is determining the prime measures to be applied against each factor as these are often subjective being based on management intuition or inspired guesses.

In order to help identify the CSF Rockart has shown that there are four sources:

Industry — CSFs relevant to any company in it

Company — large company actions generate CSFs for smaller companies in the industry

Environment — economy, consumer trends, politics etc.

Temporal — specific short term organizational factors

In addition he classifies two types of CSF — monitoring and building. Building CSFs is generally a top management concern. They not only vary from organization to organization but between managers and over time periods. It is an on-going process and consists of seven steps in three stages:

Stage 1

introductory workshops
CSF interviews
focusing workshop

Stage 2

development of system priorities
workshop on decision scenarios

Stage 3

prototype design
systems development, use and refinement

The method is quite widely used but may be more appropriate for large-scale organizations who have lost sight of their strategic directions. Interestingly, the application of the technique can show that the current IT direction is completely misplaced. A form of CSF applied to Warwickshire County Council in the UK, an employer of over 20 000 people and with a revenue of more than £235 million, identified only one of the 36 IT projects outstanding as coinciding with the 24 CSFs defined by senior management.

7.3.2 Business systems planning

Business systems planning (BSP) is another popular methodology developed and marketed by IBM. The basic philosophy is that data is a corporate resource and should be managed from an overall organizational viewpoint. The method is again biased to the large-scale MIS type of system development and is carried out within the structural framework illustrated in fig. 7.6.

We have experience of applying this technique in the Social Services Department of a large authority. A major advantage in this type of study, where individuals are not specifically aware of a need to share information in a

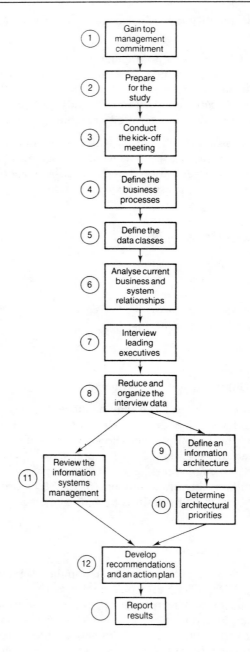

Fig. 7.6 Business Systems Planning (BSP) framework.

formal manner, is that BSP wonderfully focuses the mind on data and from there one can identify the relationships between data classes and formal processes. Figure 7.7 provides an example of one of the matrices produced during the study.

DATA CLASS

PROCESS	Clients	Referrals	Services	Costs	Employees	Voluntary agencies	Legislation	Budgets	Plans	Facilities/resources	National statistics
Strategic planning			U	U				U	C		U
Organizational analysis									U		
Strategic review and control								U	U		
Financial planning	U			U	U			U/C	C		
Budget acquisition			U	U				C			
Resource allocation				C					U	U/C	
Personnel planning	U		U		C			U	U		
Staff development			U		U				U/C		
Administration		U	U	U				U	U	U	
Community operations	U/C	U	U			C	U			U	
Social work operations	U/C	C	U/C				U			U	
Public relations	C		U				U			U	
Research			U		U	U/C	C				U/C
Service monitoring and control		U	U					U	U		C

Services { Administration, Community operations, Social work operations, Public relations }

U = Usage
C = Creation

Fig. 7.7 Data class by process showing data creation and usage: the processes are arranged in the life cycle sequence of the key resources.

Both BSP and CSF are very much the techniques employed by a large organization when they move into the integration stage described by Nolan (1979). Their large investment in and exploitation of IT may now be obscuring the route to increased productivity and there is a need to return to the basic strategic objectives of the organization before attempts are made to develop an integrated network of information services at all levels.

7.3.3 Information economics

Unfortunately, many things in life come down to a cost–benefit analysis approach. This is especially true of organizational investments. We must evaluate proposed systems against the expected rate of return. Most organizations use very simple cost–benefit approaches based loosely on the return-on-investment capital budgeting model which ignores other non-monetary dimensions. Information economics is an approach developed by Parker & Benson (1988) which tries to address these issues. Managers are allowed to select among IS investment possibilities by evaluating each project's perceived contribution to the corporate goals. Information economics uses the following techniques:

Cost/benefit analysis
Standard CBA is effective when dealing with cost displacement or cost avoidance issues and useful for tactical planning.

Value linking and value acceleration
Value linking and acceleration analysis are techniques to assess costs that enable benefits to be achieved in other departments — via a ripple effect (linking), or quicker receipt of benefits (acceleration).

Value restructuring
Value restructuring analysis assists in estimating the effects of modifying an existing job function. It calculates the value of employee/department contribution.

Innovation and investment monitoring
Innovation and investment valuation is useful for new, unprecedented applications of IT, since it considers the value and benefit of gaining and sustaining competitive advantage, the risk and cost of being first, and the risk and cost of failure.

Information economics expands the traditionally limited view of economic benefits; it shifts the focus to value and beyond the traditional CBA definition of cost-reduction to include enhanced view of return on investment, strategic match, competitive advantage, management information, competitive response, and strategic IS architecture. When combined, these six classes of benefit provide an appropriate method of assessing the importance of benefits previously classed as intangible. It is not sufficient, however, fully to define value in order to make the best choices among IS projects. We also need to consider the full dimensions of cost to include risk and uncertainty. Information economics recognizes five classes: strategic uncertainty, organizational risk, IS infrastructure risk, definitional uncertainty and technological uncertainty. These basically assess whether the IS is associated with a high risk business strategy; depends on new or untested business skills, management experience or capabilities; requires a high degree of the entire IS organization support; has vague specifications; and is using untried and untested technology.

Information economics is, on one hand, a set of simple computational tools to rank costs and benefits. But it also provides a real assessment of risk and in so doing provides a powerful framework for analyzing and allocating resources to support business strategies and performance.

This may not be the answer for everyone. Indeed, it is impossible to apply unless the IT strategy is directly linked to corporate strategy. It is also a set of techniques which can only be used effectively with the full cooperation of all the personnel involved — users, IS and IT specialists, finance and accounting advisers and top management.

There are a number of variations on this type of approach and some specific versions tailored for particular applications' markets such as Sassoni's approach to cost–benefit analysis for office automation systems.

7.3.4 Portfolio selection

IS applications are investments and also products of development. Like investments they provide more or less of return, and like products they have a life cycle. Like both, the range of applications possessed and possible can be considered as a portfolio. McFarlan & McKenney (1983) propose a matrix (fig. 7.8) for considering the portfolio as a whole and to position the company's systems. This matrix relates the impact of IT on the industry to the degree of computerized IS penetration in the organization. It is also useful, however, to consider the actual position of a specific application area on the matrix. Ward's variation on the matrix is shown in fig. 7.9.

The correlation of these matrices to the Boston Consulting Group (1970) square has already been given in fig. 7.4 where the current 'cash cows' are the profit-earning factory systems, those important for the future are the 'star'

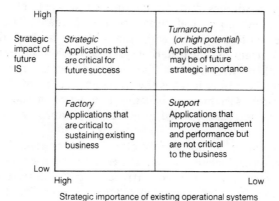

Fig. 7.8 Matrix relating the importance of IT within a particular industry to the penetration of computerized IS within a particular organization.

Strategic	Turnaround
CENTRALLY PLANNED Leading edge	LEADING EDGE FREE MARKET Centrally planned
MONOPOLY Scarce resource	SCARCE RESOURCE Free market Necessary evil
Factory	Support

Fig. 7.9   A variation of Fig. 7.8 showing the actual position of a specific application area on the matrix.

strategic systems and there are uncertainties involved in the 'problem children' turnaround applications. 'Dogs' and support systems are alike in the sense that they should only be allocated resources sparingly. Now, just as in the BCG square, applications, like products, evolve through the life cycle and will move around the matrix. So, a turnaround system can become a strategic application and, in turn, a factory system generating the high return that every organization looks for and which underwrites more risky ventures. Similarly 'problem children' can be worse than 'dogs' or they can turn into them. This is the portfolio risk.

In the IS matrix, the importance of experience in developing and sustaining complex and critical systems is as important as generating benefits for investment, otherwise, the organization will not be able to tackle the more problematic advanced systems successfully.

Strategic and turnaround systems demand a high level of resources and cannot afford to be drained by resources going into factory and support. In the 1960s turnaround applications were in the realm of payroll and accounts, demanding vast resources and no guaranteed success. Now they are the support systems with no critical impact on the company. The 1970s was the decade of the on-line system with the airlines leading the field. The strategically important on-line ordering systems which were spawned in almost every other walk of life are now the standard factory systems. It will be interesting to see how long it takes the strategic systems of the 1980s such as electronic transfer systems to become the *passé* mode of the 1990s. Undoubtedly, the increasing speed in technology improvement can lead to a short life cycle.

The portfolio choice is not simply one of cost or risk. It is also one of balance. We need sufficient factory systems to generate cash to invest in turnaround systems and we need sufficient strategic systems to generate factories. The specific balance selected will very much reflect the awareness of the organization as to the strategic value of IT. It should also reflect an awareness of the need to keep abreast of IT state-of-the-art and to maintain a portfolio of technical skills within the IT development group. Tozer (1986) suggests that the need is answered by the 'information factory' which supports a portfolio of methods, skills, resources, tools, techniques and development vehicles. This will only be realistic if there is a well developed systems requirements development selection procedure. It is to this that we now turn our attention.

7.4   Systems requirements development selection

7.4.1   Overview

At this stage, we are concerned with the definition of the specific resources required to develop the system. This may not be at the level of the specific software package to be used out of a number of available packages in the organization, but it should at least identify the classification of tools involved. It should also identify the personnel requirements and the specific project management required over the development life. In order to do this we have to look at what the user wants to do — keep fig. 7.1 firmly in mind. We also need to know what particular tools and technology can do; we need to understand the different development methods which can be applied; and we also need to look at the management and organizational aspects involved. All of these are covered in detail in later chapters in this book and so at this stage we will merely provide an overview and look at the areas which must be considered with respect to the user, the development tools and the organization and management.

7.4.2   User considerations

Users, like organizations, come in all shapes and sizes and there is no guarantee that similar job titles will produce similar degrees of intelligence, skill or charm. What it may produce, however, is a similar level of respect towards that job role. It is therefore implicit that the manager as a user will have to be treated differently to the clerical worker. At the very simplest level, we have to classify users as managers, supervisors, clerical workers and operations staff. It is also advisable to have some special categories such as knowledge workers or experts and DP specialists (who are frequently the least tolerant users). In assessing software capabilities, we find that many menu-driven user-friendly packages find great disfavour with the 'expert' who prefers to get into the system and tailor-make his application.

We also need to know how integral the system is to the user's role. Will it form an indispensable part of the work operation or is it a minor support tool? Will the user interact on a regular basis or only occasionally?

It is then necessary to look at: the usage which will be made of the system such as the class of application and the type of requests which will be made;

the workload volume; the degree of integration and interdependence; the complexity of the application; the levels of integrity and recoverability expected; the expected lifetime and maintainence required. This will give us some basis for deciding whether the system has to be built to last and whether it is feasible for the user to develop it.

We must also look in detail at the characteristics of the data since increasingly this exists in forms other than conventional file form. It may be document based, computer based or in other electronically readable form. It may take the form of an existing model, possibly micro-based or be in graphical form. Apart from these physical characteristics we need to know whether it is shared and the degree of connectivity required. Finally, we need to get some idea of the type of data which we will be processing.

7.4.3 Development tools

This area covers: the selection of a specific product or service; the development vehicle; developer; development methodology, support style. Tozer relates this again to the portfolio concept where he suggests there is a need to steer a course between:

> Overusing one product and forcing it into too many areas (very few products are that versatile)
> Ending up with a large number of similar products, confused users and a proliferation of technical support

Figure 7.10 illustrates the tradeoff between ease of use and flexibility/power.

Ideally we need to build up our experience of software, in particular categories, and relate these to specific application types. Classifications of database or fourth-generation languages (4GL) could be categorized against mainframe or micro and then ranked against specific applications such as the decision support area for the user needs required.

7.4.4 Organization and management

Finally, we need to look at the requirements of the system for specific organizational objectives. There is no point in imposing formal DP organizational standards on a user-developed system.

Indeed, we may always question the need for heavily formalized structured approaches in a modern development environment.

The issues which have to be addressed are the roles and responsibilities of DP specialists and users throughout the lifecycle of the application development. It is also important to examine the extent of management and control which will be required and where this should come from both during the development cycle and over the lifetime of the application. Just as a portfolio of development techniques exist so there are many ways to provide

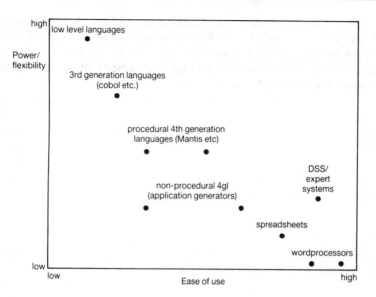

Fig. 7.10 There is generally a trade-off between ease of use and power.

organizational support. Increasingly popular is the idea of information centres which provide support and advice for user development and separate development centres for major DP developments. It can also be advisable to operate on-line help assistance for those urgent, but probably easy, queries.

7.5 Summary

This chapter has looked at the whole question of information systems requirements planning. This is not a one-off activity which is completed prior to the commencement of system development. Planning is an on-going process but so too are changes in requirements. We are not suggesting that the system can never be developed. Rather, it must be developed in a manner to allow for change and future enhancements.

There are many suggested approaches to the planning process, and many techniques which can be applied. Those which may work well within a large formalized organization structure such as a multinational bank are unlikely to be as effective in a small entrepreneurial investment broker, even though they may both make use of many of the same information services. People involved in planning for information technology usage in an organization must never underestimate the need for a full requirements analysis planning exercise to identify the specific approach which will be the best one for that particular situation.

Unfortunately, planning is the one thing we all find we never have time to do. It always has to wait until we have solved the latest crisis. This book is about how to avoid crisis and the first step is to recognize the importance of planning for the whole organization and the necessity of making IT planning an integral part of this overall strategy.

8   Information systems development strategies

8.1   Introduction

It is only in the last decade that alternatives have evolved to challenge the standard life cycle model of development of computer based systems. The proliferation of micros, development of application generators and evolution of end-user computing has rendered the formal structured approaches redundant for many applications.

This chapter will look at the many approaches which can be used and examine the situations in which such an approach can be appropriate. This will be insufficient unless accompanied by the appropriate management and organizational support models which are explored in depth in Part III.

8.2   Systems development cycle

8.2.1   Systems life cycle

In the 1960s, general unhappiness with the lack of structure in systems development environments saw emphasis being placed on formal standards and processes. Figure 8.1 is typical of the system development life cycle model which was enforced. Prominent support came from the government and military departments where the need for standardization of system products is at its greatest. The result was that professional practices became much more rigorous and an emphasis on quality rather than quantity was encouraged. It also had the effect, however, of polarizing development groups into specialist fields and giving the typical departmental organization chart of fig. 8.2.

Furthermore, it specifically introduced barriers between the users and the systems development groups and, in many ways, created a situation of distrust and unease from which we are still struggling to recover.

The life cycle model is one which is specifically oriented to the large centralized system development and in a revised form can still be applicable for this type of systems development. A common misinterpretation of the process from fig. 8.1 is to assume that the development is linear and indeed has

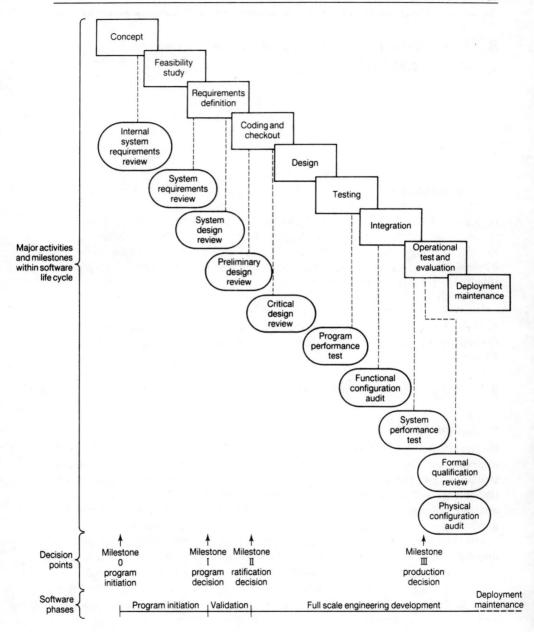

Fig. 8.1   *The systems development life cycle.*

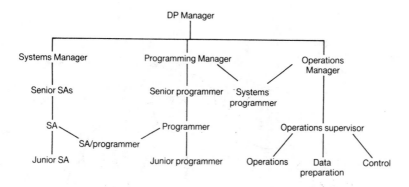

Fig. 8.2 DP departments have become polarized into a variety of specialist groups.

a single life. In fact, the model is iterative in nature and Aktas (1987) suggests this in a revised model depicting the cyclical nature where iteration of certain stages and between stages and over the whole process is anticipated (fig. 8.3).

In leaving this model we should also note the similarity to engineering models. This has had considerable influence on enhanced versions of the life cycle and, indeed, in many quarters the model is called the 'systems engineering' model.

8.2.2 Structured systems methods

The life cycle model emphasized technical expertise and created a large gap between the user and the system developer. As a result, the analysis of reasons for system failures or user dissatisfaction tended to suggest that insufficient understanding of the requirements had been obtained. The emphasis of the structured approaches has been in this area. The structured approach provides the analyst with tools and methodologies which formalize the requirements analysis process but, at the same time, provide a working interface with the user.

For the purpose of our overview discussion these methodologies are broken down as follows:

1. The incomplete
    Functional decomposition methodologies
    Data flow oriented methodologies
    Data structure oriented methodologies
2. The more complete
    Information engineering
    SSADM

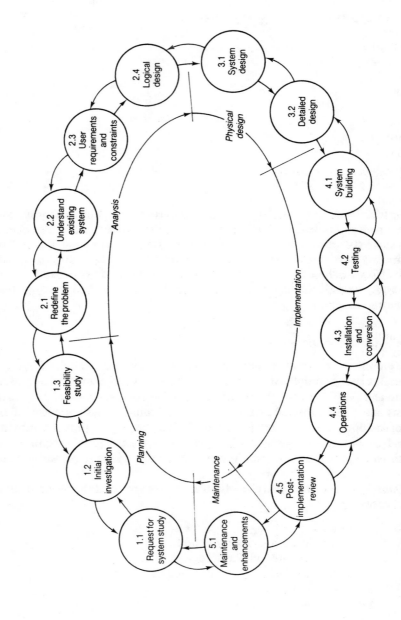

Fig. 8.3 Systems engineering model of the information systems life cycle.

The incomplete are those techniques which can be applied to a part of the overall system process and must normally interact with other development tools to complete the system. This does not mean to denigrate them. Rather the reverse, since they allow an organization to build up their own tool box as appropriate to the variety of applications and expertise involved.

Functional decomposition methods emphasize the relevant dissection of the system into smaller subsystems so that the resulting elementary systems are not so complex to understand, design and implement. System functions are considered the major concern, hence the name 'functional approach'. The most common examples are top-down and bottom-up approaches and the IBM documentation method HIPO (Hierarchy plus Input Process Output) supports this. Simple examples are shown in figs 8.4 and 8.5. All of these methods are decision analysis tools — they suggest which decisions to make first but they do not assist in how to make the decision. They are not primarily aimed at improving the analysis process, but rather at refining the design and documentation.

Data flow methods with the technique of data flow diagrams (fig. 8.6) are perhaps the best known of the structured techniques and come in a variety of forms such as the Yourdon & Constantine (1979), DeMarco (1978), and Gane & Sarson (1977) methods. These methods generally emphasize the characteristics of the data by using 'black box' processes (processes where procedures are not yet defused) and concentrating on the data flow logic between them. This process of structured systems analysis can be defined as the use of data flow diagrams, data dictionary, structured English, decision tables and decision trees to build a structured system specification.

They provide a communications mechanism between the analyst and the users. They also provide a precise means of recording the specification, so that the design can be translated into computer code and implemented. They do not provide the means to effect the implementation. Their strength lies in the analysis and design of the data and the hierarchical process used which allows the analyst to concentrate on a small part of the whole at any one time. A major disadvantage is the vast amount of data which may need to be recorded, duplicated and controlled. During the life of the system this will require constant changing if the organizational processes change.

Data structure methods can have largely the same comments made about them. These methodologies mainly emphasize the output/input data structures of the system. The functional relations between the modules or elements of the system and their decomposition are then realized in terms of the system structure. We have chosen to include two somewhat different approaches under this heading as examples: the Warnier/Orr approach to structured requirements definition (Warnier, 1981; Orr, 1977, 1981) and the Jackson approach (Jackson Systems Design or JSD) to systems design (Jackson, 1983). This will also be related to the entity-relationship model which is a logical model used in database analysis as well as in the design of information systems.

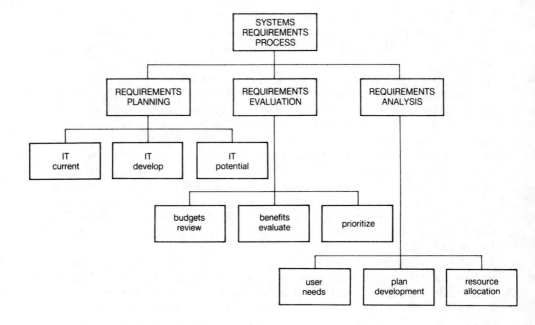

Fig. 8.4   The functional approach to systems analysis.

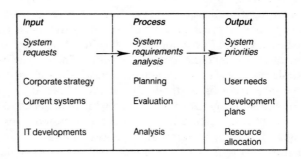

Fig. 8.5   Hierarchy plus Input Process Output (HIPO): requirements analysis process.

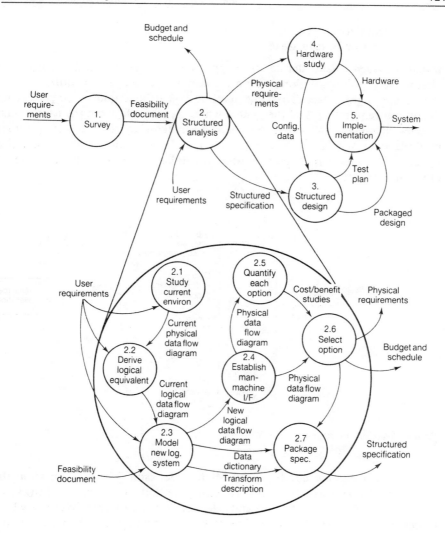

Fig. 8.6 A typical data flow diagram.

The principle followed by Orr is that system specification and design are derived from output requirements. The primary tool used is the Warnier/Orr diagram which is a series of brackets which can represent system, program and data hierarchies. Figure 8.7 provides a simple example. A second tool is the entity diagram, which charts information flows (outputs) between entities (organizational units). There are two major stages:

Logical definition stage
Physical definition stage

which between them define the application functions and results and
alternative physical solutions with a recommended course of action.

This is a highly 'user-satisfying' method given the emphasis on producing
the output requirements of the system which is, after all, what the user wants.
It does, however, fall down on the data-integration side. It can produce
multiple data files for one application and largely ignores the interactive
updating of files which may continually take place without recourse to
physical outputs.

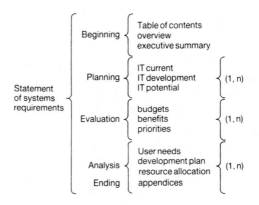

Fig. 8.7   Warnier/Orr diagram.

JSD is a technique developed by Michael Jackson following on from the
success of JSP as a structured programming method. It uses many of the same
constructs — sequence iteration and selection in the structure diagrams which
represent hierarchies of actions. The overall philosophy is to provide a model
based on the real world and one in which the time dimension is an integral part
of the model. The total process extends over six steps:

entity action step, entity structure step, initial model step, function step,
system timing step and implementation step.

This is a very 'elegant' method but, for many, introduces too many new
concepts. A simple example is the definition of an entity which in Jackson
terms is not the entity in a database but something which must exist in real life
outside the system. In a computer system, for example, the error report is not
an entity but a system output. For each entity, we have to define a set of
actions which must take place at a point in time. Figure 8.8 gives a simplified

example of a structure diagram for the entity 'system proposals file' which is produced during the requirements planning stage.

JSD is a method which is particularly suited to run-time control systems where the emphasis is on the time dimension and where control is a priority. It can, however, be very time consuming during the development process.

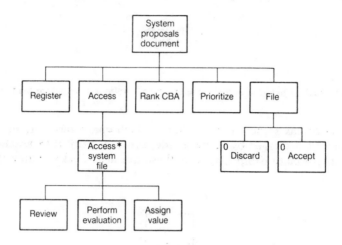

Fig 8.8 A simple structure diagram for the systems proposals file entity.

Entity–relationship (E–R) models have three elements:

> entities, relationships, descriptions of entities and relationships of their attributes or values.

This is very similar to part of the Jackson methodology but concentrates specifically on the third element and so is of particular value in the definition of data relationships for database design.

An entity is a person, place, thing, event or concept about which information is recorded. In the E–R diagram it is shown as a rectangle. Relationships may exist between entities as one-to-one, one-to-many, and many-to-many and are represented by a diamond shaped box as shown in fig. 8.9. This shows work and project leader as two different relationships between two entity types, analyst and application project. It also shows that there are N application projects, M analysts work for these projects and each project has only one leader. Also an analyst can be the leader of many projects. From the diagram we can see that project leader relationship between analyst and project is one-to-many, and work relationship analyst and project is many-to-many, meaning that each project may consist of several analysts and each analyst may be concerned with more than one project.

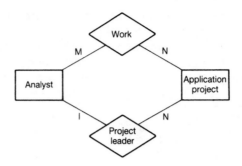

Fig. 8.9   Relationships between entities may be one-to-one, one-to-many, or many-to-many.

Every entity has some basic attributes which characterize it. For instance analyst may be described by name, grade, previous project experience and so on. In Entity–Relationship diagrams these are described as value types (fig. 8.10).

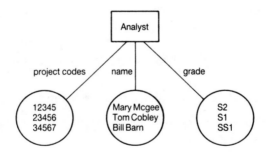

Fig. 8.10   Value types in an Entity-Relationship diagram.

These examples are only a limited selection of some of the many structured tools available. Each of them have their advocates and their own unique characteristics which may make them the most appropriate tool for a specific application. No IT development centre wants to cope with them all, however, and one answer has been to develop more-embracing methodologies.

More complete tools include life cycle development vehicles such as information engineering and methods which have been designed to amalgamate a number of existing tools such as the UK government standard SSADM.

Information engineering was first described by Clive Finkelstein and then later further developed by James Martin (Martin & Finkelstein, 1981). It is a set of disciplines which effectively encompasses the design of information systems which satisfy an organization's mission and objectives. The technique allows us to derive data requirements from management objectives, convert the raw data into stable data structures and relationships in a data model, take into account data existing in present systems and build processes and procedures from the data model. It specifically interfaces with corporate planning and strategic requirements planning. The user plays the key role throughout the system specification and design process. The method covers the following areas:

Strategic requirements planning
Information analysis with data modelling and canonical synthesis
Procedure formation
Data use analysis
Implementation strategies
Distribution analysis
Physical database design
Fourth-generation languages (4GL)
Program specification synthesis

The relationship of these in the overall model is shown in fig. 8.11.

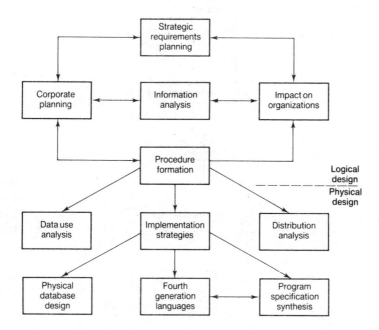

Fig. 8.11 The relationship of the methods used in information engineering.

This method concentrates on data and data relationships. It is an ideal approach where the integration of data producing stable, logical organizational databases is of prime concern. This is also a drawback, however, as the emphasis is on stability and the static data model is not a suitable one for dynamic systems such as run-time control systems. It is also a very comprehensive system which specifically orients towards the use of fourth-generation languages (4GL) although formal program specifications can be produced. This method requires a total commitment from the organization and the system users.

Structured systems analysis and design methods come in various forms. SSADM is a UK government standard methodology but there are many lookalike versions such as LSDM. It consists of six stages (fig. 8.12), and succeeds in combining a number of techniques in an almost bewildering overkill.

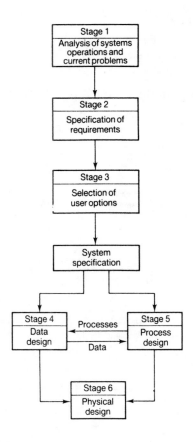

Fig. 8.12   The six stages of SSADM.

The major techniques used are:

> logical data structuring techniques, data flow diagrams, entity life histories, process outlines, third normal form (TNF) analysis, 1st cut data design, 1st cut programs and physical design control,

providing three views of the system

> the structure of the data, the data flows and the chronology of the processing.

These partial views are combined as part of the overall iterative process and so should provide a more comprehensive view of the system than that supported by only one of these tools. The method provides: an integrated set of structural standards with explicitly defined tasks, interfaces and products; procedural standards with useable techniques and tools accompanied by detailed rules and guidelines; and documentation standards.

This is a method for the brave! It is also probably exactly the type of structured method required by a huge organization comprising many disparate parts where control will always remain a major issue of concern. It is not, however, an easy tool although it can be an extremely powerful one.

Both of our examples of the more complete are supported by automated development tools, discussed in the next section, and it is this feature which may be the longer term factor to promote their widespread use.

Contingent with the use of all structured methods are three goals:

A more disciplined approach
Reliability and error prevention/detection/correction
Efficient use of resources

While these goals have been achieved to some extent, it is in the area of nontraditional development where the greatest impact has been made. This is particularly true of the prototyping approach made possible with the development of 4GLs and application generators.

8.2.3   Prototyping

Prototyping is a totally different approach from the traditional life cycle development using different tools, skills and procedures. It consists of the development of a live working system which acts as a model system on which to test our assumptions. The essence of prototyping is fast, inexpensive system building as part of an iterative design process where each new prototype will progressively perform more of the required system functions as user and designer together evaluate the match of information requirements against the latest model. The real beauty of this method, of course, is that the definition of the systems requirements is part of the on-going prototype development. The problem may be knowing when to say enough. Naumann & Jenkins (1982) define four steps in the process (fig. 8.13) and suggest that there are four components in the ideal software prototyping environment: a 4GL or application generator tool; well managed data resources for easy access to corporate data; a user who has a problem, has considered the idea of using the new tool, knows the functional area well and seeks assistance from data processing; and a prototype builder — an information systems professional versed in using the various tools and with an understanding of the corporate data resources. Unsurprisingly, the ideal size for a prototyping team is two people.

This might suggest that the method is only suitable for small system development but there are several uses of the technique.

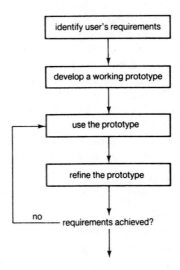

Fig. 8.13   Four steps in prototyping.

Developing the user requirement
It can provide either a simplified model of the whole system to clarify user requirements or highlight a specific part such as the main screen interfaces for the user. It may even build all the functions of the system but using techniques which would not be replicated in the working model possibly for reasons of performance or security.

As part of the life cycle
It may be used to design the system and test the feasibility of the design before being implemented using standard software techniques. Figure 8.14 gives an example of how this can be incorporated into the standard life cycle model.

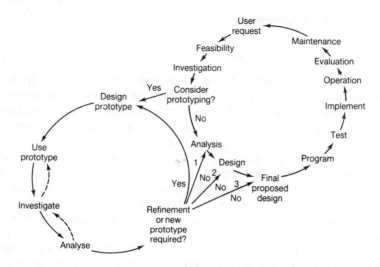

Fig. 8.14   Prototyping as part of the standard life cycle model.

As an end-product developer

In the evolutionary model, it may produce parts of the system or the total product in stages.

What does prototyping do for us? To start with, it generally gets a system up and running a lot faster. It also normally produces a very happy and contented user. Coincidentally, it improves the productivity rates in the information system development group and cuts down the backlog. So why have we spent so long looking at other development methods! The answer is that 4GL is not a panacea for all problems. It is generally not such a flexible development language as the more traditional languages and it is insufficiently specialized for some of the more rigorous software development projects. It is also true that 4GLs are heavy users of resources and can lead to highly inefficient processing. Finally there are problems with the development cycle. Prototypes may not fully explore or develop the system requirements and, in the excitement of a working system, standard practice such as the development of some sound system documentation, may fly out the window.

Our solution is to revert to the factory development approach and to suggest that there is room in an organization for both traditional and 'quick and easy' development methods. The choice of which structured approach to select (if appropriate) may be largely a question of the skills or tools which are available in the organization and we shall look at these in greater detail in the next section.

8.3   Systems development tools

8.3.1   Software development choices

There are a number of choices to be made here. The first is not to develop software at all with the wide variety of software packages available on the market this is often the only sensible solution, especially, for the small business user. Considerations to be taken into account are discussed in chapter 10 and elsewhere. Unfortunately, it is not always a successful solution.

Assuming, that we are going to develop our own software, the choice reduces to two: do we use an application development tool (ADT) or do we not. This question might at first seem something of a nonsense since all software tools are ADTs. But the term has come to mean something more specialized and refers to the range of 4GLs, database products and workbenches available. If we do not use an ADT we must use a standard programming language such as Cobol or C. The choice between these is normally straightforward since languages have generally been developed as application or environment specific: Cobol is regarded as a tool for the development of business applications while C is more regularly used for systems software. Where there is no obvious dividing line then it is usually the language best supported which is selected. The general trend, however, in commercial programming is towards application generators and this is easily explained by the productivity improvements which normally result.

8.3.2   Fourth generation languages

There are a large number of tools which may be described under this umbrella:

PC based tools such as Lotus 1-2-3, d Base III, Symphony
Query languages/report generators such as RPG-III, SQL, Intellect
Decision support generators such as system W, Express, FCS/EPS
Procedural 4GLs such as Mantis, CSP, Link
Applications generators such as Focus, Nomad, UFO
Expert system generators such as Personal Consultant

Indeed, there may be many more as both the technology and the terminology are in a constant state of flux. The overall objectives of all of these tools is to speed up the development process and, in so doing, to extend the development of the system into the user domain (Lehman & Wetherbee 1989).

A good, general purpose 4GL is likely to have several components. Those used most often are non-procedural in nature. These non-procedural components are typically backed up by a few procedural components which are usually only used to define the last 10% or so of the application. Most successful 4GLs are designed to be used in combination with a data dictionary and relational database. Both these technologies possess inherent characteristics which speed up the development process. The non-procedural elements may include: data dictionary, screen painter, report generator, dialogue specifier, complex decisions or conditions, administrative aid, guidance system, end user query and reporting languages, and graphics as well as the regular facilities expected of any modern software development tool such as back-up, security and maintenance.

Typical developments such as Application Factory (RTZ) contain a data dictionary, screen, report and menu generators, business graphics and an end-user query system. In addition, the latest release includes an implementation of action diagramming, an information engineering technique as described in the last section. This is a typical development for the future with the long-term survival of 4GL products depending on the extent to which they can integrate with design and analysis tools. This may make it realistic to build complete computer systems automatically from information gathered during analysis and design.

8.3.3   Automated design development

In the last few years, major resources have been devoted to the task of automating the automators. This has produced a series of tools variously described as analyst workbenches (AWB), or integrated project support environments (IPSE). In its simplest form an AWB may be considered as an electronic drawing board which supports shapes equating to the diagramming standards of the methodologies and is capable of drawing relationship lines. Most of the products are, however, very much more comprehensive. Apart from the diagrammatic support offered to the methodology, facilities such as data dictionaries are automatically generated along with a design database. A popular AWB is Intech's Excelerator. The basic product has support for a number of graphics techniques — data flow diagrams, structure charts, logical data models, entity relationship models and structure diagrams, and within these a number of commonly used notations are supported. All the information is stored in a project dictionary where it may be automatically reported and analysed to ensure consistency and completeness. In addition, files may be exported to other environments allowing Excelerator to interface with other development systems such as 4GLs and databases. This illustrates the potential for automation of the whole development process, although at present this is far from complete.

Certainly refinement of these tools will revolutionize the work of the information systems developer and also impact on productivity. Most suppliers suggest a minimum figure of 40% increase. The real impact will only be felt, however, when complete integration is achieved with software development. This may take some time when we consider the variety of software available on the market.

8.4   Systems development process

8.4.1   Information factory

A variety of development methods and tools are available for the systems development process. How do we ensure that the appropriate approach is used in a particular application? A sensible solution is the development of the information factory concept. Tozer (1986) suggests that it should support the following primary functions.

A clearing house where all requests are vetted and allocated to the most effective development role and method.

'Arm's length' end-user computing, by those suitably qualified and experienced.

Closely supported end-user computing.

A rapid development shop where more complex but urgent needs can be met by a joint development.

A more conventional development centre where major applications can be built.

An architecture definition and control group to maintain the overall 'blueprint' of the organization's information systems.

This would clearly need a portfolio of methods, skills, resources and tools as described in the preceding sections. It would, therefore need to establish criteria to:

Select development approaches for the system

Assign development to user

These would be related to the requirements for speed, cost, control, quality and flexibility of the system. A number of alternatives will be evaluated against these criteria and selected according to the priorities of the organization, and specific users experience.

There is a major area of development still untouched: the question of how we deal with existing systems for maintenance and redevelopment.

8.4.2   Maintenance and redevelopment

Many DP managers feel trapped by their existing systems. In the early 1980s when 4GLs appeared on the market the most common excuse given for not introducing them to the organization was the existing commitment to Cobol. While the pattern is changing, there are still a great number of applications in existence using outdated techniques which cost a large amount to maintain. Sprague & McNurlin (1986) suggest five options for improving old applications

Restructuring. Clean up the internal structure of an application so that it is more efficient, more maintainable and more understandable.

Refurbishing. Add some facility or functionality to an application with enhanced input, output or data handling capacity.

Rejuvenating. Add enough function to an application to give it increased value to the firm.

Rewriting. A complete rewrite using current development methods and tools.

Replacing. A complete replacement with a purchased software product or package.

All of these are viable alternatives but the selection of a particular option should relate to the impact of this system on the overall corporate strategy. It must also relate to the effect it may also be having on the effectiveness of the IT strategy. The cost of maintaining a system with out-of-date techniques, especially where there is a need for connectivity with other systems, may in itself justify a complete replacement. The maintenance and redevelopment process should be conducted as a result of the regular review of the systems in operation and, as shown in fig. 8.1, provide feedback directly into the strategic planning model of the systems requirements planning process.

8.5 Summary

This chapter has examined the various ways by which a system may be developed or re-developed. It specifically suggests that the organization require criteria to select a product or service, development vehicle, developer, development methodology and support style, and that this can best be achieved by adopting an information factory approach to the development process. The other very important part of the process is the development of the information technology strategy in line with the overall information systems requirements of the organization. It is this we will look at in the following chapter.

9   Strategies for information technology

9.1   Introduction

In many organizations the ability to assimilate and implement information technology lags far behind the available opportunities offered by the use of IT. It is important that new technologies are adopted in the most efficient and effective manner to enable the achievement of corporate goals through implementation of new technology in an optimum fashion. The most important issue in technological assimilation is probably the exercise of control over its diffusion through the organization so that a balance is struck between stagnation and uncontrolled adoption of the newest technology.

Managers need vision to articulate a view of the future which must be broad, flexible, and simple enough for everyone to remember and follow. Technology is changing too fast to be specific. Managers must be aware that managing information as an asset is important and understand the importance of the integration of business and information systems planning. Many senior managers do not need to be convinced of the value of information. Their problem is often that they do not know how to go about searching out information technology. There is no specific solution. Innovation and ideas can not be pre-engineered. Most of the time they are spontaneous and unplanned.

In the next section a model is described which has been created to show the stages of evolution many companies go through in the implementation of IT. Learning from others' experience is often very useful in avoiding reinventing the wheel. In his book *The information weapon*, Synnott (1987) describes some strategies used by a number of companies interested in getting to grips with the use of IT and trying to get the best out of the technology. He stresses the importance of the education of senior managers to promote better understanding of IT and describes this as a critical success factor. Large corporations such as Citibank and Kodak apportion funds specifically to allow groups to look at new ventures in the use of information services.

9.2   Planning for information technology — what to expect

McFarlane & McKenney (1982) have created a procedural model to enable organizations to manage the diffusion of new technologies. This model identifies four stages of the innovation process. It is of interest since it gives strategic planners some food for thought and helps to prepare organizations for potential problems depending on their own organization's current state of development. The four phases are as follows.

Phase 1: Technology identification and investment
At this stage users have no experience of using IT. This appears to be a crucial phase. Participants can often fail to grasp long-term implications and benefits of the new technology. If they have a bad experience in trying out something new for the first time they may well form negative opinions which severely impede progress and adoption of new possibilities. A person who has no experience of the value of using word processing can easily be put off the idea for a long time by unfriendly commands. When we first learned one of the most popular microcomputer-based word-processing packages, we certainly found that typing 'control' (identified in the training guide as ^) simultaneously with K followed by D was not exactly an easy way to remember how to save work. Many users have persevered with this horrendously unfriendly user interface because the software is really very useful when you have hacked your way through the jungle of exotic commands and achieved what you want. Not only does badly designed software put people off and create negative impressions, it also deters them from migrating on to newer and better products which appear later. Many users are reluctant to write off their hard-won expertise as they think (erroneously) that having taken so long to learn to use one word processor, it is likely to take roughly the same effort to learn another.

Phase 2: Experimentation and adaptation
In this phase users learn through using computers and become more aware of the possibilities offered by new technologies. With this comes an increased demand for their use. Requirements for staff, costs, and the requisite skills are of concern at this stage of development. Strategic applications within an organization will evolve and be identified during this phase, often differing very significantly from what was originally envisaged. Very often IT is brought in to an organization in a piecemeal way. A corporate champion in senior management spearheads the drive and perhaps different departments acquire separate systems which are appropriate to their individual needs. Examples of several word processing systems being used simultaneously in one office are common. When the first one was bought it may well have been a turnkey system which stored documents in 8″ floppy diskettes. A year or so later microcomputers which could be used as wordprocessors and for much more besides came along with $5\frac{1}{4}$″ disks. Later systems were brought which used $3\frac{1}{2}$″ disks. It is not at all uncommon for organizations to have several totally incompatible systems being used in one office. Rapid developments in

hardware and ever more powerful word processing software makes it difficult to avoid this situation, despite the undesirability of this in the day to day operation.

A real life example illustrates how this situation can develop. An excellent Wang dedicated wordprocessing system was in use (with 8 ″ disks) for several years, at a time when there were still three or four times as many electric typewriters in the office as there were word processors. Gradually, as time went on, several Wang microcomputers were acquired as dedicated word processing systems which used $5\frac{1}{4}$″ disks. In the publically funded organization where this was happening write-off periods are fixed by the accountants. Equipment must be used for a certain number of years before money can be spent on replacing it. This meant that the microcomputer Wang word processors were used in parallel with the older large format Wang machines till the latter could be written off.

Problems of document transfer from one disk format to another were handled with careful planning but again technological change was posing a new dilemma. All the users of the typing pool had now been provided with their own personal IBM compatible computer on their desk. There was not enough money till the next financial year to install a network so the machines were all standing alone — temporarily. Users now started to draft documents on their own machines and pass the disk to the typing pool for further processing, letter quality printing, and so on. Individual users typed their work using a wide variety of word processing packages — Word Perfect, Symphony, WordStar, PC Write and so on. To allow formatted documents to freely pass from the users' computers to the typing pool and back again meant the adoption of standard software — and more retraining for either the staff of the typing pool or the users of their services or both.

It was clearly impossible to expect a typing pool to be able to handle several word processors with equal competence so Multimate was chosen as the office standard. This meant that files could pass between the Wang microcomputers in the typing pool running Wang word-processing software, and the IBM PCs in the staff offices using Multimate. The files were all still in a machine readable format when eventually the typing pool Wang machines were phased out and replaced with the same IBM PC compatibles that the staff used. The installation of the network linking all the staff offices with the typing pool would present few problems since all elements in the system were fully compatible.

What has been described in this example is the evolution through phase 2 into phase 3.

Phase 3: Rationalization and management control
This seems to be a consolidation phase where short-term efficiencies are a goal, often achieved by means of management control. Staff expertise and skill in using IT consolidates and reaches generally acceptable levels, creating possibilities for further projects and cost-effective use of IT. This is a phase of

confidence in the new technology together with (or created by) increasing ability to use it. Here are two examples of how companies manage their IT planning at this phase.

In one instance a small Resources Committee was established which controlled the equipment budget for a department. The amount of money in the budget was known at the beginning of the financial year and proposals for future funding could be passed to the central management during one financial year to allow rolling plans to be implemented into the next year. Requests for hardware and software were solicited from all staff and were welcome at any time. They had to be costed and justified in terms of detailed proposed usage. Evaluation was also encouraged by allowing requests for the purchase of new products to be granted on condition that a report on the product was produced and circulated to all interested staff for their consideration within a short period. This enabled many staff to learn from the work of their colleagues and encouraged the implementation of new ideas widely throughout the staff as all were kept informed of the potential value of newly evaluated products relative to the specific needs of that department.

Another model was adopted by an engineering consultancy firm where a computer manager was responsible for providing technical and accounting services for the organization. A Computer Users Committee was formed to bridge the gap between the computer expertise in the Data Processing Department and the technical needs of the engineers using the systems. New packages essential to the technical needs of the engineers in the company could then be thoroughly evaluated in terms of their functionality. At the same time checks could be made on important aspects of decision making. Could the new packages run on existing equipment? What was the effect on response time on other applications? Were new 32-bit workstations really essential? Could a cheaper solution be adopted which would allow the packages to run on existing 16-bit computers with the addition of extra processors? Could the company's mainframe be the appropriate machine to run the new application?

From these two examples readers may see how confidence and skill in an organization increase over time as ways of coping with the increasing use of IT are found which best fit with company requirements.

Phase 4: Widespread technology transfer

The learning phase for the organization appears to be over by now and there exists significant corporate expertise enabling the spread of IT throughout the whole organization.

This is an interesting model. According to Raho *et al.* (1987) the model can be viewed as 'forming the connection between the micro and the macro aspects of organizational assimilation'. From the standpoint of the organization this model suggests that the process of adopting IT is extremely complex with the realization that an organization must go through a (somewhat painful) learning process.

In an interesting study conducted by Raho *et al.* (1987), problems encountered in personal computer integration were identified in a survey of membership of the Data Processing Management Association (DPMA). The nature of the problems enabled the researchers to classify the respondents' state of IT assimilation according to the four phases of McFarlan & McKenney's model. Problems associated with the first phase of assimilation related to lack of management attention, support for users, official policies, and the rate of technological change affecting both hardware and software. This illustrated a basic lack of understanding of the capability of a personal computer and how it might affect the organizations. It relates to the initial consideration in the model on technology identification and investment with particular reference to building staff skills.

As assimilation within an organization progressed to the second phase, the type of problems which were encountered became associated with problems of organizational constraints in areas like finance, manpower and hardware together with a diffusion of responsibility and user perceptions of personal computers. Specific concerns included users having a stand-alone mentality regarding personal computing, lack of clear definition on what should be personal computer or mainframe functions and general usage of equipment. One director of information systems was quoted as saying that 'User needs outstrip available solutions'. As user awareness increases they realize all they did not know at phase one. Technical issues are better understood and previous experiences are used to make judgements and implement pilot projects.

By phase 3 problems encountered relate to operational policy development such as establishing guidelines for the acquisition and use of particular hardware and software technologies with a view to: maintaining cost effectiveness; maintaining compatibility to mainframes and between personal computers; applicability of software; and issues such as software licensing. This is a standardization phase when problems created by developments from earlier phases can be cleared up with the greater expertise now gained and future strategies can be worked out with more confidence in establishing useful and acceptable guidelines. Controls to monitor growth can be developed.

In the fourth phase when widespread adoption of technology is apparent, types of problems (if any) deal with issues like data security and end-user education. The whole organization at this state is benefitting from a widespread understanding of how technology can be best used.

9.3 The relevant issues

9.3.1 Strategic

Having discussed the phases one can expect in adopting IT within an organization it is appropriate to reiterate briefly the strategic issues related to IT planning. Every organization, whether profit-making or not, will consider

COPING WITH STRATEGIC ISSUES
ALIGN 'IT' AND ORGANIZATION PLANNING
ADOPT COST EFFECTIVE STRATEGEMS
AVOID 'INFORMATION OVERLOAD'
SUPPORT FUNCTIONS OF THE ORGANIZATION
SUPPORT NEEDS OF USERS
SUPPORT FORMS INFORMATION USERS NEED

cost control and improved productivity as heading the list of management priorities. Together with the ability to respond to the needs of those it serves this will enable an organization to increase its competitiveness and growth potential in an environment which supports better quality decision making.

In implementing any IT policy decisions, the major strategic issues which concern the organization as a whole cannot be separated from those relevant to any IT planning. The IT strategy has to match up the functions within the organization which will use information technology — the needs of the users and the various forms the information takes — and put together an electronic solution which both aligns with the strategic goals of the organization and also facilitates them. Cost-effective stratagems should be developed to allow the adoption of new technology as it appears while avoiding the creation of a situation of 'information overload' in which it becomes necessary to know about or refer to an ever-increasing amount of internally and externally generated information.

Fortunately, suppliers of IT devices and services are also aware of the relevant strategic issues which should concern users. This is not a surprising situation since the suppliers most likely to succeed in business will be those who offer the best services and best understand their users problems and needs. This has led to developments in integrated office systems encouraging the migration of technology from the Electronic Data Processing (EDP) department to the desk top. Support is provided for the central goal of providing decision makers with better information. The emphasis is on quality, not quantity, of information.

In planning for the adoption of IT it is imperative to avoid computerizing any badly designed system which already exists. It is also vital to strive to maintain flexibility. This has been shown in studies conducted in the UK to be essential to achieving the maximum benefits of the use of IT.

9.3.2 Tangible and intangible benefits

An important benefit of the use of IT is that there will usually be a reduction in the number of support staff needed. In most organizations this can be reached

---

COPING WITH TANGIBLE AND INTANGIBLE BENEFITS

EMPHASIZE BETTER QUALITY

CONSIDER ADDED VALUE BENEFITS

ADAPT TO LOCAL CIRCUMSTANCES

OPPORTUNITY HOURS

---

through natural wastage. More important benefits should be clearly understood to lie in the better quality of work which can be achieved (for example through the use of word processing, local area networks etc.) thus giving added value benefits to the users. The improvement in quality of work made possible by the integration and implementation of IT into an organization should be strongly emphasized as an advantage to be gained with probably lesser emphasis on any cost savings through reduced staffing levels.

However, this justification may be different from one country to another depending on the employment situation. In Hong Kong for example there is full employment, a situation which is not new to the territory. This means that due to a scarcity of skills in certain sectors, entrepreneurs have no choice but to adopt labour-saving technology since they are faced with a labour shortage which means that there are simply not enough people to do all the work required to meet full order books. With little fear of redundancy, workers will be much less reluctant to embrace fully the advantages of new technology. In other economic climates where fears of unemployment are common, job security is very important because many workers know that if their present job disappears they will not easily find another one nearby. In this situation the prospect of jobs being replaced by technological innovation will usually meet with strong user resistance.

Another unquantifiable benefit of adopting IT is in its ability to create more time. Time is a businessman's most scarce commodity and any technology that provides him with a way that he can spend a greater proportion of his time thinking creatively will be of direct value to the organization. Activity analysis schedules of specific departments can often highlight how much time is spend on non-productive work.

A simple example is the use of the telephone. If you connect on the first attempt only 50% of the times you try, then, out of every ten calls you make, five are wasted. Some of this wasted or non-productive time could be regained through the implementation of electronic mail. Photocopying and document retrieval are other obvious areas where useful time can be readily gained. Even with the services of a secretary the time delay an executive experiences between asking for a copy of a document to be retrieved from a file, photocopied for him and then delivered to his desk and actually being able to read the information he needs represents wasted opportunity and with it lower quality of activity.

9.3.3 Selection and identification of needs

In selecting IT devices which support the overall strategic aims of the organization it is essential to have a team which is aware of the latest developments. This will ensure that the technological developments and new products can be related to the needs of the organization and their consequences for the organization can be assessed in terms of costs, ease of conversation, and ease of use.

With the convergence of computing, office systems and telecommunications, the integrated office will enable managers to be more productive and do a better job. Communication of information is enhanced through electronic telephones, facsimile transfer, linked word processors and so on. In justifying the adoption of IT the key issue will be to define the user's needs as the basis of the strategic plan and then establish an implementation strategy that will meet these needs and have a reasonable chance of success.

Bair & Nelson (1985) suggest that the first task in implementation is to identify workers for whom an increase in productivity would provide the organization with the greatest return on investment. This premise therefore does not point to the usual group of secretarial and clerical workers at whom automation efforts have often been directed. Instead it puts greater value on supporting the knowledge workers, including managers and professional people whose function it is to interpret information and make decisions. A series of studies done by Bell Northern Research (BNR) looked at this problem. This 'activity model' accepts the fundamental premise that the actual products of knowledge workers are intangible so must be measured qualitatively rather than quantitively. They also accept that improvements are obtained for the organization if there is a reduction in the non-productive time. Needs of knowledge workers were classified in three main categories: communications, information processing and personal support. These needs provide a strong justification for the adoption of information technology devices since IT facilitates the satisfying of many of the stated areas in which improvements were desired.

The BNR cases studies showed that knowledge workers had needs in three areas.

Communication needs
Reduce interruptions especially those caused by the telephone
Reduce delays in producing written communications
Reduce unsuccessful phone calls
Increase flexibility of contacts
Reduce unnecessary contacts; reduce misunderstandings
Find people easily
Reduce travel
Make more convenient records of meetings

SELECTION AND IDENTIFICATION OF NEEDS

READ ABOUT LATEST DEVELOPMENTS

WHAT DO THEY COST?

HOW EASY ARE THEY TO USE?

HOW EASY ARE THEY TO USE IN *YOUR* OFFICE?

RELATE THE PROBLEM BACK TO THE NEEDS OF THE
WHOLE ORGANIZATION

INCREASING WHOSE PRODUCTIVITY BEST HELPS THE
ORGANIZATION?

Information processing needs
Increase access to remotely stored information
Reduced redundant information
Reduced irrelevant information

Personal support needs
Reduce uneven workloads
Support writing
Support personal calendar management
Support routine calculations

To adopt IT successfully we have to meet these needs. Delving in this area should be done carefully since asking people to list their needs from IT will not uncover the real situation. This is due to the 'fallacy of perceived needs' which means that it we apply IT on the basis of reported needs then we are not likely to achieve the optimum increase in productivity. Those questioned may be ignorant of the full potential of IT devices although superficially they are aware of the functionality of IT products. Successful implementation must avoid determining needs simply on the basis of availability of an attractive product. Better management policies may be much more relevant to the achievement of strategic objectives than buying an 'all-singing, all-dancing', full colour spreadsheet package. Questionnaires and interviews on actual work habits and work conditions of people will provide better data on which to base IT implementation devisions.

9.3.4   Summary

Successful implementation not only requires a good understanding of user needs but also special attention to the factors critical to success discussed here and in the next chapter. At the strategic level the organization should analyze current information management problems and follow that with an attempt to answer how IT can help solve them and raise the quality of work and productivity. Pilot experiments may be undertaken to help an organization move through the various stages of the McFarlan and McKenney model to gain hands-on experience, increase understanding of available technology, build up some evaluation experience between different types of workstation, user system interfaces and so on. At the same time the impact of the introduction of IT into an organization may be investigated. One of the most difficult balances to achieve is between avoiding being a test site for brand new products and the possibility of unnecessarily delaying the acquisition of newly available technology which offers attractive capabilities. The assessment of the benefits offered against costs to be incurred cannot be entirely objective.

9.4   Justification in terms of gains

As many hard facts as possible should be collected to attempt to quantify expected user advantages and disadvantages, costs and savings, impact on cash flows, profitability, productivity, employee morale and so on. Normal pay-back periods of say 5 years for capital equipment may be quite unrealistic for IT devices given the rapid advances seen in the recent years. The National Computer Centre's publication *Office Technology Benefits* identifies and discusses several types of benefits which should be considered in the justification process.

9.4.1   Piggybacking

This means getting additional benefit from a system you implemented for some other purpose. An example of piggybacked development in banking is the rapid increase in automatic teller machines in branch offices which could be cost-justified as a piggyback advantage gained when branches were linked to their main central computer systems for the purpose of customer account recording. If the installation of automatic teller machines were to be costed on a stand-alone basis then the service would be too expensive to install, but given the existing network of computer banking systems the relatively low additional costs of the ATMs is easily justified in terms of customer convenience and increased provision of services. The use of an integrated software package which allows the user to do word processing, use an electronic spreadsheet, store information in a database and create graphics vastly increases the utility of a personal computer. In our experience this has led to the implementation of desktop publishing as well as the potential to benefit from a digital scanner to integrate picture- as well as computer-produced words, numbers and graphs. Buying a laser printer and being able to justify it in terms of greatly enhanced quality of documentation is one of the many spin-off benefits being derived from piggybacking more uses on to personal computers originally justified on the basis of word processing alone.

JUSTIFICATION IN TERMS OF GAINS

DOUBLE BENEFITS OF PIGGYBACKING

THE *RIGHT* PERSON GETS THE *RIGHT* INFORMATION
AT THE *RIGHT* TIME

ALLOWS FREE ACCESS TO IMPORTANT DATA

SAVES PAPER

CREATES TIME

MAKES BETTER USE OF TIME

INCREASES PRODUCTIVITY

CUTS DOWN INTERRUPTIONS

ENABLES BETTER MANAGEMENT

9.4.2   A faster flow of information

Nothing is more useless than yesterday's newspaper. Every piece of information has a decreasing utility of value to its user as its age increases and it becomes ever more relatively out of date. IT provides up-to-date information on demand. With well thought-out updating procedures every time you access electronically stored information you should have a very high likelihood of it being totally up to date. Many banks now have displays of current rates of exchange and leading stock prices running in all their branches so that customers may receive fully up to date information. In Hong Kong it is common to see large crowds standing outside money exchange dealers windows watching the latest share prices come up in real time while they check out their latest portfolio in their lunch break.

9.4.3   Easier access to information

We all buy certain books which are useful only if we have a personal copy. A dictionary held in the local public library would not be much use in helping us to solve today's crossword puzzle. Easier access to information makes us better informed and so we make better decisions and are more productive. However, some information is only useful to us very occasionally and we operate a scale of judging ease of access against cost. We may have the *Shorter Oxford Dictionary* at home but we go to the library to refer to the CD-ROM version of the 12 volumes of the *Complete Oxford Dictionary*. IT devices offer ease of access to vast areas of knowledge and information — but at a price.

9.4.4   The elimination of paper

Not only will the elimination of paper in the office save some trees but it will also reduce storage costs, rental costs, and associated costs of handling, ordering etc. It should also be easier for users to find the information they need which might otherwise be buried in pages of less relevant data.

9.4.5   Opportunity hours

'If only I had known the boss was delayed in Brazil by an air ticket reservation mix-up, I wouldn't have finished that report on Sunday afternoon, but I'd have caught up on my golf swing practice'.

Information — provided *at the right time* — allows people to make better use of their time and IT devices can offer a way to increase opportunity hours. Because you only received the message about your boss being delayed when you got to the office on Monday morning, the opportunity to benefit from the information was lost. A delay in obtaining relevant facts can have devastating consequences for a business but even on a daily basis fast accurate data regularly provided creates opportunity hours which otherwise are lost.

9.4.6   Productivity

IT devices certainly enhance productivity in certain areas, given that the user is well enough trained to benefit from the capabilities of the technology. By the use of a word processing system with name and address merging capabilities a clerk could produce personalized promotional letters for customers living in a certain area in a fraction of the time it would take to sort out the list of recipients manually, then type separate letters.

9.4.7   Fewer interruptions

One of the nice things about electronic mail (which is discussed in detail in chapter 14) is that people can communicate with colleagues *when they want to*. For those who have personal secretaries the possibility of uninterrupted work in the office becomes merely a matter of saying 'Hold all my calls this morning'. However for most people the interruptions caused by the telephone are often unavoidable with consequent loss of concentration and disturbance to one's train of thought which is not easily regained. Electronic mail offers one way to reduce interruptions caused by callers with questions which can wait for an answer.

9.4.8   Better control

Better control often means better cash flow, greater profits, better service and other advantages of direct benefit to a business. Information provided when it is needed, say on stock levels in a warehouse or rate of usage of a particular stock item, allows managers to exercise greater control and again make better decisions, and cope with increased volumes and higher peak loads. Without good stock control a retail outlet runs the danger of overstocking slow moving items, which needlessly ties up capital, and risks running out of stock with consequent loss of business and customer continuity.

It is interesting to note how, as an organization evolves through the phases of development described in McFarlan and McKenney's study, then the benefits and gains of using IT are more and more realized.

9.5   Summary

This chapter has emphasized the importance of a holistic approach to strategic planning. Planning for the strategic goals and planning for IT are related since the organization will not achieve its goals without a suitable IT adoption strategy. An IT strategy can only be designed to facilitate the achievement of the overall strategic goals.

Justification must be in terms which relate to the organization's objectives and IT should be implemented where there is an opportunity for increased productivity either positively or by reducing non-productive time. The work of most professionals is typically unstructured, dynamic and unpredictable — by definition is is loosely defined, with tasks being difficult to describe, and hard to predict. The word professionalism implies the use of judgement and decision-making skills which are largely intangible. Any useful definition of productivity which we wish to measure for the purposes of helping with strategic IT decision making must basically revert to those that impact on the organization's bottom line. Improved company image through the adoption of new technology is important to the future of a typical business enterprise but much more to the point are developments which can lead to improved revenues and reduced costs.

The most important point to strive for in the implementation of an IT strategy is to incorporate the use of information technology in to an ongoing concern *to derive the implied benefits*. The successful adoption of IT is initially designed to meet and sustain the organization's objectives but an attempt to measure these also ensures that crucial issues are given the careful planning they warrant. Again, we are taken back to the needs for requirements analysis discussed in chapter 7. Requirements analysis provides an ongoing framework to measure success, monitor and control the use of IT in an organization and ensures alignment with major strategic objectives.

10   Implementing information technology

10.1 Planning for change

Any good IT implementation and selection policies will be robust and flexible. The essence of achieving this is for them to be designed for change. Changes in any business bring with them a need for changes in the technology employed in the organization. IT planning, acquisition and implementation are expensive in terms of time and money. As far as possible IT implementation strategies should avoid unnecessary development costs and the time taken to implement desirable changes. One of the problems we discussed earlier in chapter 9 related to the changing needs of users as they become more familiar with the use of IT. Any IT system which cannot change easily becomes a hindrance and an obstacle to growth. IT systems should provide users with what they need, in a timely and convenient fashion, for the entire life of the system. From the point of view of efficiency (both in time and money) low maintenance strategies adopted at the design and selection stage will facilitate this. The costs of fixing errors during the 'thinking and planning' stage is obviously minimal in comparison with the effort and inconvenience of discovering that the system is inadequate after it is in place. Not having a crystal ball, the IT planner can only look into the future with the same degree of certainty as any other mortal.

10.1.1 Causes and effects of change

Changes are inevitable and are caused by:
> External forces (a large customer goes bankrupt)
> Changes in performance requirements (the company opens an office in Japan and the systems now have to cope with sums of money running into 30 digit figures)
> Staff turnover and different philosophies (the Chief Accountant retires and his younger replacement has been waiting for years to try out his 'new fangled' ideas which his predecessor was too obstinate to consider)
> Removal to new premises.

Whatever causes the change, the IT system will be affected as aspects of the organization change.
> The data being processed may change (a new branch may mean dealing with a new currency)

The procedures may change (the Hong Kong Government has been threatening to introduce negative interest to discourage people from keeping too much money in savings accounts)

The interfaces between parts of the system may change (a new laser photocopier, scanner and printer combined may allow us to throw out our old nonintegrated stand-alone devices)

The available resources may alter (for the better or worse)

The implementation environment may change (if we buy the new desktop publishing system a member of staff will specialize in this new work thus taking him away from his existing job and creating a knock-on effect in terms of needs for redesign of internal procedures)

The quality of work provided by the system may also change as work measurement monitors the implementation of the new system and potential improvement areas are identified.

10.1.2   How to cope with change

Having discussed what kind of changes will happen it is important to point out how to cope with these as efficiently as possible. The general answer is for planners to be aware that such changes will occur. They will create implications for the IT-based part of the organization. These will best be handled through a careful process of analysis requirements allied to an informed approach to hardware and software selection.

10.2   IT selection advice

When purchasing an IT item the best way to ensue the right choice is to go slowly, step by step. Learning about the technology is covered in chapter 6; then, with some ideas on how IT can be used the next step should be to choose a system which matches the needs of the organization. A thorough needs analysis will have been done and appropriate information systems design strategies followed, as described in chapter 8. The nuts and bolts of proposal evaluation, decisions on whether to buy, lease, or hire, installation planning and detailed implementation strategies are well covered in many texts on the subject of computer management. However, those involved in strategic planning of IT systems should also be aware of the major considerations in hardware and software selection. The prime consideration must be *suitability for purpose*.

Let us take this a step further: what purpose? The answers are fundamental to the tasks of those employed in any organization. People need information to take decisions. This can be retrieved from a myriad of sources and the purpose of obtaining the information and the type of information needed depends on the job to be done. IT systems must be easy to use. Many people say that this is the most important aspect of IT selection. Together with functionality and reliability these criteria ought to guide all IT selection decisions.

Many multi-function machines perform several functions which together make them easier to justify. An example of this would be a personal computer which could be used as a word processor, a terminal to a remote computer system, a facsimile terminal and so on. The user can do more useful jobs on this one piece of equipment and the total number of machines will be fewer than if one piece of equipment had to be purchased to fulfil each individual function.

The further evolution of standards for commercial IT products will make integration and comparisons easier but where standards do not yet exist, or are not universally adopted, the issue of strategic planning becomes more complicated. Areas in which IT standards are of particular interest are in open system connectivity, local area networks, keyboards, and information retrieval command languages. General considerations of response time are of particular importance in real-time system applications.

We have had some interesting learning experiences in installing and managing a fairly large local area network which was the first of its kind in the country. Unfortunately response time problems were only resolved after the installation of significant additional hardware and a long period of tolerating far from satisactory system performance. The problem was caused by believing the advice of the equipment supplier. The supplier had no experience of supporting a network of this configuration and had never done this kind of work, although he was the local agent for the product. We were installing a tried and tested networking system of worldwide reputation supported by a history of successful performance going back over several years in other countries. Unfortunately this lack of local expertise, resulting in the user acting on advice which was quite misleading, only became clear when the system was installed and attempted (and failed miserably) to operate under a production environment. It is cold comfort to be able to retrieve proposals which promise certain performance characteristics when the system does not in fact achieve them. What would have been much more satisfactory for both parties would have been a much more cautious sales presentation where the vendor admitted his lack of practical experience ignorance. Both parties should then have gone forward together in a spirit of controlled experimentation.

The lesson this example gives is that, if you are a naive user of a particular technology, even if you assess your needs well and specify them clearly, it is not always straightforward to get the system running. It is always a good idea to obtain as much information as possible from other organizations who have dealt with a particular supplier in the past. They will give useful opinions on how reliable the service is and how happy they are with their installation.

This is not, of course, foolproof. One person may be very happy with a standard of service that another finds quite unacceptable. However, it may be better than nothing. Certainly, some suppliers will provide lists of other organizations who have successfully adopted a particular product. It can be very helpful to talk to staff in these other companies although unfortunately, in a competitive business situation, this type of information may represent 'the competitive edge' and you may get little of value from other companies in the same business.

10.3 Selecting packages

In purchasing packaged application systems, trade shows, professional journals, books, magazines and catalogues all provide useful sources of information to inform the final decision. Demonstration disks are sometimes available from software suppliers and these can offer a good hands-on experience of using application software. Sometimes these have to be purchased and prospective customers should ensure that the cost of the demonstration is deducted from the cost of the purchase price if a sale is made. Some general guidelines for purchasers of software follow.

Ease of installation
If software is badly documented or requires the installation of a special board or other piece of hardware then you may want to think twice about buying it. Some software has been marketed with extensive copy protection achieved through the installation of a special additional chip or board in to the owner's machine. This can be a real nuisance in a small system unless it is placed in a slot you will never need for anything else and it never needs to be removed.

This is just one example of the type of problem you will discover only if you try out the package from scratch; you would probably not discover this if you tried it out in a shop as the installation will have been done well away from the customer and by a professional.

Time for the software to load
Usually this is not very important for major applications such as word processing since the chances are that the system will only load once a day anyway. However in the case of a multi-function workstation which is likely to be used for alternating applications this is a point to consider. Loading time is non-productive time — an anathema to business efficiency.

Ease of learning
More detail will be given about this later when we discuss training with respect to implementation of IT systems. However, beware of the fallacy that the more power you have the easier it will be to solve your problems. The power of any software has a direct effect on the learning curve associated with it.

Fortunately you can often get a package to do all you want without learning how to use every feature it offers. Do not buy on the basis of whether a package is easy or complex. Check how easy it will be for you or your staff to learn and what training facilities are available.

Ease of operation

This is another trap for the unwary. Demonstrations at many exhibitions we have visited have left us with the impression that we could design for Boeing or NASA if we could only sit in front of most microcomputer-aided design systems. Unfortunately it is not as easy as that. The true level of difficulty (or ease of use) for software can only be ascertained in a real-life application such as the user will want to implement. Salespeople have undergone extensive training in the use of their products. The demonstration applications are the result of the best brains in their marketing department. This gives no indication of how easy *your* staff will find it to use. The answer is to try it out.

The consistency of the command structure

This is important mainly in avoiding errors in use and in shortening the learning time to achieve a useful degree of proficiency in utilizing a package. Consistency in command structure can be a two-edged sword — it can also create problems which are not easy to uncover at the selection stage. The letter E in Symphony can stand for at least two commands — 'Erase' and 'Exit'. If you hit the function key F9, and then press E, you exit from the system. However, it you want to erase a typo you press E after selecting the F10 key (which is just beside the F9). This consistency of command structure can lead to entire documents being lost by the operator exiting from the system instead of just deleting one character. In aiming to present a consistency in command structure it can be difficult for the interface designer to reconcile the need for commands to be easy to remember but still keep them sufficiently different for them not to get confused.

The average response time

This is important in maintaining user friendliness for the system. People are very impatient and become irritated waiting more than a second or two for the computer to respond. Response time say between saving one document and starting to create the next one can be fairly slow. But think about what the operator is doing at this time. He is probably putting away certain papers and organizing himself to start on the next piece of work. At this stage in the process he doesn't need a fast response time. On the other hand when scanning through a document, fast paging and scrolling will be highly desirable. Response time therefore is important but the length of time that is acceptable between certain steps in a process is not rigid and depends on what the user is doing in the meantime.

The range of functions offered by a package

This is difficult to assess. When buying a new sewing machine you may see the top-of-the-line model with its vast arrays of fancy stitches but eventually opt for the more restricted range of options available on a cheaper model because you know you will never need to embroider socks! Conversely, if your car does not have power steering you will not feel deprived until you have the experience of marvellously parking in a multi-storey carpark, when you borrow a friend's car which does have it. The range of options which you *think* you will want or need is coloured by your knowledge at the time you make the purchase. Later on, your knowledge may change and you may find features useful which you could never have imagined wanting.

Ease of data entry

This is important in avoiding errors and speeding up the work to be done. If data is difficult to enter then the operator will do it more slowly and also make more mistakes. The type of data you want to enter determines whether or not a certain keyboard or package gives you ease of entry. A separate numeric keypad or the use of a hand-held scanning device are a couple of alternatives which may help in certain circumstances.

Error handling

Error handling is important. Take the example above from Symphony where we discussed consistency of command structure. Even if you select E for 'Exit' when you really want E for 'Erase' the software pops up with the confirming question before allowing the user to exit the system.

This is a nice touch in error handling but is often very difficult to assess when you are not familiar with a package at the initial selection stage.

On screen help

This facility is common to many packages. If you forget how to use a command then a set of instructions can be called up to the screen to remind you. This is a good idea especially when you are past the stage of looking at the manual all the time. On-screen help is only of short-term use and once a degree of competence is achieved in using an application, the help facility should be deleted from the system because it is probably just wasting valuable disk space.

Standard of documentation

The standard and presentation of the documentation which supports the software is particularly important. If the instructions are clearly written with the right level of detail, many of the major problems of training, user education and maintenance can be avoided.

Portability

This refers to whether a package can run on different types or models of hardware. Portability allows users to avoid being tied in to buying hardware from one particular supplier so it is generally desirable. However, occasionally a product comes out which runs superbly because it uses the capabilities of a particular piece of hardware to the full. If a product does everything a user wants and is evaluated to be distinctly superior to its nearest rival then the fact of being tied in to a particular manufacturer may be of little consequence. In fact, many first-time users prefer to buy well-known brand names, which give them confidence, and like to be tied in to one manufacturer by choice.

Maintenance

Maintenance is important in keeping a package up and running and providing users with latest versions. Together with this we should mention the desirability of obtaining a software guarantee in which the vendor agrees to fix faults or refund money if the product fails to do what was promised. In evaluating a prospective software purchase it is important to check whether new versions are supplied free or at a reduced price to registered users. Some very expensive microcomputer software is sold on floppy disks and this storage medium is very easily corrupted. Even if your diskette does not get dirty or scratched it can be rendered unreadable by programmer error or a faulty disk drive head. Make sure you are able to get replacement copies of expensive software by returning the corrupted original, either free or at a low cost and check on how long replacement will take.

Software licensing

This is the last and certainly not the least important consideration in obtaining software. You should not expect to be able to make copies of a package unless you have paid some additional fee. Site licences can sometimes be agreed to allow large customers to use an application package on various micros freely within the organization.

It is not expected that the user will be able to modify the system without endangering the warranty. Software suppliers will have their own terms of sale and these should be carefully considered (with the help of legal advice in cases of significant expenditure) to ensure that the terms are clearly understood.

A general benefit of buying ready made packages is the fast implementation they offer, with no waiting time while development and testing takes place. This gives better planning and scheduling and greater likelihood of achieving target implementation dates within the estimated budget. It also ought to offer better quality software products because the specialist software developers should be able to afford research and development since the costs of these can be offset against a wide range of products and a large customer base.

10.4   Ergonomic factors

Other considerations are important to successful implementation and adoption of IT within an organization. If a system fails to achieve what it was designed to do it can be for a variety of reasons. Most often failure will be a result of user rejection. To give any system the greatest possible chance of fulfilling the requirements of the users it will be necessary to pay special attention to the physical environment in which the technology will be used. Improper lighting, badly designed workstations, uncomfortable chairs, and poor ventilation all put the user in a poor frame of mind and make him feel bad when using the technology, no matter how excellent it is. Ergonomic factors help facilitate user acceptance of new technology and with this goes a higher probability of the organization achieving its objectives of greater productivity. The keyboard should be adjustable to suit the personal comfort of the user, with matt grey keys to avoid eye discomfort. It should be on a work surface high enough to allow sufficient clearance for the user's legs under the table.

The legibility of the display screen is its most important feature. It should be adjustable to various angles and glare-reducing features used to help reduce reflected light. Unfortunately the optimum lighting levels required for work using display screens is considerably lower than that required for normal office tasks. One answer is to install individually controlled lamps which operators can personally adjust to make their workstation right for themselves. A document holder reduces strain on neck muscles.

The chair is very important to comfort and avoidance of back strain and height adjustability is essential. The environment of the room is often not easy to alter radically. Windowless work spaces can exacerbate workers' negative feelings about monotonous tasks and restricted movement. Good air conditioning systems ensure that comfortable air temperature and humidity levels are maintained.

10.5   Training

10.5.1   Why train?

The key to successful use of IT is undoubtedly training. Without user acceptance of the system productivity cannot be improved. The emphasis should generally be on training staff in user applications. In the longer term, training helps to raise productivity levels by giving the users a better understanding of how the technologies work, aiding the easy transition into using IT and contributing to professional and personal growth. Often, training is not given a proper place in planning for information technology implementation. A recent survey of 100 users in 200 large and medium corporations showed that companies are simply not meeting the training needs of their staff. In many firms technology, rather than the training to use it, was given the highest priority.

One reason for training not being given its proper emphasis is because of the difficulty in measuring its cost effectiveness. Many training benefits are intangible. When a company purchases some equipment it can be capitalized and depreciated over a 5-year-period. The underlying philosophy is that hardware is free. Unless there is a malfunction the equipment will always be available for its useful life. People become ill, have holidays and, worst of all leave the job taking with them all their expensive training.

The results of a survey on the key issues facing MIS managers (referred to in chapter 6) rated the three most important issues to be: the alignment of the MIS with the business goals; data utilization; and education of senior personnel. This indicates the importance of demonstrating to top management the value of a responsive MIS in accomplishing business goals. The intrinsic value of training senior personnel is not obvious but the survey shows how important it is that decision makers understand what information systems can do so that key decisions about IT can be made in coordination with corporate strategic and tactical objectives.

Given the problems associated with costing training, it is nevertheless imperative for organizations to train their staff if they are to achieve projected savings in using IT. In order to make training as effective as possible, a total approach should be adopted to ensure that long-term planning includes employee development. This will assure the optimum use of all resources. The aim should be to improve the quality of work by considering both business and human factors. Training will speed up the acceptance of technology, increase employee motivation, improve work quality, impart new skills and imbue staff with a feeling of personal and professional development.

Since the implementation of IT often creates a great deal of change in the way work is done, there is often a strong resistance to it from users. The associated restructuring of ways of working which often accompanies the introduction of IT can provoke fears of unwanted change in job nature or status. Fears of failure associated with the unfamiliar, especially in people who have a low opinion of themselves, all surface. Training both prepares people to use the new technology and also can help to allay their fears. By giving them proper training workers will feel prepared and ready to undertake new ways of doing jobs and will have a positive attitude as well as improving work quality by having additional knowledge of how to use the technology.

10.5.2 What to train for

If there is inadequate availability of skilled manpower then growth in using the new technology can be greatly hampered. This means that training must also include keeping staff up to date. Some of the areas in which training may be provided include:

Understanding how to set up and adminster a database

Understanding information technology principles and capabilities

The management of the change process to ensure smooth innovation and implementation

Expertise in work and job design including an understanding of the human factors involved

The use of electronic filing and electronic mail

Only through a thorough understanding of the potential and limitations of information technology systems at all levels in an organization will technology be able to be effectively introduced and conflict avoided.

The first step in meeting a company's training needs is to identify those needs. One method which had been tried is to use a questionnaire to rate employees computer-related abilities.

The employees themselves are the best people to know their existing skill levels and they also know what they have to produce. They can more readily identify the areas in which they would like to receive additional training. Items from the basic-abilities questionnaire can be added or deleted as new skills and technologies become integrated into the organization. After administering the questionnaire on a periodic basis the organization can take steps to remedy the shortfall in skills by arranging appropriate courses or seminars.

10.5.3 Sources of training

In the survey previously mentioned it was discovered that self-training was found to be the most dominant source of training. Certain types of training were found to be the most useful in building particular abilities. For example college training was recommended for developing an ability to program, and to use certain proprietary application packages. Vendor training was good for helping managers understand the use of specific application software packages, data communication and hardware concepts. A variety of ways of obtaining training can be considered according to the training needs. Various types of training will be more suitable depending on factors like whether or not there will be an on-going need for training, the numbers and level of staff to be trained, and so on. Other approaches including following a philosophy of anticipating user demand, responding to users' requests, or helping users to develop their own courses.

Courses, lectures, and seminars are the traditional approach to the distribution of knowledge but these can be expensive in many ways. The presenter will have to be paid only for his time in giving the course, but also for his time spent on preparation. When the course is being run a room will have to be provided or rented, and while attending the course employees are taken away from their normal productive work. Courses tailored and created to the individual needs of just one organization will often be very expensive although they appear to be the perfect solution. Using the service of local colleges for in-house training is an attractive option for employers who want to have good quality training tailored to their own environment at an affordable price.

Obtaining training from the product vendor is often an attractive proposition since he will (or certainly should) know his product inside out. He will often be prepared to include training in the purchase price of the technology, and he may also provide a classroom and equipment for employees to use while receiving their training. For smaller applications (such as learning to use integrated application packages for microcomputers) there is often a real problem for the small business which wants to implement such a system in quickly training the staff to a level at which they can use the package productively. Nowadays in-built tutorials are often included with packaged software and these training utilities can be run on the organization's existing equipment (thus piggy-backing on existing machines which were primarily bought for production work but can also act as a means to deliver training in-house). The advantages of this computer-based training are obvious: it is available as and when required; it can be followed on an individual basis at any speed; and its use requires no formal timetabling of courses, booking of rooms etc. However, when a microcomputer is being used to deliver training it is taken out of the mainline production process.

Computer-based training is an extremely attractive option to both small and large organizations. Small businesses can use ready-made training packages and have a quality and flexibility of training material delivered bespoke at an affordable price. Larger organizations can deploy resources to create computer-based training material specific to their needs. Banks, for example, have a continuing need for programmes to train new tellers. This is due to staff turnover, expansion, and adoption of new procedures. By developing a computer-based training package, tellers at any branch can learn to use the new procedures without taking time off for travelling. They can avoid accommodation expenses. Importantly, the local branch manager is given the flexibility to train new staff according to his own branch needs, without having to wait for the next course to be organized centrally. An additional advantage offered by this method of delivering training is that it can be used to help individual staff overcome personal weaknesses or difficulties thus avoiding embarrassment. Finally refresher sessions can be offered in a totally flexible way.

10.5.4 Expert systems for training

Although the artificial intelligence (AI) revolution implied by the 'Fifth Generation' research is still in the future nevertheless significant results have been achieved in specialized areas such as AI-enhanced computer-based training systems. Indeed it has been suggested that AI research may offer a new or different way to think in general, and about training in particular.

There are different ways of representing knowledge in AI but all have the property that they make the stored knowledge available to inferential procedures. Several areas of AI are relevant to training since they might affect the supply of, say, a scarce specialist skill. Knowledge representation is important in all conventional training which is really about transferring knowledge from one person to another. AI research into learning may be useful to trainers in helping them to gain insights into what is involved in learning. It may also be useful in the area of knowledge engineering, in extracting from the 'human expert' the essence of his expertise while recognizing that subsections of the knowledge are interconnected, related and contrasted in highly complex ways.

The concept of an intelligent tutoring system is of a computer program which will be highly adaptable to cope with individual differences between students. Such a system must be efficient, and allow the student to control the interaction wherever possible. Computer-based training in its current form has problems since it is limited in the ways knowledge can be represented. It lacks the ability to represent the state of the student's knowledge of the subject matter. Therefore it cannot use this assessment as a basis to decide how to proceed with the tuition. In recent years a number of attempts have been made to address these deficiencies through the introduction of 'machine intelligence' into the computer-based tutoring system.

Implementations of these ideas have covered application areas as diverse as arithmetic teaching and electronic trouble shooting for the US Air Force. AI has a great deal to offer training in the future so long as the system can explain its reasoning in terms that are meaningful to the student by incorporating sophisticated methods of knowledge representation.

10.5.5 Tax benefits

Tax relief may be available for training expenses including both training received from external institutions and in-house training. Employees receiving training which gives them skills or knowledge necessary for their job do not have to pay tax on training expenses. Various other tax benefits are available to encourage employers to implement training schemes.

10.6 Access, security, and control and confidentiality

The questions of access, security and confidentiality for information technology are important because of the spread of microcomputers and a trend towards open and distributed systems. In general, organizations using IT become increasingly dependent on it. An ever-increasing number of managers have sensitive information in their desktop computer.

The threats to consider will vary from one company to another and the seriousness of the threats will to some extent also depend on the nature of the application and the nature of the work in which the organization is involved. Unauthorised users may be able to read confidential files through local area networks. Databases used to support management decision-making may become vulnerable to corruption by unsophisticated users or to deliberate sabotage by a disgruntled employee. As an organization becomes more dependent on IT to conduct its business, reliability becomes increasingly essential. (Have you ever tried booking an airline ticket when the computer is down?) Computer security covers any eventuality which might result in the computer system becoming unavailable or the integrity or confidentiality of the system and the data it contains being affected. IT based systems are valuable corporate resources and should be protected as far as possible. Some ways of doing this include having duplicate back-up hardware available for certain key parts of the system or alternatively arranging a mutual back-up agreement with a neighbouring organization to allow each other the use of equipment (after office hours usually) necessary to maintain essential systems while repairs are awaited. Performance reliability criteria can be built in to systems and together with a regular programme of scheduled maintenance (just as a car might be serviced every 6000 miles) offer preventive maintenance which provides a very high degree of reliability.

Security precautions built into software such as access passwords, file back-up procedures, fireproof cabinets to store back-up master files, extra copies of important data stored away from the place of business (say in a safety deposit box) are all easy measures to adopt. Compared to the loss to the business caused by a fire or theft or major system failure these measures cost little. Security features built into a computer's operating system are usually hard to evade. The cost of developing and maintaining adequate software security features can be very high. Usually a balance had to be struck between achieving a desirable level of security and spending an acceptable amount to achieve it.

Physical security can be greatly enhanced by selecting a good site for the strategically important systems. This is often not possible. Weather and its consequences can affect IT devices and the impact of wind, rain, lightning, earth tremors, and landslides can all affect the reliability of computer systems. An unreliable power supply not only cuts off the computer but also the air conditioning — often standby generators are bought to protect essential systems against disturbances in power supply and motor alternators are useful in areas where the voltage fluctuates.

Fire in the building is a great danger to all (including IT devices) and since some computer installations are designed without windows (for security) special thought should be given to taking precautions against the accumulation of heat and smoke. Smoke and fire detectors and appropriate types of fire extinguishers should be available and staff shown regularly how to use them.

Access control can be achieved if necessary by employing a security workforce, using mechanical locks or various electronic systems. Employing secure and trustworthy people is a good way to begin any security programme. Much can be done in selection and recruitment to improve security standards and reduce risks. Proper training and treatment of staff grievances should help to minimize the chances of bad relations interfering with the computer systems.

The avoidance of sole control of security sensitive operations is easy to adopt in large organizations but poses problems in small companies. Similarly, segregation of duties may be workable for large companies but completely out of the question in small organizations.

Risk management tries to produce and implement a plan of countermeasures in the best interests of the security of the organization. The tasks involved include: finding out about how the organization operates; identifying and assessing risks to assets and resources; and designing, planning, implementing and monitoring countermeasures.

In '*Risk Analysis and Control*', Wong (1977) identifies vulnerable areas within an organization which has computing systems including:

> The nature of the business
> Economic and physical environment
> Supply of essential services
> Company structure and organization chart
> Physical siting of computer-based functions
> The flow of information within the computer department and between the computer department and other departments

Dr Wong explains how to undertake a detailed analysis and assessent of risk with the aim of decreasing annual loss exposure. This is done by selecting a set of countermeasures which is estimated to cost the least but give the greatest protection against losses. Not all threats can be insured by counter measures. A judgement must be made about how serious the threat is (i.e. how much harm it would do to the organization if it occurred) and how likely it is to occur. The theories of risk management ensure that corporate decisions regarding the value of implementing security are taken on a sound basis.

10.7 Summary

The successful implementation of IT can only be judged by whether its adoption actually creates opportunities which would otherwise have been impossible. To achieve the utmost from IT means planning for change so that technology can meet the needs of the organization and be suitable for the purposes to which it is put. Many criteria determine how to make the best long-term decisions to ensure that IT implementation aligns with the strategic plans of the organization but careful selection and training ensures less risk surrounds the implementation of information technology into any organization.

Part II   Summary

In this section we have taken an in-depth look at the way we can develop a system. Once again we have emphasized that the critical stage comes during the planning for information systems development. A number of methods can be used which assist the organization to understand the key results areas and hence critical success factors for the organization as a whole. These should underpin the information systems development plans. The plans should themselves be subject to detailed evaluation and matched against a portfolio of applications development appropriate to the strategic plan.

A very large range of development tools exist and must be considered in concert with the technology which can support it. There may be little point in buying a relational database management system if it is incompatible with your current hardware. At the same time, consideration must be given to the overall standards applied within the organization — you cannot afford to support all technology in the marketplace or to develop expertise in every new software product. The answer we have suggested is to develop an information factory approach where a range of options are acceptable and should be chosen to develop an application according to the nature of the system, its users and the technology required.

Depending on the information architecture, a range of systems-development methods can be applied. These will relate to the experience of system development personnel as well as the nature of the system. An organizational system integrating a number of departmental systems will require fairly formal structure in its design and implementation, but no one method is necessarily appropriate for every circumstance. Certainly the advent of end-user computing has brought with it a complete new set of development methods most notably prototyping. This has proved successful in both small and large systems developments.

A case study follows which briefly reviews some of the issues discussed in Part II and relates them to specific applications.

Case study: Executive Office Equipment Ltd

This company is a major producer of high quality office equipment which retails throughout the world. Essentially the business can be seen as three separate functional areas: design, manufacture and retail. Within these there are a large number of other functional groups such as warehousing, stores and distribution, and overall we have the normal administrative and product/service management groups of purchasing, marketing, accounting, personnel and information services.

The business mission is to retain the level of profits currently enjoyed and to hold its market position in three areas:

Executive office furniture. The company is one of the top three companies designing and supplying the ultimate executive image. They intend to become the leader in this market, mainly because it is largely price insensitive. If you want a Porsche then you will pay the price and nothing else will do. Similarly, if you want the Goldexec range then that is what you will pay for. In this market, it is quality of design and materials which count.

Open plan office design. In this area the company niche is in the provision of a flexible modular range of office furniture which is in the mid-price range and largely aimed at large corporations. The key to success in this area is to be able to offer a complete supply with fast delivery. Much of the selling in this range is completed through catalogue ordering.

Take-away offices. The last range offered is at the cheaper end of the market with take-away desks, chairs and filing cabinets. Most of this is sold through their retail outlets and is highly price sensitive rather than quality dependent.

Within each of these markets there are very different critical success criteria and therefore we have very different systems needs, very different users and necessarily a different set of criteria to be used when selecting system development methods.

In the design group, we have a set of highly professional design engineers who develop models of the equipment and test the design materials. Application systems such as computer aided design packages (CAD) can be developed either by the designers themselves (many engineers are already computer literate) or by prototyping with the assistance of information systems professionals. There is no point in developing such a system from scratch when a number of excellent packages exist on the market from mainframe to microcomputer environments.

In order to calculate a cost for the design, the costing department need to have the breakdown of parts and quantity required but this also has to be integrated with the likely demand to identify breakeven points of sale and profit forecasts. Given the nature of the business the Goldexec can be excluded from the standard costing and supply system since completely different emphasis is required; the remaining markets, however, are very dependent on price and fast, efficient delivery.

A parts database is linked to the orders and stock systems: automatic ordering from suppliers takes place and automatic repricing takes place when costs increase. This is also directly linked to the marketing system: forecasts of demand and projected impact on sales can be calculated. A system such as this essentially becomes critical to the effective performance of the company and requires a high standard of professionalism in development of operations. This is particularly so in this example of a multinational operation in a distributed computing environment.

At the retail end, the company have installed a direct link from the shops to other shops and through to the warehouses: checks can be made to find out if an item not available at one outlet is available elsewhere. The system offers a simple menu to the retail salesman. In fact, though, it fronts a complex search over a distributed database network. This network is also linked to a delivery costing system which can calculate whether the time and cost of goods transfer is feasible.

In order to cope with the variety of system requirements involved, the company have had to acquire a variety of technology since computers which can support fast decision support are not necessarily the ideal for a CAD system or an integrated manufacturing database.

The type of hardware which the company will use is likely to be based around a powerful mainframe machine which supports the core of the MIS application environment. In integrating the CAD systems with the points database, compromises may have made complete compatibility impossible. The needs of the designers for CAS utility and flexibility in a system may not necessarily be met by a product which will also readily integrate with the company's existing hardware or way of storing and retrieving data. It is very common to see powerful but separate systems addressing the needs of managers and designers in a manufacturing and retailing business but true integration of the entire process is not readily available in a robust tried and tested system to suit all needs.

Part III   The management of information technology

This third part of the book essentially relates the theory and techniques of specific applications and also examines how we manage this process. A number of different types of system exist, for example strategic systems, decision-support systems, small business systems, office automation. These are all examined and examples given showing when these would be the appropriate model for systems development. In particular, chapters 14 and 15 consider the integrated application of technologies and their role in the small business environment. The last chapter considers the overall issues of how to manage the IT environment given the variety of methods, technologies and systems which can be adopted within any one organization and also looks at reasons for failure in the use of IT. Part III summary reviews these issues and examines a case application where all are highlighted before summarizing the concept of the book.

11   Strategic information systems

11.1   Introduction

There has been much written about 'strategic systems' in recent publications but no real unanimity of definition as to what these are. Is it a strategic system when you are first in the marketplace with the idea? Is it strategic when it appears to generate a great deal of additional revenue?

What few writers point out is that a system can be strategic and a huge failure. Too much of the literature equates success with strategy. There is no guarantee in any system that it will lead to corporate success although we have tried to point out during this book that there are ways to shorten the odds against failure. This is a risky area since failures are generally more spectacular than successes and extremely costly. It is undoubtedly, however, the area where organizations should now be focusing their IT directions. We are now considering stage 3 of the evolution of the organizational use of IT (fig. 11.1).

STAGE

Use \ Function	1 Automating basic processes	2 Satisfying information needs	3 Supporting or shaping competitive strategy
Transaction processing	MIS		SIS
Query and analysis		MSS	

Fig. 11.1   The organizational use of IT evolves in three stages.

Strategic information systems can be defined, tautologically, as those which address the fundamental strategic factors in an organization. There are several ways of achieving this:

An information system which attacks the key strategic issues in the competitive marketplace and is designed to provide a competitive advantage; a specific example is the TOP system implemented by the UK-based Thomson Holidays tour group.

An information system which provides a significant impact on strategic issues but is not necessarily designed for competitive advantage; examples of this are collaborative Electronic Data Interchange (EDI) systems.

An information system which addresses the strategic issues in an organization and has an impact on strategic decision making; examples are the use of computer conferencing and high level decision support systems.

An information system which unexpectedly realizes competitive advantages so that it becomes a strategic system; an example is the McKesson drug usage database which was an unforseen byproduct of their ordering system.

Most of the literature concentrates on the first category, because it is easier to identify specific advantages generated through increased market share or profits. Many of the systems which are generated in the last category become the model for the rest of the market place and so move into the first category. All of these systems will, however, affect the way organizations are structured, the way work is accomplished and the way information is used. They connect the islands of information usage that McFarlan & McKenney (1983) calls the 'information archipelago'. They change the focus of information usage, which has evolved from efficiency to effectiveness, to innovation.

Drucker (1988) goes even further. He suggests that it heralds the coming of the new organization which he calls an 'information based organization'. He specifically sees impact on three areas.

Policy making. The availability of information transforms analysis by opinion into diagnosis based on a rational weighing of alternative assumptions. In the area of capital investment this new information transforms the opportunistic financial decision governed by the numbers into a business decision based on the probability of alternative strategic assumptions. So, the decision both presumes a strategy and challenges its assumptions.

Organization structure. Almost immediately, it becomes clear that both the numbers of management levels and the numbers of managers can be cut as their only function is to act as 'relays' — human boosters for the faint unfocused signals that pass for communication. Coincidentally, there will be a need for more specialists at operations level and a flatter structure will develop more closely resembling organizations of the last century.

Nature of work. A good deal of work will be done differently in task-focused teams, with specialists from all areas working together in synchrony.

These are the major impacts of information on the organization and this —
building the information-based organization is the challenge of the future.
The question for us is whether we can identify the opportunities.

11.2 Opportunities and impacts

11.2.1 Where they are

A number of industry-wide studies have taken place which identify typical
characteristics of leading companies in their use of IT. A survey of UK
organizations in 1985 found that the failure of companies to align IT strategy
with business needs was leading to a continuous waste of resources (Kearney,
1985). Furthermore, it stated that companies lagging in their use of IT were six
times more likely to have a poor financial performance within their sector than
the companies leading in the use of IT. The report identified a set of
characteristics appropriate to leading companies but also a separate list for
lagging companies. This covers the whole organizational and management use
of IT and is a good starting point for an organization wanting to examine their
role. The key features are identified in fig. 11.2.

Leading Companies	Lagging Companies
Better than average ROCE	Lower than average ROCE.
Exploiting IT for competitive advantage	Lower than sector average spending on IT
Requirements determined by board with clear success measures by application	Requirements and priorities determined at departmental level
Detailed and realistic cost/benefit analysis available	Overall spending sanctioned by board
Priorities and spending sanctioned by board	Top and middle management involved in implementation
Top and middle management control project	Large scope for cost-justified investment
Cost/benefit monitored on implementation	Significant barriers perceived
Little further scope for investment	Unaware of use – but possibly aware of spending of competitors
Few barriers perceived	Reports to finance director
Aware of competitors' use of IT	Arm's length supplier contact
Reports to an appropriate board member	
Strong links with supplier	
'Literate' managers	
Emphasize implementation skills	

Fig. 11.2 Characteristics of companies leading or lagging in the use of IT.

A more recent study completed in the US looking at the insurance industry found similar correlations and showed that the most profitable firms are most likely to spend a significantly higher proportion of their non-interest operating expense on information technology. This is particularly relevant in an industry where information technology largely drives product innovation for production, distribution and service functions. Harris & Katz (1988) state that the ability to provide flexible investment based products at the lowest possible costs (using IT) has become a critical success factor for the industry.

Those areas which might be described as being the greatest opportunities providers are normally in the areas where Electronic Interchange of Data (EDI) is possible; Electronic Funds Transfer (EFT) is an obvious example for which many of us are grateful.

A further survey conducted in the UK by Butler & Cox (1987) highlighted the role of EDI in providing strategic opportunities. They found that EDI can impact on the organization as follows:

> It can win or lose business as in the case of six machine toolmakers in the UK where five collaborated on the introduction of EDI to their customers and the sixth experienced a 24% drop in orders within 3 months
>
> It can change the market structure — 'Big Bang' in the London stock exchange is a good example
>
> It can change relationships with trading partners — in one case invoices under query between airlines and travel agents were reduced from 30% to 5%
>
> It can change the internal organization of the company — 'just-in-time' ordering redistributes the function of a warehouse and causes staff and organizational changes

They match EDI usage in industry against the four levels applied by McFarlan to measure organizational maturity of IT usage as follows:

Mature — banking and airlines
Key — motor industry, manufacturing, aerospace
Pacing — insurance, transport, chemicals
Emerging — government, construction, energy

The opportunities are, it seems, never ending with exciting new possibilities in CAD/CAM, cartographic work, bibliographic interchange, graphics and design, and the whole area of trade data interchange. This latter development has also opened up the question of security and standards. A number of countries refuse to exchange data with those where there is no legal safeguard for the handling of electronic data.

Faced with the remarkable benefits which can be achieved the question is really how to choose a specific application.

11.2.2 How to find them

This is not a cheap investment although the returns can be enormous. There are some obvious areas where EDI will have maximum impact:

A system with highly structured messages
A system where speed, reliability and precision timing are required
A system with remote recipients
A system where several organizations process the same data; an example here might be freight forwarding

One way of identifying the specific opportunities is by using an opportunities search framework such as that developed by Feeny (1987) (fig. 11.3).

	Low	Medium	High
1 Perceived product differentiation	Look here first Add service	Maximize hit rate	Segment database Illustrate value
	Owned	Dedicated	Shared
2 Sector channel structure	Seek alliances	Support optimize	Structure bias
3 Relationship between need and product	Unclear		Clear
	Guidance system		
	Low		High
4 Frequency of purchase decision	Customer tracking		Deliver decision parameters
	Low		High
5 Frequency of delivery within contract			Build relationship
6 Buyers access to IT resources	Poor		Good
	Provide service		Seek partnership

Fig. 11.3 An opportunities search framework.

The first question in the framework asks how much the product is differentiated from its competitors. It suggests that where this is high, for example, the use of a market database to target customers might give high value returns. Where low, the answer may be to develop other services. A particular example is that shown by the McKesson drug company. By providing terminals to pharmacists to enter orders and hence improving order levels, they also found that they were gathering information on drug usage which they could sell back to the pharmacists.

A similar approach is used to analyse the rest of the framework and all of these can point to specific IT opportunities. An alternative approach returns once again to the portfolio. This time Synott (1987) extends the use of the Porter model through six stages for business and systems integration (fig. 11.4).

The approach applies standard portfolio analysis to defining the strategic business units of a firm. It identifies the areas where IT systems should be developed with specific emphasis on lead and niche. At the final stage, the specific competitive business strategy to be used in developing this strategic area is identified according to the Porter (1985) model as one of cost leadership, product differentiation and market focus, and related to the specific IT strategy which will support it; productivity, technological innovation and product or information support.

The IT planner need only look around at the enormous number of applications which are now making strategic contributions to the organization to realise what they can do.

11.2.3   What they can do

Strassman (1985) has compiled an analysis of how IT has or has not achieved the objectives of improving efficiency and management effectiveness. He finds that in terms of competitiveness, improved efficiency of information processing may reduce some direct and indirect business costs but that the contribution to overall profitability is at best marginal. Using an effectiveness approach to productivity has greater potential if achieved in order to improve long-term competitiveness. This is an area where measurements are very hard to obtain. The Strategic Planning Institute has recently extended the database of its product impact of marketing strategies (PIMS) programme to include a study on management productivity and information technology (MPIT) and attempted to analyse how an IT contribution can be measured as part of a value-added approach to assessing managerial performance. As yet, limited results are available but Strassman also suggests that there is in fact unlikely to be a pattern since there has been very little focus for deploying technology within an organization and instead a preoccupation with piecemeal efficiency seeking cost reduction.

To some extent we are forced to take the suggested benefits and impacts on trust, supported by the many examples of organizations where such benefits have been achieved. There is, however, no reason to believe that the strategic use of IT will differ from the strategic use of any organizational resource and hence a number of highly influential publications have produced articles which suggest how IT can be the key to achievement in:

Redefining the boundaries of the industry and removing constraints to growth

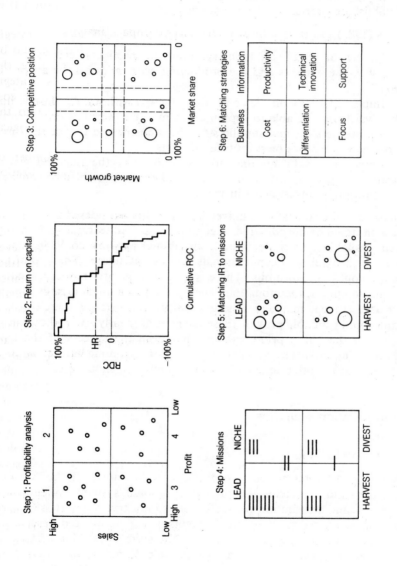

Fig. 11.4 Six stages for business and systems integration.

Developing new products or services

Realigning the balance of power in the supplier/customer relationship

Changing the basis of competition between existing rivals

Establishing barriers to deter new entrants

Parsons (1983) proposes a three-level strategic impact analysis

1. Impact of IS/IT on industry: how the products/services of the industry, the markets and the production economics can be altered by IS/IT.

2. Impact of IS/IT on the competitive factors within the industry: how the rival firms are able to exploit IT to increase their business leverage over customers of, and suppliers to, the industry and reduce the threat from new industries or substitute products.

3. Impact of IS/IT on the business unit: how the required generic strategy of low cost differentiation or niche can be enabled or enhanced by appropriate investments in IS/IT.

Consider this in the context of a university (generally considered a non-profit-making venture). The introduction of computer-assisted learning programmes and their availability to students on a distributed network could be further enhanced by providing cheap terminals for use at home. The production economics would be enormous. There would be a greatly reduced need for faculty and campus accommodation. There would be a much greater capacity for increased student numbers. The university would steal a march over its rivals and could probably provide these facilities at greatly reduced cost in the long-term. In the UK a prime example has been the success of the Open University, using off-peak television as the transmission media. Let us take a look at some of the other applications in a number of industries.

11.3   Application scenarios

11.3.1   The airline industry

The Apollo and Sabres systems are the most well known of the American airlines reservations systems — interorganizational systems which control market access and distribution channels in their industry. A report to Congress on these systems claims that travel agents using automated reservations systems make use of one or the other of the systems in 65% of cases on average. The Apollo system for example, provides domestic and international travel agents with information and reservations on over 640 airlines, 15 000 hotel properties and 22 car rental companies, as well as a multitude of travel-related products such as theatre and train tickets, travel insurance and currency conversion. Apollo, together with American Airlines' Sabre, Texas

Air's Systemone, Delta's Datas and TWA's Pars, provides automation to an estimated 95% of the 31 000 US-based travel agents.

These systems are highly competitive and are constantly trying to improve their lead over rivals. The Sabre system has now been extended to include hotel bookings and to provide travel agents with accounting facilities, thus cementing their relationships with the airlines still further. Delta airlines monitor over 5000 daily changes in the air fares charged by their competitors and can respond to their rivals' pricing decision within 2 hours.

Sabre was the first system developed and gave American Airlines (AA) a clear lead over rivals. It provided support for the 'AAdvantage' (sic) program launched in May 1981 which offers discounted or free travel to customers who fly high levels of mileage on AA flights. This was the result of over 7 years development resting on technology. AA developed software to adminster the programme before the introduction of the service. Traffic details on their reservations network, serving 41% of all travel agents in the US at the time, were automatically captured on a database of all their customers. All the other airlines were forced to follow, but without the system support they had to institute labour-intensive manual tracking of flight data. Even with computerized systems developed for all their competitors American Airlines still hold the lead with enrollments on their AAdvantage program far outnumbering any competitor. Their load factor, percentage of seats filled, has also improved by 4%.

Robert Crandall of American Airlines recognizes the contribution when he stated 'the data processing business is going to make a substantial contribution to the corporation's profits, to the order of $100 million in 1986'.

The impact of these systems is not restricted to the US but effects the world market. In an analysis of the airlines battle for supremacy, Gilbert (1988) described the dynamics involved using Porter's five force model (fig. 11.5).

While as yet there is no real threat of substitiution for air travel, except possibly teleconferencing, there are challenges on all other fronts. In

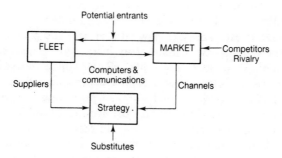

Fig. 11.5   The five forces model applied to the air travel industry.

particular, he cites the need for access to GDS (Global Distribution System) by all international carriers. Examples of the use of Apollo and Sabre can now be found around the world and such systems have potential long-term effects for all countries who rely on tourism for a large part of their GNP.

IT applications continue to emerge and over the next decade the application of expert systems will have substantial impact on the whole air travel industry (Doll, 1989).

11.3.2 Banking and brokerage

Examples of strategic systems in banking abound since they were early pioneers of EDI with electronic fund transfer (EFT) systems and also brought banking into the street with the installation of automated tellers machines (ATM) for customer service. Today, there are about 60 000 ATMs in the USA and each ATM transaction costs about one-quarter of a paper cheque transaction.

The movement, however, is to go beyond this stage and replace ATMs with EFT terminals. Many of these systems have been developed in conjunction with retailers since there are obvious advantages from their point of view, with faster transfer of funds and a restriction of physical cash flow.

This is an area where large investments have not always paid off. The introduction of an Easy Pay System (EPS) in Asia was a marketing failure. Because of a charge levied on the retailers there was no incentive for retailers to use it. The target customer market of young upwardly mobile professionals were a group far more impressed by cash in hand than by a plastic card, especially as many of this group did not qualify for standard credit cards and had not built up their plastic money consciousness.

Perhaps, a more exciting development than any of these was taking the bank into the home. The UK-based Homelink was the world's first public home banking service. It is a composite business venture between Nottingham Building Society, British Telecom, the Bank of Scotland, Thomas Cook, Thames TV, Scrimgeour Vickers, Comp-u-card, the British Medical Association, Hill Samuel Investment Services and others. Homelink provides its services through Prestel, the UK viewdata service, and provides a vast range of facilities to the general public apart from instant movement of money from bank and building society accounts. The collaborative links allow stockbroking access, investment services, travel arrangements and some rather weird and wonderful activities aimed solely at providing fun for users — real banking was never like this! The system cost around £3 million but the society estimated that in free publicity alone they had recouped this within one year!

In the US, Citicorp and Chemical bank have launched similar schemes but in the absence of a nationwide videotext service such as Prestel there is a far smaller chance of success. Very large investments by these corporations have yet to provide any returns.

A further area where the banks have perceived a strategic advantage is in the development of cash management accounting systems (CMA). This is not solely the province of the banks since the most famous example is in fact the CMA system developed by a brokerage, Merril Lynch. The system allows a full range of cash management facilities to be enjoyed by the customer whilst Merril Lynch gain increasing shares of customers' assets. The CMA account service grew from 190 000 accounts in 1980 to 580 000 by the end of 1981, providing $33 billion in assets. Currently, they have over 1.2 million accounts. They were the first in this field, and have remained preeminent. It took over 5 years before any similar CMA service was offered and although the specific figures cannot be easily obtained it is believed that there is no competitor with over 200 000 accounts as yet. This is a case where no return on investment (ROI) analysis took place because, no-one knew what the investment would be, far less the return. It was a deliberate planned move, however, to use a technological innovation to change the marketplace and one which succeeded beyond all their expectations.

11.3.3 Trade data interchange

One area which is set for massive growth in the use of networking and electronic data interchange (EDI) is in the area of international trade. Here there are normally three principal sectors involved: the exporter and customers; services such as transportation and finance; authorization groups such as government bodies. An overview of the principal paths of communication in international trade is shown in fig. 11.6. These transactions involve a great deal of paper and a large error factor — UK banks estimate error rates in letters of credit at around 52–57% at a high cost in lost interest. The objective of a trade network is therefore to bring together some of these parties so that the information which is needed to allow the physical movement of goods from seller to buyer can be processed electronically.

Some trade networks already exist but are concerned with limited aspects of the trading transaction with for instance, finance, transport or customs. Some examples of trade networks are described below.

LACES was the original London Airport Cargo EDP system replaced by ACP 80 and ACP 90 at Heathrow, Gatwick and Manchester.

SWIFT is the financial communications network and stands for the Society for Worldwide Interbank and Financial telecommunication.

IATA was developed by CARGO-IMP jointly with ATA (Air Transport Association of America).

MEMA (Motor Equipment Manufacturers' Association) *Transnet* links automotive spare parts suppliers to their wholesale distributors and transmits in excess of 40 000 orders per month to over 2500 different locations.

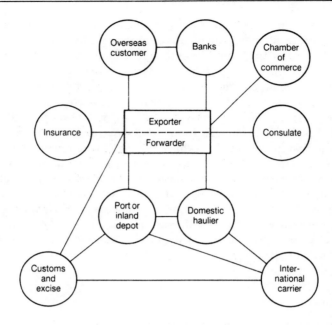

Fig. 11.6   Principal paths of communication in international trade.

These were pioneer systems in the field with recent development in the 1980s centring around retailing, transportation, customs, finance and banking. Data interchange for shipping and direct trader input ports are being developed and, perhaps, most significantly of all, a trial system is underway with the US customs authority involving three multinational companies, Phillips, ICI and Texas instruments.

This latter development is one of the few attempts to create a national network. Very few — bar examples like SWIFT — operate internationally. This is where real developments will take place as countries develop systems to eliminate paper processing and costly time delays in their trading networks. One of the first countries to make such a breakthrough is Singapore with a system known as TRADENET (fig. 11.7).

This system has been initiated by the Singapore Government primarily to improve the efficiency and productivity of government but is also open to private sector participants. It has been deliberately undertaken to improve Singapore's competitiveness as a regional trading centre and to attract multinational business. Singapore has the advantage that it is small with limited international terminals for sea or air and so the concept of a comprehensive international network is infinitely more easy to develop than in the UK or US for example. Such systems will undoubtedly be developed however, over the next few years as countries compete in the international arena for increased

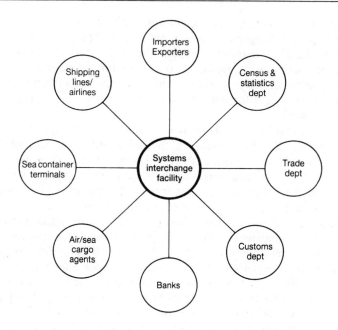

Fig. 11.7   The Singapore trading network TRADENET.

trading and the emphasis is on reducing costs and time delays. The present growth for EDI in trade related activities is variously rated as between 35% and 50% per annum over the next decade. EDI is at the centre of such developments and as we have seen is central to many other strategic areas.

11.3.4   No EDI, no business!

EDI's 1987 domestic market volume has been put at between US$75 and 90 million for network-processing services, software and professional services. It has been predicted that there will be a US$1.3 billion domestic market by 1991. On the international front, US user expenditures is expected to rise to US$220 million in 1992 from US$2.5 million in 1988, an annual average growth rate of 147%.

The cost savings and the speed of doing business are just two selling points that customers hear from suppliers. Sometimes the message comes over loud and clear as in 1984 when General Motors gave its suppliers until 1987 to get on-line with EDI or get off-line with GM. Estimates from IBM suggest that their 37 worldwide plants will be doing business with 2000 of the company's largest suppliers by EDI in 1991. That represents 80% of the company's production. Estimates are that EDI will save IBM US$60 million over the next 5 years.

While EDI may never replace paper entirely, its use has become mandatory in many companies, requiring those who wish to sell goods and services to comply with the EDI mandate. Implementing EDI is not solely a case of buying the right equipment, however. It also requires organizations to change the way they think in order to change the way they do business. This in turn means that the existing information systems have to be redesigned and the EDI software integrated.

For those companies who have already taken the plunge, savings can be enormous. Some 200 EDI users in the oil industry processed 7 million transactions in 1986 at a gross cash flow saving of US$40 million. This is a mere drop in the ocean compared to the savings they expect to make in the future with the development of a joint interest billing system between Amoco, Shell, Arco and Exxon. Joint interest billing is the industry's method of allocating costs in a drilling consortium. No oil company actually drills its own wells — it is too expensive. The lead partner in a consortium sends out monthly joint interest bills itemizing each partner's costs for that particular well. A lead partner usually spends 80 hours per week entering each partner's bills into its computer system. What formerly consumed hours will now take minutes and is an excellent example of how even the fiercest competitors are forced to trust each other to derive economic benefits from EDI.

EDI changes the way in which organizations work and sometimes the nature of the business in which they operate. It cannot just be added on to an existing system but requires a complete rethink and detailed planning for implementation. The impact of EDI is such, however, that most organizations should be including this as part of their corporate strategy in the near future and giving consideration to the need for collaborative development in order to reap maximum benefits.

11.4   Summary

This chapter has examined the role of strategic systems in an organization and emphasized that this is an area where maximum returns can be obtained. It is also an area of high risk and may often involve the use of high technology, large scale investments, untried marketing concepts and a great deal of innovation coupled with strong nerves!

One of the major problems which arise in the development of a strategic system is the lack of management experience in this area. Experience in the management of payroll systems or even management information systems does not provide the appropriate background for the management of systems at this level. Often, it will be the marketing skills which are the most important. This is where it becomes crucial to develop IT applications in concert with corporate management overall. The full force of the organization has to support the system and also believe in the importance of its success.

This is especially true of systems using EDI where by its very nature the system must be collaborative between the organization and its customers and or suppliers and occasionally also with trading partners or industry competitors.

Strategy implementation is a fast-paced high risk enterprise. As companies seek to renovate their systems to support new strategies, they must also develop comprehensive test plans that can prove the reliability and integrity of these systems. While in principle we all support the theory that IT strategies should flow from corporate strategy, we must also accept that information systems can be a major impediment to strategy unless they are managed in a very different way. This experience is reinforced by events in the oil companies over recent years. With oil prices plummeting more than 100% and long-term exploration plans shelved, refineries have been shut down and supply contracts rescinded. The channels of trade and distribution costs have been substantially altered. In response, strategies for decentralization were set and expedited to allow for a more competitive and flexible petroleum industry.

One major company spread operations across three divisions and formulated new management structures. Performance systems and goals were redefined and a directive to dismantle the computer system issued with the intent that each division should build and operate its own computer systems to meet its individual needs. Some 60 major computer systems had to be moved out to divisions and after 18 months not only was no end in sight but there was absolutely no way of knowing when or if the end would ever be reached. Furthermore the senior management had no way of telling whether the new systems would serve the new strategies or simply compound previously existing problems.

Projects such as these require a clear definition of objectives and success criteria. The organizational complexities need clarification with regard to the active parties, liaison parties and management. For each, certain skills may be required and an appropriate operating structure defined such as team structure, or committee structure. The overall management must be the responsibility of a senior manager who understands the key objectives of the strategy as well as the role of IT. In addition, complex systems need expert involvement from functional departments. One large company implementing a new inventory system for retail outlets discovered to its horror that the retail inventory method used in the system was incorrect. This was after testing was nearly completed. A functional expert had not been involved.

The ever-increasing complexities of strategic systems mandate a multi-disciplinary approach to systems development, implementation and management. The advent of expert systems, computer-integrated manufacturing (CIM), EDI, nth generation languages and advanced communications systems require an intensive collaborative team of experts.

Strategic systems demand strategic management at all levels.

12   Management support systems

12.1   Introduction to management support systems

The concept of management support systems (MSS) has evolved from developments converging from several fields. The first of these is decision support systems (DSS) an area which originated as a systems concept from MIT in the beginning of the 1970s. It emerged out of the many failures in the application of computers to problems in managerial decision making, many of which are ill structured and cannot easily be represented algorithmically. The reorientation of such systems away from the management science approach whereby optimal solutions can be obtained from a fixed set of alternatives was precipitated by studies of organizational decision-making at Carnegie Institute of Technology in the 1960s with Newell & Simon (1972) producing seminal work for the definition of the concept. This was further developed by many others. The key issue in DSS is support — they help the user to come to a decision but they do not automatically make the decision.

The same time that developments were taking place in DSS also saw the emergence of artificial intelligence (AI) concepts and the coining of the phrases expert systems and intelligent knowledge based systems (IKBS). Initially, AI was concerned with product-oriented research and the expert system concept represented a paradigmatic change in this research. Prior to this change most AI research was concerned with generalized strategies of problem solving. It was recognized, however, that human beings develop expertise not because they have learned a problem-solving method but because they have acquired domain specific knowledge. In order to develop computer systems that can handle complex problems in the real world, the computer system must contain a knowledge base where the domain specific knowledge can be represented as well as reasoning models. This requires a process known as knowledge engineering where a suitably skilled person, a knowledge engineer, is responsible for talking to the expert and transferring the information to the computer. This knowledge transfer process is the most crucial stage of building an expert system. The expert, called the domain expert, has to be able to describe accurately all the factors, constraints and reasoning that contribute to the decision-making process — not an easy task. Very often experts are unable to say how they reach a decision. A typical case involved a biologist who when asked by a knowledge engineer how he could tell a cell was anaemic replied 'Listen, I have been studying cells for 20 years. If I tell you it's anaemic then it is anaemic!'

Many current DSS are in fact, IKBS. Because the knowledge was elicited from experts they are called expert systems rather than just systems with intelligent support. As developments continue in this field the line betweeen a system with an intelligent knowledge base and a so-called expert system becomes very fuzzy and it is only those heavily involved in research in this area who choose to differentiate between them.

For the remainder of this chapter we shall use the terms indiscriminately to mean any system with an intelligent support.

Readers should keep in mind, however, that while an expert system is also always an IKBS the reverse is not always true as the intelligence can have been built up historically from an analysis of events rather that through elicitation from expert sources.

A further development which impacts on MSS is the growth over the last decade in office automation and office support systems. The workstation concept has brought computer support on to many managers' desks and the proliferation of spreadsheet software has provided them with the facility to perform 'what if' decision queries up to a fairly sophisticated level. This has been further enhanced by the expansion of computer graphics and the ability to produce instant pie charts and graphs for management reporting.

Finally the largest growth area of all — communications — has not only provided for integrated office applications but also provided the technological environment for group management decision-making both in the teleconferencing mode and group decision support systems (GDSS). The ultimate development, of course, is that of the intelligent organization: an organization which is efficient at learning and deciding. This intelligent organization information system should be a system monitoring the internal and environmental status of an organization in a manner which supports attainment by the organization of a goal state. In particular, an intelligent computer-based organizational information system should actively plan and initiate acts which will result in the realization of organizational strategies.

Having said all this one might reasonably expect every organization to be a thriving MSS environment. The reality is still not so although much progress is starting to be made. For too long there has been a great deal of hype concerning DSS and expert systems. Neither, to date have actually made much impact on the way that real managers make real decisions. One of the reasons that expectations of researchers in these fields greatly exceeded delivery was the role of management in making use of them and also, in the area of IKBS, of contributing to the design. The lack of faith on the part of the manager that there could be any tool which could help him to make decisions is also often supported by his fear that there might be one which could usurp his decision-making role in the organization. This has resulted, in part, from the journalistic licence employed when describing expert systems which have often been represented as thinking machines with minds of their own. The truth is that these systems are the ultimate management tool in the sense that they allow managers to enhance their decision-making skills by presenting them with more rational choices and associated risk probabilities. All of these essentially, however, are developed from parameters specified by management themselves so it is in their hands that ultimate control lies.

This chapter goes on to examine DSS and the role of expert systems. It also surveys the developing use of graphics in management support and summarizes the concept of the intelligent organization.

12.2 What are decision support systems?

DSS provide decision support. Sprague & Carlson (1982) give a definition that captures the key aspects. They define DSS as computer based systems that help decision makers confront ill-structured problems through direct interaction with data and analysis models.

The last two items have become the basis of the technology for DSS, what Sprague & Carlson call the DDM paradigm — dialogue, data and modelling. They make the point that a good DSS should strike a balance among the three capabilities. It should be easy to use to support the interaction with non-technical users; it should have access to a wide variety of data; it should provide analysis and modelling in a variety of ways. Many systems claim to be DSS when they are strong in only one area and weak in others.

The conceptual framework for DSS basically consists of three components: model base, data base, software component for managing models, data and dialogue.

Due to the ill-structured nature of the problem-solving task to be supported by a DSS, and the sharing of information processing between man and computer, the human-computer interface is of key importance to a successful design (fig. 12.1).

A typical DSS consists of analytical models and numeric data with problem-solving methods defined prior to model solving. Its analytical capabilities comprise functions for: scenario-building (what if?), means-ends analysis (goal seeking), sensitivity analysis, risk analysis and optimization.

DSS were initially developed in the financial area for investment decisions but have expanded into the area of marketing analysis, forecasting, consolidated reporting and analysis. Typically a DSS in marketing would address the following questions: what has happened? why did it happen? what will happen if?

In other words, a large base of data has to be collected from various sources and relationships examined. One of the major problems, of course, is in isolating variables and identifying that strict causal relationships exist. This, to some extent, is why the popularity of DSS was first founded in financial

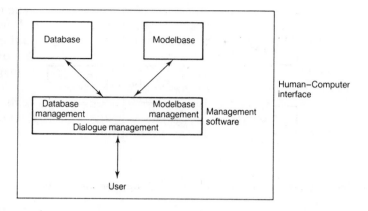

Fig. 12.1   Conceptual framework for decision support systems (DSS).

systems where there are fairly strong relationships defined between cost and pricing variables.

Such DSS tend to be aimed very much at the organizational support rather than personal or group support. Hackathorn & Keen (1981) describe three types of decision making with respect to the number of people and the way they participate in the decision making process:

Independent decision making is where the decision maker has full responsibility and authority to make a complete and implementable decision.

Sequential interdependent decision making is where a decision maker makes only part of a decision and then passes on to someone else.

Pooled interdependent decision making is where a decision results from negotiation and interaction among several decision makers.

These can be described respectively as

personal support, organizational support and group support.

Personal support requires the full commitment of a single manager and, of course, direct interaction with the computer system. This is steadily growing as managers become familar with and comfortable with the use of personal computers and the software packages available such as LOTUS 1-2-3, Symphony, IFPS. These are, in fact, tools for the flexible building and modification of a DSS without expert programming knowledge and are called decision support generators.

Group support is only recently becoming a possibility with the growing use of networked communications and is still largely at the research stage.

One further area which is worth mentioning as a DSS category is that of multiple criteria decision support systems (MCDSS). The major software components of an MCDSS are shown in fig. 12.2. Even though they include

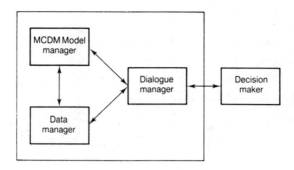

Fig. 12.2   The major components of a Multiple Criteria Decision Support System (MCDSS).

the same basic components as other DSSs they are distinguished from them by the kind of mathematical models they use and, therefore, the nature of the decision making environment to which they apply.

The following are the essential features which distinguish MCDSS from classical DSS:

They allow analysis of several criteria at once

They allow subjective evaluation of the criteria alternatives by weighting and ranking them

They support interactive decision making such that the reactions of the decision maker at any stage influence the criteria definition

They use a variety of multiple criteria techniques to compute the efficient solution

In other words the DSS has to interact as an expert and so will include an expert system base which allows the model to identify and explain the inconsistencies between the two perceptions — that of the decision maker and that of the MCDSS in a learning process.

An example of the use of such a model can be found in a leading European car manufacturer. The company is interested in building an adaptive DSS intended to help make better and faster decisions concerning:

The launch of a new model or model version on the market and its potential consequences on the clientele

The withdrawal of an existing model from the production lines

The development of a 'health diagnostic' — that is the assessment of the suitability of a model from the marketing point of view (sales volume, quality of distribution, maintenance facilities, competitive vendors) as well as from a technical point of view

The modification of the existing strategy according to the results of the 'health diagnostic' (reduction of production volume, review of some components of a product, introduction of new technologies, definition of a new commercial approach)

The mathematical models involve MCDM and data analysis such as factor and regression analysis methods. Figure 12.3 provides an example of six quantitative criteria characterizing ten reference cars and this forms part of the relational data base which supports the data manager identified in fig. 12.2.

Similar models can be applied in any manufacturing sector and, in fact, the major developments in this area today are in linking these models to a computer automated design and manufacturing process (CAD/CAM).

Model	Maximal speed: km	Consumption in town: l/100km	Consumption at 120km/h: l/100km	Horse power: CV	Space m²	Price: francs
1	173	11.4	10.01	10	7.88	59,500
2	176	12.3	10.48	11	7.96	56,700
3	142	8.2	7.30	5	5.65	42,100
4	148	10.5	9.61	7	6.15	49,150
5	178	14.5	11.05	13	8.06	74,700
6	180	13.6	10.40	13	8.47	85,700
7	182	12.7	12.26	11	7.81	78,593
8	145	14.3	12.95	11	8.38	65,000
9	161	8.6	8.42	7	5.11	45,200
10	117	7.2	6.75	3	5.81	34,800

Fig. 12.3 Six quantitative criteria for ten different cars.

12.3 Expert systems

The basic components of an expert system in the 1990s are shown in fig. 12.4 as inference engine, knowledge base, data/knowledge dictionary and database. The inference engine is in effect the reasoning system.

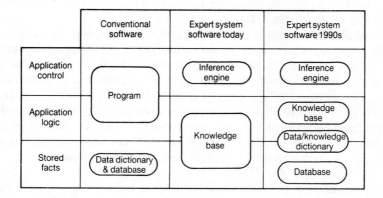

Fig. 12.4 Comparison between conventional software and expert system software.

In some descriptions of expert systems we find the database representing factual information as part of the knowledge base. The most common representation mechanism for knowledge is production rules. Data are represented as associative triplets; objects, attributes and values. The reasoning system, or inference engine as it is sometimes called, reasons about a problem by applying rules on the data base either stored in a database or provided during a consultation with the user.

A typical expert system is concerned with symbolic inference. It reasons about a problem by searching a solution space for a solution which can be discriminated by logical rules or constraints. It may also increase reasoning effectiveness by heuristic methods. Most commonly, it exhibits intelligent behaviour by applying knowledge (rules) in a context (problem). This is a dependent manner; other methods exist, however, such as frames and semantic nets, which may be more suitable for some problems.

The functional capabilities can be classified into consultation and explanation. A broad generic framework of application categories comprises problems of interpretation, prediction, diagnosis, design and planning.

Just as we have DSS generators so we have tools for building expert systems, commonly called shells. A typical shell is generally built around the following technology:

A representation language for production rules

A control structure for reasoning (forward/backward chaining)

Host programming language (LISP, PROLOG, etc)

Systems controlled dialogue (question/answer type)

Natural language interface

Personal computer tools are also available such as the Personal Consultant system developed by Texas Instruments, Goldwork from Gold Hill computers and Twaice from Nixdorf. These products are capable of operating on a base of between 400 and 1000 rules and allow for the development of a number of expert systems simply by changing the knowledge base (although this is the really difficult part) (fig. 12.5).

This is, of course, very similar to the concept of the 4GL as an application generator discussed in chapter 8. Indeed, many of the latest offerings on the software market combine some of these concepts offering decision support and expert system support within the application generator environment. We will look at a typical offering in the later section on generators but fig. 12.6 indicates the very broad range of expert systems software currently available.

There have been incredible claims for some expert systems, for example that they can outwit any human expert. What they certainly can do is combine knowledge from a variety of sources and so provide experts with a much greater base of support.

Applications have been particularly successful in the medical field for both diagnosis and consultation such as MICKIE developed in the UK and CADUCEUS developed in the USA. Growing interest is being shown in the financial sector

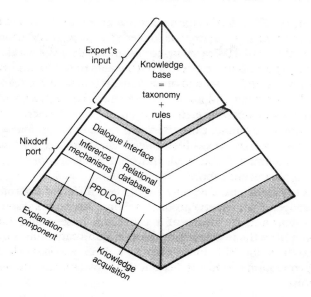

Fig. 12.5   The knowledge base for an expert system can be changed.

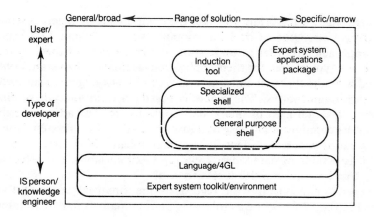

Fig. 12.6   Range of expert system software.

for banking, insurance and investment decision support, although as yet, only a few systems are operational. Digital Equipment Corporation use XCON, an expert system to help configure VAX computers. DIPMETER ADVISOR is used to interpret data taken from oil well bore holes such that they can deduce the type of earth fault that has been penetrated.

In Singapore, the Port Authority is using an expert system to make it more efficient. For shipping companies, the longer that ships spend in port the less time can be spent on voyages carrying goods and companies would like to see that time cut. The port authority, for its part, wants to use its equipment to the maximum advantage and so among other aims, it wants to reduce the amount of time to find a container and load it onto a ship. Also it wants to make sure that all its cranes are working efficiently. An expert planner from the Port Authority provided the human expertise as the domain expert and worked with a knowledge engineer from Texas Instruments who mapped this knowledge on to an advanced computer. The result has been a halving of the time a ship needs to stay in port at Singapore.

Thus, expert systems and DSSs are simply two different approaches to the support of managerial (or expert) problem solving. An expert system simulates expert human reasoning by means of a knowledge base containing inference while a DSS amplifies the manager's decision-making capabilities by providing data and analytical models. Furthermore, a DSS accommodates learning through its open man-machine interaction. Real power comes in merging these two applications.

12.4   Knowledge-based decision support systems

Knowledge engineering brings together the components of expert systems with the analytical strengths of decision support systems. Figure 12.7 shows the overall approach. In order to understand the real power of these systems we will look at a typical area for their application — finance. Konstans (1982) has described a model that can assist an analyst in identifying financial problems in business organizations. The model is based on ratio analysis of financial statements, a target area of many DSS applications. The advantage of ratio analysis is its computational ease and Konstans takes this one step forward by grouping ratios which can identify certain problems. Now look at fig. 12.8. You will see a table of data where rows represent variables and columns time periods. Just how meaningful is this to you?

An expert's conclusion with regard to the financial state of the firm described in fig. 12.8 may be as follows: 'The company is undercapitalized; its management of receivables and inventory are questionable; its operations are inefficient, or it is operating at below break-even point; assets are being diverted from uses productive of revenue. These factors all result in a liquidity problem and a general decline in the company's financial condition.'

How would he arrive at this set of conclusions? Methlie (1984) distinguishes three tasks in financial analysis as:

Intelligence, where information relevant to the problem domain is collected and interpreted

Quantitative analysis, where income statements and balance sheets are

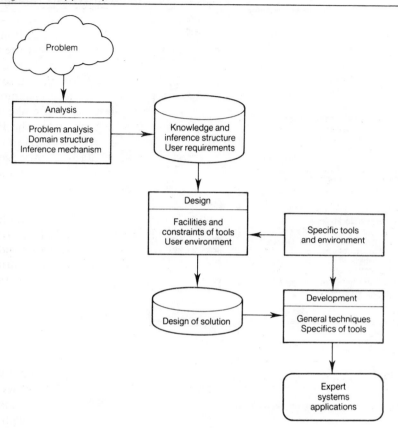

Fig. 12.7 Knowledge engineering.

processed into key variables, a set of standard ratios

Quantitative reasoning, where the figures are dealt with in qualitative terms based on logical rules and constraints

In the traditional DSS approach the computer system performs the computations and the analyst performs the evaluation or diagnostic of these data in order to reach a conclusion. This diagnostic reasoning is the target area of expert systems, where once the computer system has been provided with the knowledge on how to interpret the figures, the expert system can employ a process of symbolic reasoning in addition to computation.

A number of potential applications exist in the financial sector: money transfers, credit rating, personal financial planning services, portfolio management and business loan applications to name only a few. Several prototype systems have been developed and fig. 12.9 expands the concepts in fig. 12.7 to illustrate the type of systems architecture which has to be defined

	1968		1969		1970	
	Firm	*Industry*	*Firm*	*Industry*	*Firm*	*Industry*
Margin						
1 Net income/net sales*	7% .	3.0%	loss	2.3%	loss	2.7%
2 Gross profit/net sales	2.0	22.0	22.0	22.0	21.0	20.0
Turnover						
3 Average collection period* (in days)	69.0	36.0	75.0	38.0	82.0	41.0
4 Days sales in inventory*	71.0	35.0	72.0	34.0	79.0	22.0
5 Net sales/stockholders' equity* (times per year)	7.9	5.3	6.8	5.0	6.4	4.9
6 Net sales/total assets* (times per year)	2.2	3.7	2.0	3.6	1.8	3.6
7 Net sales/net fixed assets (times per year)	19.0	21.1	13.4	22.0	14.1	20.0
8 Net sales/net working capital (times per year)	17.5	7.2	25.7	6.8	28.8	6.2
Balance						
9 Fixed assets/stockholders' equity plus long-term liabilities*	41.0%	9.1%	51.0%	9.2%	45%	9.4%
10 Current plus fixed assets/ total assets*	96.0	96.0	93.0	95.0	90.0	96.0
11 Current assets/total assets	84.0	85.8	78.5	86.3	78.0	85.7
12 Current liabilities/total liabilities	99.0	44.0	99.6	47.8	99.5	47.3
13 Total liabilities/stockholders' equity	257.0	134.0	244.0	152.0	250.0	166.0
14 Accounts receivable/current assets	45.0	45.0	48.0	46.5	48	46.9
15 Inventory/current assets	52.0	41.0	51.0	40.0	51.0	37.0
Liquidity						
16 Current assets/current liabilities	1.2:1	1.6:1	1.1:1	1.5:1	1.1:1	1.5:1
17 Acid test	6:1	1:1	5:1	9:1	5:1	9:1
Solvency[†]						

*Denotes a primary ratio
[†]Ratios could not be derived from the data provided

Fig 12.8   Data for a financial analysis.

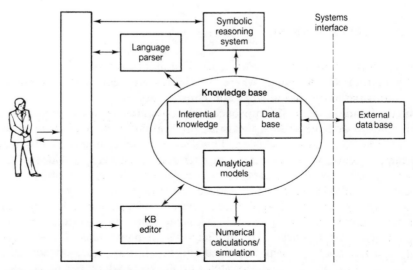

Fig. 12.9   The systems architecture needed for financial analysis.

for financial analysis combining quantitative analysis, qualitative reasoning and information retrieval.

Figure 12.10 shows part of a model of a prototype system for business loan applications, where the reasoning system is determined by a reasoning mechanism of goal-directed backward chaining. Using this we would start at the top of the inference table and then perform an exhaustive in-depth first search. The example shown is the goal structure for part of the credit assessment search based on the bank's risk assessment, amount of current assets and liquidity of current assets.

Such systems are now being implemented, albeit cautiously, in many financial institutions and throughout the business community at large. One DSS development area which is not yet impacting greatly on the business world as yet is the group decision support systems (GDSS) discussed briefly in the next section.

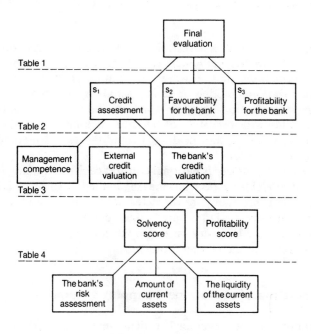

Fig. 12.10   Part of a model of a prototype system for business loan applications.

12.5   How viable are group decision support systems?

The viability of GDSS has related almost entirely to technological considerations until fairly recently. The growth in communications links has removed the constraint and allows for three basic styles of GDSS environments:

Face-to-face-conferencing This GDSS incorporates a conference room with terminals for each participant and any decision making which takes place in this environment is conducted in a certain space of time. This type of GDSS is often referred to as war room.

Face-to-face-teleconferencing This GDSS takes place under similar conditions to the first system with additional links with other groups at remote sites. Examples of this type include teleconferences and videoconferences.

Interfaced conference Here participants communicate through their terminals, whether they are in close proximity or not. Participants may interact at the same time or through a system such as electronic mail allowing comments and replies to be stored until participants are ready to deal with them. This type of GDSS may be encompassed in an electronic mail system, computer conference system, distributed computing network or through such software packages as FORUM.

Obviously, there is still a constraint with regard to the organizational settings required and the very high cost incurred when introducing them. Perhaps even more important, however, is the appropriateness of the GDSS to particular organizational models of decision-making and to particular types of decisions. The organizational culture which we discussed in chapter 3 may be completely at odds with this style of decision-making. Certainly it is hardly conducive to the wheeling and dealing, behind-the-scenes methods favoured by many large corporations.

Another factor to consider is national culture: decision-making in Japan has a very different model from decision-making in the USA: thus GDSS may well have a future but probably in restricted applications and in very large organizations. However, DSSs are quite definitely part of the MSS environment and there is a very large growth market in the development of generators to facilitate such an environment.

12.6   A generation of management support systems

Initially, products were developed which were solely marketed as DSS generators, such as EPS/IFPS, System W and Wizard. These were developed from both mainframes and micros. Increasingly, however, other products have entered the market with an overlapping role. As we mentioned in section 12.4, software to generate DSS and expert systems is increasingly integrated within an application generator environment. Also, the development of more sophisticated PC software, such as Visicalc and integrated packages such as Symphony, means that decision support is provided through spreadsheets. This section concentrates then on these two areas — application generators for the larger scale computer environment and PC based software, specifically spreadsheets.

12.6.1 Packages for larger systems

Typically a package for a larger system will contain the following: a database, a structured query language and an application generator (procedural, non-procedural or both). In addition, it may also include an expert system generator. One such package is produced by the software house Cullinet and is built around the IDMS database and the structured query language SQL (fig. 12.11).

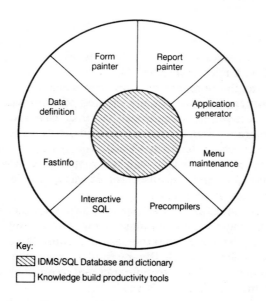

Fig. 12.11 An expert system generator: 10MS/5QL productivity environment.

The application generators include KnowledgeBUILD which enables the developer to paint layouts for data entry forms and reports and transforms these into efficient BASIC, COBOL, or FORTRAN in a matter of minutes. In addition the package includes Application Expert based on EMYCIN as a rule-based expert systems shell. These two can be totally integrated and so provide us with an intelligent knowledge based decision support system (IKBDSS).

One particularly noticeable feature of this package is the generation of third-generation code (3GL). In fact, one of the major problems with 4GLs is their high resource demand. The generation of 3GL code gives us the type of information factory environment which we recommended in chapter 8.

Products such as this are more than sufficient to meet most of the current needs of organizations for MSS; we might call them semi-expert systems. They also allow for very rapid development of systems and can produce a 'quick and dirty' DSS in a matter of hours. In many cases, this is all that is needed. There are, however, cases when obviously this would be inadequate especially in the area of non-rule-based expert systems and highly specialized decision-support environments. For these, more specialized packages are available. Also, many such generators are custom written for the applications.

At the other end of the spectrum, there are a large number of applications where some decision support of the 'what if' variety is needed without very sophisticated statistical analysis or expert help. These are well provided for by a range of spreadsheet software.

12.6.2 Spreadsheet

In contrast to the packages described in the previous section, spreadsheets are commonly based on a microcomputer. The spreadsheet is the one tool which has probably led to the purchase of more microcomputers than any other. Electronic spreadsheets were originally created to automate the rows and columns of an accounting spreadsheet so that changes in data would automatically generate recalculation of related items. The first electronic spreadsheet for microcomputers was Visicalc which was originally developed for the Apple II computer. One can only speculate how many Apple computers were bought purely because Visicalc was available, but the number is probably in the tens of thousands.

Today many other spreadsheet packages are available; they are mostly very similar to each other and users can quickly adapt from using one spreadsheet to another once they have mastered the basics. Because the underlying design of electronic spreadsheets so closely resembles tasks like profit and loss statements, personnel files, budget summaries and so on, they are a useful tool in any organization. The electronic spreadsheet becomes a template or model of relationships which can be used over and over again. It is also easy to modify to fit a variety of situations and can be used to search for records which satisfy certain criteria. An example of this might be if a salesperson had entered all his customers' orders into a spreadsheet and wished to make special follow-up calls on those who had placed orders in excess of \$10 000, he could then issue a simple search command like ORDER > 10000. The records of such customers would be highlighted and could also be printed out as a report. This is not a very sophisticated application of data retrieval but it illustrates how electronic spreadsheets are extremely easy to use and can easily generate more than just lists of figures.

As a decision-support tool, spreadsheets come in to their own in enabling decision makers to perform 'what-if' analysis. By altering the underling model in the electronic spreadsheet, many hypothetical questions can be posed and answered. An example would be in projecting growth in sales of a product and estimating the output capacity required from the production line. 'What if sales grow at 5% next year? What will be the effect on raw materials requirements? Can our warehouse facilities cope? What if we have a boom year and sales grow by 20%? Could we cope then? What is the maximum figure for growth that we could handle with our existing production capacity? Let's look at the effect on related factors of growth of 5%, 10%, 15%, and 20%'. The example spreadsheet in fig. 12.12(a) illustrates this point.

A factory produces Gadgets. The underlying model or rules which the factory owner describes are:

Each Gadget require 1 m^3 of storage space when it is finished and packed for distribution.

The company has to maintain warehouse capacity for 30% of its production of Gadgets pending distribution to sales outlets and to meet orders quickly.

The raw materials needed to produce one Gadget require 0.5m^3 of storage space.

The company policy is always to store enough raw materials to produce 20% of its annual production volume of Gadgets. This ensures that production is not disrupted even if deliveries of raw materials are held up.

Existing warehouse capacity is 10 000m^3.

Gadget production	Growth %	Storage for completed gadgets	Storage for raw materials	Existing warehouse capacity	Spare warehouse capacity	
22 000	0	6600	2200	10 000	1200	
23 100	5	6930	2310	10 000	760	
24 200	10	7260	2420	10 000	320	
25 300	15	7590	2530	10 000	−120	
26 400	20	7920	2640	10 000	−560	(a)

Gadget production	Growth %	Storage for completed gadgets	Storage for raw materials	Existing warehouse capacity	Spare warehouse capacity	
22 000	0	6600	2200	10 000	1200	
24 200	10	7260	2420	10 000	320	
24 420	11	7326	2442	10 000	232	
24 640	12	7392	2464	10 000	144	
24 860	13	7458	2486	10 000	56	
25 080	14	7524	2508	10 000	−32	
25 300	15	7590	2530	10 000	−120	(b)

Fig. 12.12 A typical spreadsheet: the relationships between the entities has been defined and if one is changed the others will be affected.

By embodying these rules into formulae underlying the spreadsheet the inter-relationships between the entities are defined.

A change in one will automatically result in a relative change in associated factors. The resultant spreadsheet might look like fig. 12.12(b).

The decision maker now has a tool which allows him to explore various scenarios based upon different assumptions. An additional feature of many spreadsheets is their ability to display two parts of the spreadsheet simultaneously on the screen through different 'windows'. This allows the user to change an assumption within a financial balance sheet and simultaneously see the effect of the alteration on the bottom line. Spreadsheets can easily be printed out and utility programs enable even very simple printers to print spreadsheets sideways thus allowing a spreadsheet going over many columns to be printed completely even on fairly narrow paper.

12.7 Graphic support

Our discussion on spreadsheets leads logically into the presentation of data not just in rows and columns but also in graphical form. Spreadsheets usually have an option to allow users to draw pictures directly from the data in the electronic spreadsheet. One of the advantages in this integrated approach to decision-support is the ease of use which is greatly enhanced by having one program do many related things. The user only needs to learn one set of commands and time spent referring to user manuals is therefore lessened. Business graphics is an area currently experiencing high levels of growth. Systems are now readily available at an affordable price which can display and print graphics relating to the increasing volume of data with which many managers have to cope. By summarizing pages of facts in a simple chart, information becomes easier to understand and retain. Graphs aid comprehension by explaining complex information, highlighting key points, showing comparisons and showing relationships. Business graphics usually take the form of pie charts, bar charts, or line graphs. The type of presentation used depends on individual preference and on the type of data to be graphed. Two simple graphs based on the data in fig. 12.12 shown in fig. 12.13. They illustrate how the need for warehouse storage space increases relative to growth in projected Gadget sales.

Business graphics as a support in making better decisions can undoubtedly be justified in terms of time saved. The speed with which a manager can comprehend data will be greatly enhanced by displaying the data effectively in a graph. The use of graphics in presentations gives the audience the feeling that the presenter is well prepared and professional and is generally more convincing than if no visual materials are used. When graphs are produced by computer they can be easily updated to include current data. They can also

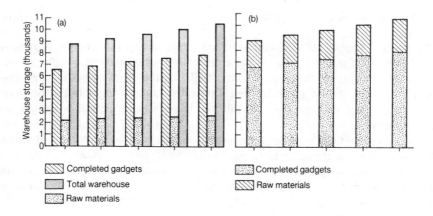

Fig. 12.13   Graphs based on the data in fig. 12.12 showing how projected sales growth results in a need for more warehousing space.

help illustrate 'what-if' scenarios (discussed in the previous section) when created by an electronic spreadsheet which also has a graphics capability. The cost effectiveness of slide and chart production is significantly improved with the use of computer-based systems. Slides can now be produced by presenters in-house, saving time and money as well as the extra effort of going out to an external graphics art company.

A summary of where graphics can be used within business decision making is provided in fig. 12.14. A wide variety of graphics can be displayed but it is important to include easily readable text.

Reports: black and white graphics, bar charts, time series graphs
Presentations: colour graphics, 35mm slides, overhead projector foils
Command and control: military, public services, transport maps
Design and manufacture: CAD/CAM packages
Planning critical path: charts trend analysis, management charts
Conferences: teleconferencing, videotex

Fig. 12.14   The use of graphs within business decision-making.

Graphics can play a very large role in decision-making in an organization but the users must know what to ask for. They must be aware of the issues which will be affected by management changes and possible roll-over effect. This implies a level of awareness concerning the threats and opportunities throughout the business. Ultimately, it leads us to examine the possibility of the intelligent organization.

12.8   The intelligent organization

The concept behind all MSS is that of improved decision-making that is based on better information and a more thorough examination of the choices involved and their probable outcomes. Utilizing the types of system described in this chapter should not only help the individual manager but should also necessarily impact on the overall decision-making capabilities of the organization.

The concept of the intelligent organization was born in a paper produced by Huber (1984) and christened in a later paper by Huber & McDaniel (1986). The concept is that of an organization which becomes efficient at learning and deciding. In providing the organizational support for this we enter into the world of organizational support systems (OSS) where information systems actively plan and initiate acts which will result in the realization of organizational strategies.

Paradice (1988) notes that there are four ways to use OSS: communication tool, information enhancer, information reactor and information anticipator. The last level is where the OSS reacts to messages within its environment based on consequences generated by a model that predicts a future state given the current environment. Obviously, as the system moves through these four levels it will rely further on memory and 'intelligence'. How do we arrive at such a state? The ultimate information model of an organization is still very far from a reality in even the most innovative users of information technology. There is also the question of whether such an ultimate is achievable or even desirable at all, given the essentially social nature of an organization.

Nunamaker (1987) suggests that if intelligent organizational behaviour is important at all it is most important at times of crisis. Survival itself may depend on an organization's ability to make and implement intelligent decisions — decisions which are timely, appropriate and successful. Organizations that decide to improve the effectiveness, or intelligence, of their crisis decision groups need to acquire expertise in using cognitive, computer and communications technologies.

Intelligent behaviour in organizations requires being able to acquire information and to use that information to make and implement effective decisions. Intelligent organizations, therefore, have the following characteristics:

> *Learning centred.* They focus attention on learning because consistent, effective decision making depends on their ability to acquire knowledge.
> *Technologically supported.* They must use computer and communications technologies to support an environment of applied cognition.
> *Collaborative organizations.* They require group efforts because of the diffusion of responsibility across multiple individuals in an organization.
> *Information literate.* There are three aspects to this: information/

knowledge needs, information systems assumptions and limitations, information technology sophistication.

In a crisis situation, the intelligent organization must respond out of deliberation rather than desperation. Nunamaker, has, therefore, developed a framework for a crisis-management environment which is designed to identify those situations which, if unchecked, would wreak havoc on the organization. The organization must be able to acquire the knowledge and tools required to anticipate, manage or forestall crises. It must allow trained, flexible decision groups to be developed. It must be able to evaluate and learn from its crisis-management experience. Figure 12.15 portrays integrated computer- and communications-based processes required for crisis management, as well as the command centre in which crisis groups would meet to make and implement decisions.

Systems such as these are only possible in organizations where strategic

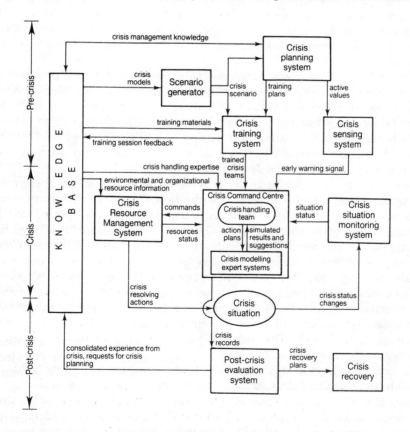

Fig. 12.15 Model of a crisis management environment.

planning is a well-developed activity involving all the decision makers within the organization. Managers have to be aware of the goals of the organization and be able to identify threats and opportunities. Most importantly, they must understand how fundamental information is to the effective conduct of their business.

12.9 Summary

This chapter has been concerned with management support systems and their role in improving the quality of decision-making within an organization. In a sense, this should be the obvious goal of any information system but, in practice, the information is often presented in such a way that it becomes meaningless to the manager. This is where PC software and graphic displays may have a major impact on managerial perceptions of the usefulness of computer-based information systems. Similarly, the new generation of integrated application development tools beg for user involvement and with fast prototyping methods an interactive DSS can be developed in a very short time frame.

The real joy of such tools is that they help the user and the system developer to understand the actual decision-making processes involved. Often we do not know how we arrive at certain decisions. Even more commonly, we cannot identify our real information needs without knowing what might be possible. MSS are all about discovering how we do this and also how we might do this better. When used effectively, they generate excitement and creativity in both the manager and the system developer.

This is an area which can be developed only with the total co-operation of the senior management within the organization. Organizational awareness of decision-making processes is also necessary. Much of the routine decision making is just that — routine and rule based. Where this applies, management are far better employed in handling exceptions and overall policy decision making. An example, standard to many banking organizations is in letter of credit authorization. One large bank employed 18 credit assessors and two senior credit assessors whose sole job was to assess the status of letters of credit for overseas transactions. It was found that the work could be reduced to a rule-based system of 140 rules. Exceptions were left for the two senior assessors to deal with. This released the other 18 staff to concentrate on developing new business.

In order to develop this sytem the credit assessors had to be willing to provide an analysis of their decision-making and to accept that such a system would allow them greater opportunities to use their expertise for the benefit of the organization as a whole but also for their personal job satisfaction. This required a totally participative development approach but also one where the system developer was familiar with the business processes and the role of the managers.

In many organizations it is becoming more usual to employ IT specialists with a particular business background to bridge the gap between users and technology. In this case, instead of the MIS department being organized into specialist technical units such as programming, systems design and so on we find specialist units centred around business expertise such as finance, marketing, personnel. In such a situation it is more and more important that the IT manager should have a thorough understanding of the business environment and the information needs.

The organization of today has to accept that it is an information organization and that it needs to build up intelligence related to information and the systems which can support it. The organizations that fail to do so today may not be here as the organizations of tomorrow.

13   Office information systems

13.1   Introduction

The paperless office may be an interesting phrase which appears attractive to many of us surrounded by books, files, correspondence and the like. Rather than getting rid of paper all together, what is much more sensible is to aim for the reduction of volume of paper passing over our desks. We should concentrate instead on improving the quality of the information on which we base our decisions and fulfil our function within the organization.

One way of achieving this is through the implementation of the various office automation (OA) tools available today. A paperless office may be a utopian dream but the truly electronic office remains an achievable goal. It will be essential to utilize the enormous power of new desktop machines like those based on the 80386 processor chip which are designed as single user workstations. These generally have an enormous excess capacity which can be utilized only in an integrated office environment. To gain the full benefit of an integrated office all functions have to work together in an integrated way which means that there has to be ready communication between the component parts.

This chapter will discuss the various services available to users of office automation technology. It will look at some of the ways in which these can contribute to an organization's productivity and the achievement of its strategic goals. The key to success in utilizing OA will be to take an integrated approach to its adoption. With a careful needs-analysis combined with a good understanding of the various technologies available and their individual pros and cons, users of OA should easily reap the expected benefits.

13.2   Strategic planning considerations

Strategic planning for office automation is essential if company-wide needs are to be met. The purchase of incompatible systems within the same organization is a problem many of us have already encountered. Individual departments can address their own problems but without a strategic plan the benefits to be gained from an integrated electronic office will be lost. The need for a strategic plan must be emphasized. But flexibility and adaptability to the changing technology are also essential ingredients in the planning process.

New opportunities created by new products are regularly becoming available because of rapidly changing technology. Constant review will allow the OA implementation to maintain its alignment with the strategic plans of the company and allow opportunities to benefit from increasing experience in its use in the organization. Since OA affects all the workers in an organization it also makes changes necessary in many working procedures. These changes can only come about smoothly if accompanied by retraining and a systematic approach.

The OA strategic plan should provide a rationale for the adoption of any new technology into a process. This means looking at what is being done and analyzing *why* it is being done. There is a danger of taking an approach which merely computerizes processes. This is the wrong approach. Defining where automation can best help is essential to ensure the benefits of its use are gained. By concentrating on the type of information needed and why it is needed, an OA strategy can be defined to meet the needs of the organization and avoid the pitfalls surrounding a piecemeal approach to OA use.

Chapter 7 discussed some strategies to define an organization's information systems requirements. The point to remember is that the successful use of OA is dependent on a careful study of the essential information flows in an organization. Responsibility for the automation project should be assigned clearly. Overall long-range planning should accompany, rather than precede, practical developments. Clear goals should be developed which refer to the future needs of the organization. The investment strategy should detail a clear range of options alongside an evaluation of expected benefits with careful attention being paid to the importance of training if success is to be achieved (see also chapter 10).

13.3   Testing the strategy

Various strategy testing options are available. Experimentation through pilot projects appeals to many new users of various technology. This approach allows hands-on experience to be gained which in turn makes final purchasing and implementation decisions better informed. The reaction of employees can be assessed and this in turn helps to plan future training requirements. Areas for which pilot projects are suitable may be selected with a view to informing the cost-justification process in identifying where savings and productivity gains can be made and in quantifying their values. Referring back to points made in chapter 10 about intangible benefits is relevant in this context since the value of opportunity hours and the better quality of work done by knowledge workers in an automated environment is hard to quantify. By providing users with a taste of what is possible, these intangible benefits may be easier to describe based on experience within the organization.

Care must be taken in designing a pilot project. For example, the success of electronic mail depends on whether or not you can reach enough people to make your job easier. If only a fraction of your contacts are possible by electronic mail then it may be more of a nuisance than a benefit since you will have to work with your existing system plus the new electronic system at the same time. There is a critical mass which is essential to ensuring that a new technology can be properly piloted. If you design only a small pilot project it may fail simply because it was not extensive enough to allow users to experiment with the full range of services the technology could provide.

For organizations already using word processors, their experience in this application can be useful in providing a basis for future development. As an established concept in the organization, the value of integrating new technologies can clearly be seen to make sense. The piggyback effect of using existing equipment to gain additional benefits which could not be individually cost-justified may create opportunities for the simple adoption of electronic mail and so on. The cost of workstations capable of not only word processing but also acting as decision-support systems for managers is falling. This will allow managers to use decision-support software easily as they become aware of the potential advantages available to them.

The issue today is not really whether benefits can be realized but rather if the costs will be exceeded by the benefits enough to justify the investment. The benefits can be realized by:

> reduced time spent on less productive activities, increased quantity of work produced, improved quality of work products and improved worker satisfaction.

Evaluating costs requires that you have a rough model of the system you are evaluating which can be used to analyze impact on time saved in the various activities affected. Not all office automation projects have the same objectives but all should be carefully evaluated before purchases are made.

Impact and system adaptation evaluation to determine the effect of electronic support systems *after* they are implemented is helpful in ensuring that a system *continues* to meet the needs of the organization. The more that is learnt about the impact of the results of planning, the better the planning becomes in the long term. Also the organization is enabled to adapt the system to take better advantage of its benefits and overcome its shortcomings. Impact evaluation can be built into the planning phase. To measure impact you need a starting point, so you need to collect baseline data before the technology is introduced.

Conrath (1985) provides some useful guidelines to assist in planning for the successful adoption of OA.

Start with a problem, not a solution.

Think about people before technology.

Focus on support not automation.

Remember that support implies integration.

The key to the system is the organization; people and technology are merely components.

Good management can survive without office technology. The reverse is not true.

Effectiveness is essential, not efficiency. Worry about doing the right thing before doing things right.

Following guidelines such as these will ensure that a system evolves which provides the service the users need.

13.4   Office automation systems technology

Office automation (OA) devices are well known to hundreds of users and it would be redundant to describe applications generally widely understood and well documented elsewhere. What follows is not by any means a complete rundown of OA technology but rather a selection of some of the more interesting features and some of the characteristics which should be taken into account in ensuring that planned systems remain flexible and adaptable in the face of changing technology.

13.4.1   Digital networks

Any office environment is characterized by intensive communication activity. In some offices communication takes up to 80% of office workers' time.

We have seen extraordinary growth in office communications in the last 10 years. In telecommunications there are numerous long-distance networks based on computers. TELENET and TYMNET in the USA, DATAPAC in Canada, TRANSPAC in France, and PSS in England are examples. In addition satellite channels are starting to be used for high bandwidth communications around the world and in the next few years there will be submarine fibre optic cables right round the world enabling high speed, high quality transmission of all types of data. One of the problems, of course, is allowing different types of computer to communicate with each other. In the USA the original research on this produced the Government-sponsored ARPANET which now connects hundreds of universities, Government sites, industrial laboratories, and other networks.

In chapter 6 we discussed network protocols. In the office environment the session layer (layer 5) embodies most of the functions traditionally included in a network-oriented operating system. Thus it should be considered in close relation with the operating system running in various workstations and servers when designing an electronic office system. Until now no standard operating system has been properly merged with the layers in the ISO/OSI model. Now the trend is for operating systems to provide extensions to link the external operating system function with the session layer functions. In the UNIX operating system the network functions generally match with the protocols defined in the ARPANET and in personal computing there are now versions of MS/DOS which include layers of protocols. IBM has adopted an open architecture SNA (Systems Network Architecture). This evolved from a layered architecture that focused on synchronous data distribution as it is generally required in the distributed data processing application to a layered architecture that provides a means for exchanging data asynchronously in distributed office systems.

Wide area networks

Wide area networks (WAN) are the basic transmission foundation for building a distributed office system over a wide geographical area. ARPANET, which was sponsored by the Defense Advanced Research Projects Agency of the Government of the USA, was the first of the major influential vehicles for pioneering work in wide area networking and today spans all of North America, Europe and Hawaii. Other networks have been developed for experimental purposes to provide extensions to ARPANET.

Public data networks

People in the business world are mostly familiar with telephone and telex services which put them in touch with the rest of the world. However, with an increasing dependency on speedy and frequent movement of market- or transaction-based information the capabilities of voice and telex networks are often not sufficient. This has resulted in the emergence of dedicated data networks throughout the world, which enable terminals and computers to communicate accurately and economically both locally and internationally. Both direct circuit and dialled telephone access are available and the benefits to the users include:

> Easy incremental growth of service capacity at host computer
> Economic and secure data transport network for computer-based services
> Multi-speed communication between terminals and host computers
> High levels of availability
> Comprehensive network management facilities
> Ability to send FAX messages direct from your personal computer or word processor through the provision of a service to convert ASCII files from your terminal for delivery elsewhere

Switched services are high quality data transmission services and will comply with international standards for asynchronous (known as X.28) and packet (known as X.25) access. Usually customers who use switched services will send a lot of data regularly between different parts of their organization or between themselves and their customers. *Non-switched services* are circuit based data networks which can provide complete end-to-end data transmission facilities for users with less need of the costlier high speed services of switched services. They offer customers a low cost option which allows users to enter the world of data communications with the minimum of investment and risk while preserving an easy migration path to switched services as their needs develop. The type of connection employed will very much depend on users' requirements. Options available include the following.

Network user's identity (NUI). A secure code or password which ensures accurate network billing to customers where shared access is used. Dial-up customers can employ the NUI facility unless they are accessing a computer-based service which offers the reverse charging facility.

Direct call. Where only a single destination is called it is not necessary to conduct a call set up routine every time. Automatic connection can be made to a pre-determined location when the terminal is activated.

Call redirect. The automatic redirection of calls to a nominated alternate address. This is useful as a backup or automatic standby or as a diversion facility for premises which are not in full-time operation.

Closed user group. A private restricted access network within a public data network which allows group members to communicate freely but bars all other calls to and from the group. Variations in access restrictions are available to suit individual requirements and it is possible for terminals to be members of more than one closed user group.

Charging. Reverse charging can be arranged whereby all calls are billed centrally against the service rather than to individual callers. Statements showing number of calls, overall duration and amount of data sent with separate totals for local and international calls can be provided.

Commercial networks are called common-carrier networks. Some of them provide services and are therefore considered as value-added networks (VANs).

PABX

The first PABX (private automatic branch exchange) systems in the 1970s replaced the old electro-mechanical telephone switches by offering enhanced telephone services since they included a computer which could be programmed to perform all sorts of functions. PABX offers additional features to a simple local area network (LAN) such as mail, teleconferencing and databases. Extended features such as abbreviated dialling, forwarding on busy or unanswered telephones and audio-conferencing are commonly available now as a result of the evolution of the PABX through four generations. Recent PABXs are all digital and do not require a modem for communication. Voice and data are processed together and voice and data equipment can operate simultaneously through PABX. The major characteristics to note for planning office systems are the number and type of terminals, the number of simultaneous channels, the maximum rate accepted for data, the expandibility, the gateways to allow connection to public networks, and the services which are provided.

ISDN (Integrated services digital network)
Present industrial society is in the midst of an information-handling evolution in which the need to transfer various types of information between organizations is increasing. The telephone network will assist the convergence of computers and communication technology when the telephone network is switched to a fully digital network. Although digital networks can be set up locally within a company to integrate computers and communications, the full benefits will only come when the network can be extended to the outside world.

In particular the adoption of integrated services digital networks (ISDN) facilitates advantages in this area. The use of electronic mail, discussed below, is growing fast and already many people are sending messages through their phones but the transmission process is slow and clumsy since digital information is translated into audio signals and then sent over the telephone system to be received and re-converted back to digital form at the other end. When data can be sent directly, far higher transmission speeds will be possible, the quality of voice transmission will be improved and FAX will be faster.

The ISDN standard (defined as the X-21 protocol) specifies the way the user transmits data in digital form. This uses three channels and has the capability to allow data to be passed between computers and a voice commentary to be sent at the same time. Ordinary voice communications just become another data stream and computers and telephones will gradually merge together. Office PABX systems will have to be replaced by digital versions which can handle ISDN and analog telephone exchanges will have to be replaced by digital systems. The strategic importance of the whole ISDN standard is enormous since it is the foundation for allowing computers and communications systems to merge worldwide. Pilot projects are underway in many countries. ISDN is available in four cities in Japan and will be available across the country by 1997. Full services are estimated to appear in the UK and France by 1991–92, in Switzerland by 1993 and West Germany by 1995.

The type of possibilities which will come are functions like voice dialling. This is being developed in the USA. You speak the name of the person you want to call and the number is dialled automatically. The implications for OA are that the convergence of the various networks existing today will offer a wide range of feasible new telecommunication services which can easily be integrated and to which users will have easy access through multipurpose devices. The international standardization of the open systems interconnection (OSI) layered model will allow communications between any types of user systems and networks and this will lead to further rationalization of equipment which should be to the benefit of the purchaser. Figure 13.1 shows how these services can link up to provide a variety of facilities for the information users.

13.4.2   FAX and telex

Telex is often considered old-fashioned in the light of new telecommunications developments. However, despite this general belief, the use of telex is still growing both in the number of subscribers and in minutes of transmission time. The new telex machines have modern detachable keyboards, visual display screens, memories, separate printers and even disk drives. This means they can be used for not just sending and receiving telexes but also for the preparation of other office correspondence. Telex transmission has been limited by its slow speed and the fact that messages could only be sent in capital letters of the Roman alphabet. However telexes can now be sent at 4.5 times the speed they could previously and can now contain upper and lower case letters. There is now a printer available which can convert coded information through telex and automatically print it out in Chinese characters. With the dearth of high quality data lines in China telex will be the standard written means of communication there for a long time to come.

Facsimile systems (FAX) are currently growing much faster than the older telex systems. Since this is a visual medium, a document is transmitted line by line as an image rather than a series of characters. Handwritten work, or the character sets of any language, can be transmitted with equal speed. A typical page of A4 FAX takes about a minute to send, which is fast compared to telex. A dedicated stand-alone FAX machine consists of a scanner, modem and printer and the popularity of FAX in Japan is having the additional effect of encouraging the related development of scanner technology. Once you have a network of computers set up, the cost of adding FAX and telex is quite small.

A PC telex card incorporating the necessary telex modem is available and this allows the user to do things like store messages and send them at cheap times of the day. Single user FAX boards for personal computers with built-in high-speed modems are fairly inexpensive. Also available are multi-user FAX boards which can support up to eight users.

Even if he does not have a scanner, the personal-computer owner can use his PC to convert text and images into FAX format without having to print them out first. Optical character reader (OCR) software can also be run on a PC to convert incoming FAX messages into ASC11 code. Group 4 FAX machines have been announced, which will provide higher resolution of around 300–400 dots per inch. When these are available OCR in conjunction with FAX will be much more reliable and therefore more useful. High speed facsimile transmission machines are marketed which come with the telephone component built in so there is no need to attach a separate instrument. These devices can memorize many phone numbers, can be programmed to transmit

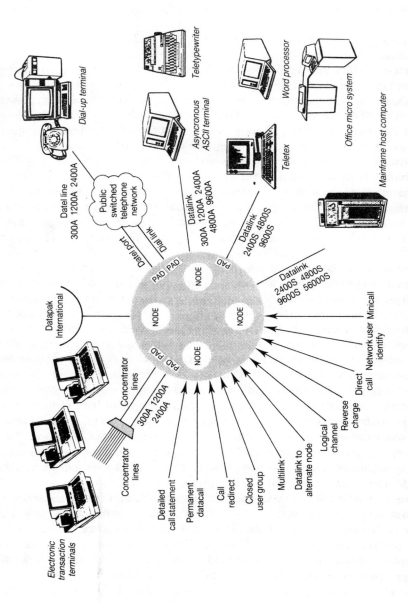

Fig. 13.1 Telecommunications services can link up to provide a variety of services: the Hong Kong Datapak service.

at a preselected time and call one or more fax machines and command them to transmit the contents of their automatic document feeders. Other telephones are available which can be connected to FAX machines and other office equipment to provide an optimum communications network for a small office. Really small lightweight FAX models are also being marketed for personal use. Small enough to fit into a briefcase, they can handle up to A4 size documents. Some can be plugged in to any compatible telephone jack for instant fax communications anywhere.

FAX provides a greater degree of consultation to be possible between geographically separated people but telex currently has many more users — about 2 million users worldwide in over 200 countries. Although it is fairly slow (with a top speed of about 60 words a minute) it is still the most established real-time hard copy business medium and this enormous existing user base will mean that telex stays around for quite some time, especially in facilitating communication between countries which are not advanced in their planning for digital telephone network systems.

13.4.3   Electronic mail, filing, and bulletin board services

Electronic mail is really a computer-based message system. It provides buffered communication between groups of individual users whereas a system like telex links station to station. A single electronic mail message may be addressed to many recipients because electronic mail systems provide facilities like distribution lists. The interactive submitting and delivering of messages by electronic mail means that speed and user convenience are emphasized. In the truly integrated office, electronic mail systems should be able to connect into unified networks. This internetworking is vital because of its critical mass effect since the effectiveness of an electronic mail system depends to a large extent on how many people it can reach. Since many potential correspondents will be users of different electronic mail systems, interconnection will be the only way to achieve maximum utility.

Some electronic mail systems name their users by means of attribute-based naming schemes. Others use short numeric codes or variable length string names. Distribution lists identify logical groupings of people who should receive certain sets of messages; if a distribution list is used as the recipient of a message then everyone on the list will receive the message. Problems can arise when two or more distribution lists are used as recipients for a message and they contain duplicate entries (one person sits on two committees, for example). Prospective users of electronic mail systems should consider finding out how their proposed purchase deals with this type of situation.

Users of electronic mail systems must have confidence that the system will make messages available to the intended recipients and no one else. Also when a message is received it is vital that the recipient can determine whether the message actually came from the originator specified. In the local mail context these assurances are relatively straightforward but become much more complex issues when internetworking is involved.

Generally, electronic mail systems increase speed of communications within and between locations within an organization. Work done in mail rooms and labour-intensive paper-handling tasks can be significantly reduced, especially when electronic filing and document retrieval is also implemented. Meetings between parties linked together through electronic mail can be readily scheduled if all parties keep their electronic diary available on the system for others to see when they will be free. Electronic filing enhances electronic mail and wordprocessing by enabling the storage and retrieval of messages and documents electronically. At the same time it ensures confidentiality of sensitive information and allows multiple access to both public and personal files.

Bulletin board services (BBS) can be a part of an electronic mail system or a separate service to which the user connects his computer through a telephone line and a modem. Many general purpose office automation and electronic mail packages can perform bulletin board functions. A simple BBS can provide some of the features of electronic mail for a minimal cost. The hardware required can be as simple: usually only a PC with a hard disk, and some bulletin board software. Since BBS are very popular ways to share public domain software there is plenty of free or low priced BBS software available. Running a BBS requires an operator who has to perform various housekeeping functions and periodically backup the system. BBS allow users to share software and leave messages for each other which can either be read by all users (an exchange forum for ideas and so on) or be sent to individuals for private communications.

A report on the use of a BBS for electronic communications in Coca-Cola Foods describes how it is used to support electronic mail between regional sales offices and their headquarters. It also serves as a document distribution centre. Coca-Cola Foods' need for electronic mail was not well defined and by using a BBS they were able to establish likely traffic patterns and gather more information on how much such a system was likely to be used.

13.4.4 Desktop publishing

Desktop publishing (DTP) is a fairly recent addition to the range of products available to users of OA. The advent of scanners, laser printers and page makeup and composition software together give even a small organization the opportunity to produce professional quality documentation in-house. This allows users to produce higher quality documentation, as well as saving them time and money and giving them the chance to produce time-sensitive documents such as price lists and technical publications. A company's product catalogue, which has textual descriptions of products, pictures and diagrams, together with price information, all of which may be stored on the company's central computer system illustrates the value of integrated systems. Price changes, new product lines and so on can be easily included in a new catalogue. This can then by typeset in the office at minimal cost compared to traditional typesetting techniques but with little sacrifice in quality of the finished product.

Desktop publishing is not entirely problem free. For a small business it has advantages over conventional typesetting in terms of quick turnaround and savings in time and money. However, it is not suitable for very high quality documents. The problem with the print quality is the resolution. Laser printers commonly used with desktop publishing systems have horizontal and vertical resolutions of around 300 dots per inch. Compare this figure with the performance of typesetting machines which have resolutions of up to 2540 dots per inch. Desktop publishing handles word processing, and graphics can be integrated from files stored in memory, created by other programs, reproduced through digitizers from photographs, drawings and live and recorded video. Page makeup software allows the operator to position text, columns, headlines, illustrations and captions anywhere on the page which is displayed on a monitor. When the appearance is approved the operator can save the document or print it straight away. In most systems the printer reproduces the page exactly as it was on the screen: this is known as What You See is What You Get or WYSIWYG. Digitizers or scanners can be used to add illustrations to a page layout. This device scans the illustration and converts it into a collection of bits which form an image to represent the scanned material. During scanning, some digitizers picture the result on the screen of the computer to which the digitizer is connected. When scanning is complete the digitized picture is available for placing on any page being composed. Digitizers should be carefully evaluated before purchase as they have no grey scale capability which means that they are capable of dealing with photographs in only a rudimentary way.

13.4.5   Hard copy output choices

Laser printers are becoming commonplace in offices and will print at about 6 pages a minute, or more or less, depending very much on what you want to print. Beware of using sales specifications to estimate how fast a printer can work — like the top speed of your car, the maximum speed of the device and the average speed actually found in use are often rather different figures.

A laser printer creates an image of the entire page to be printed by a process similar to that used in copying machines. Text and graphics data is transmitted to the printer. A wide variety of speeds are available for laser printers; they work very much faster than daisy wheel printers. They are very versatile in what they can produce, offering advantages such as many different fonts, sideways printing and duplex printing (sequentially printing on both sides of the page). The key to selecting a laser printer should be the manufacturer's recommended monthly average page volume since reliability will be a function of volume on a given laser machine. Because laser printers use non-impact technology they run much more quietly than impact printers. Internal cooling fans and paper handling mechanisms create noise though, so listen to how a printer works before selecting it. Non-impact printers reduce the cost of preprinted forms. By permitting users to control typography, graphics, and other aspects of document production, laser printers have greatly increased the effectiveness of computer-printed materials. Other advantages have been gained through progress in page description languages, which make the job of moving images from the screen to paper much easier. In high volume applications laser printers can be said to be the most economical and fastest way to generate documents.

If requirements include the production of multiple copies, the handling of multipart forms, the printing of self-stick labels, the use of wide paper or the use of materials which accept oil-based inks better than toners, then impact printers are a better choice. At the micro level *dot matrix printers* often are the best choice since getting popular application packages such as accounting packages or spreadsheets to drive a non-impact printer can sometimes be a troublesome task. The power and the flexibility of the laser printer necessitates clever software and this is not always included in business application software.

For printers in general the cost per copy is a function of consumables (basically the paper and ink), service costs and depreciation. Price versus performance should be the purchasing guideline. Serial dot matrix printers offer a low price, but slower speed and poorer quality appearance. They are currently the most popular printers for office use and can be used for business graphics, emphasizing text, and, at a push, can act as a pen plotter replacement. They use impact printing technology and have obvious drawbacks in noise and print quality. However, they are cheap, increasingly fast and improving in quality; 18 and 24 pin models offer much more acceptable results than the traditional 9 pin models.

Daisy wheel printers are noisy, though acoustic hoods can reduce this nuisance. They also have limited graphics capabilities. Changing font can be difficult necessitating the replacement of the daisy wheel — an obvious inconvenience during printing a document. However, these printers are popular for use with multiple part stationery and some users consider that a daisy wheel printer gives better print quality than a laser printer for ordinary correspondence work. Overall, daisywheel printers offer excellent quality for the lowest price.

Colour printing is quite another consideration. In colour printing (as in most things) you get what you pay for. The process of combining colours is mechanically tricky. With the exception of ink-jet printers all colour printers separate the printing function for each of the subtractive colours — cyan, magenta and yellow — overlaying colours in several passes. Registration is critical as each pixel must line up precisely with the corresponding pixel from the previous pass.

To date *pen plotters* are the most popular colour output devices for office applications such as business graphics and presentation materials. These are mechanically intensive devices which move under software control so that pens can actually write to generate graphics and associated text. They have varying levels of accuracy measured by how close they can place dots to each other. These are fairly slow devices and desktop plotters can take easily 5 minutes for simple business graphs.

Electrostatic plotters have advantages over pen plotters; they are faster, quieter, give high resolution output, and are more suited to operate unattended. However they are very expensive.

Thermal transfer printers are particularly effective for area-fills since the density of the graphic does not affect print speed in page systems. They too produce colour prints through multiple passes of the subtractive primaries and offer the least expensive colour printing currently available. However, the cost of supplies may be offputting and the appearance of the shiny paper needed in these printers may not be acceptable to some users.

Ink jet printers print colours in a single pass and tend to be more costly than thermal printers. This is a truly non-contact technology but has had development problems which have given these printers a reputation for questionable reliability.

Needs and applications are the first starting point in deciding what is the best printer for an information system. The kind of questions to ask are:

How much speed and quality to I need?
Are there any specific applications requiring scientific notations?
How much operator attention does this printer require?
Is an alarm provided for paper jams?
Are different fonts easily used?
How easy is it to change ribbons?
What are running costs?
Are supplies readily available locally?
Is the printer compatible with the intended computer?

13.5 Human factors in office automation

The successful use of OA owes as much to careful consideration of the human factors involved as to selecting the appropriate technology. Foulkes & Parizek (1985) pose the question 'By what criteria is a system deemed successful?' In OA, they say, 'There is one simple definition; return on investment. OA must provide a visibly improved return on investment, must improve efficiency, must have capabilities of providing useful information'. How much, and how well, these tools are used depends on the people. They identify the keys to OA success as training and motivation. Motivation to exercise creative thinking is important if all the capabilities of the hardware and software provided are to be utilized. Training includes basic hands-on sessions for clerical staff and abbreviated courses for managers and professionals. They have found that after completing the course a manager will almost always realize another way in which the system can be used in the business. Advanced training is given after 6 months and both clerical and management staff receive spreadsheet training. User meetings are held for exchanging ideas and experiences and additional training is provided when changes or improvements to the systems are necessary. The section in chapter 10 on training is relevant to the successful implementation of OA systems.

The social aspects of the introduction of OA are very relevant to the people involved. A secretary's power derives from his control over peoples' access to his boss and from the information he sees which is going to and from his boss. With the adoption of electronic mail many staff may be in direct communication with the boss, completely by-passing the secretary. The nature of his job is changed because he no longer necessarily has access to all the correspondence his boss has. Centralized wordprocessing services within a department replacing secretaries working for two or three individuals can create a loss of morale both for the manager and for the secretary through the removal of personal contacts.

Centralization may even create more work for the manager who now has to write out his instructions instead of giving a verbal instruction like 'Just send an apologetic note like we sent to XYZ company last week' which takes only a few seconds of his time.

Gaffney (1983) discusses what we really mean by power and comes to the conclusions that since power is transaction specific (i.e. power exists only in its application), therefore providing resources is a major source of power. Since a major resource of the future is OA, those who provide and control access to OA will exercise power. Whoever controls the creation and flow of information controls the distribution of power. Since three commodities are necessary for accumulating productive power — information, resources and support — an information system may embody all three in one form. This, Gaffney concludes, is why OA systems have an unparalleled potential for providing an individual with the means of accumulating productive power. Such potentially disruptive effects on traditional patterns of work mean that the care attention paid to the human side of OA can only be well-spent effort.

13.6 Summary

This chapter has looked at the strategic planning issues important in office automation. It has covered some of the newer technologies and emphasized how important it is to consider people when bringing in OA to any organization.

14 Thinking offices?

14.1 Integrated office automation

As we have seen in the last chapter, the talk of office automation is all-pervasive: from specialist publications to the daily press, we are assailed by news of the technology revolution. But how far are the claims of manufacturers justified, and can their products be applied to our business environments? More importantly, do we need them and are they affordable?

If the systems described in chapters 11, 12 and 13 are going to impact on an organization in the way we have described, then we have to be assured that integrated automation is both possible and practical. Before you decide to take the leap we would like you to consider the following scenario and distinguish fact from the hopeful fantasies of vendors. How much of what follows is happening today, and what is a projection for tomorrow?

14.2 A case of convenience

George Lee, a high ranking executive exployed by a large multinational in London, sits at home in the South of France. His working day begins as he goes into his study and checks his FAX/copier for messages and turns to the desktop computer. This has been left on overnight and signals that there are several messages to be seen. He reads the messages, puts one FAX into the PC through a scanner and dumps all the electronic mail but for one item. This he amends and sends on, through a modem and the telephone lines, to a colleague working in Rome.

Today George wants to check on some new engineering research and, using his PC and modem, he accesses two database libraries in the USA and downloads the relevant papers into his system. At the same time he calls up Profile in London and downloads the Financial Times to read over coffee.

An hour later, needing a stroll, George walks to his travel agent. Getting in the lift, he speaks the floor number and is taken there. Entering the office he finds three girls sitting at terminals with clean desks and no shelves of literature on the walls.

George explains that he wants to travel for a week or so, either to the Maldives or the Seychelles as he hasn't seen them. Which destination is better for his holiday?

The travel agent seats George at a workstation and puts a video disk in the player. She shows George how to summon up pictures of the hotels available and how to use the controls to be shown room interiors, facilities and whatever else he needs in the order that he needs.

Satisfied that the Seychelles would be a good idea, George asks for brochures to show his girlfriend. The agent uses the workstation to send images to a colour printer and produces within minutes a brochure showing the items that George requested and omitting the rest. George makes a flight reservation and specifies vegetarian food for his girlfriend, books the hotel room and arranges for a hire car to be waiting on arrival. He decides not to book a restaurant table for dinner as he doesn't yet know whether he'll eat on the plane.

Strolling back into the street, George drops by the supermarket where he collects several items and goes to an unattended checkout point. Passing his goods through the scanner, he hears the price repeated aloud by the electronic teller and the total given at the end. George slips his card into a slot and taps out his code number to authorize immediate transfer of funds from his account to that of the supermarket.

Returning home, George sits down at his desk and continues to prepare his report. He has been working on this assignment for 8 months and wants to finish it before taking his holiday. This time, because the report will be a reference standard for some time to come, George will put a copy onto a laser disk (similar to his music collection) and mail it in addition to sending a preliminary copy by modem to the company's mainframe computer. The company has suggested that he consider downloading to microfiches, but George has always resisted this out of conservatism: he doesn't want to clutter up the office with another input/output device for his workstation.

Before leaving on holiday the following week, George considers being out of touch except by telephone, but realises that he might miss important social as well as business calls. He instructs his FAX and PC to forward messages to his hotel. Collecting his girlfriend, he slips away—without notifying his employer. He remembers that his daughter at university in Toronto will need another installment of cash before he returns and, using his terminal, transfers enough to keep her going for the next term.

Arriving at the chosen holiday hotel, George shows his passport and is issued with a plastic card functioning as room key and payment authorization within the hotel facilities and shops.

The lift here is old-fashioned and George has to press a button to operate it, but once within the room he sits in a comfortable chair and snaps his fingers. At the sound, the television trolley moves across the room until it is 6 feet in front of him. At the same time, a small computer terminal also moves across on its table to stop at his right hand side.

Pressing a few keys, the guest looks at the dinner menu, makes his choice and tells the management at what time he would like to eat in his room. He then tells the bathroom to run a bath for him at his favourite temperature. He selects a film to watch for the evening and decides at what time he will see it.

Although on holiday, George makes no distinction between work days and non-work days: he is paid a retainer by the multinational company and is also paid on a project basis. He is also free to work on other projects for other companies.

On the third day of the holiday, George's girlfriend gets up in the morning feeling unwell. She uses the room terminal to access the hotel doctor who asks her questions about her condition and symptoms in the form of multiple choice questions on the terminal screen. On answering these, the medical diagnosis program displays to the doctor the likely causes of this distress. The doctor then invites the woman to his consulting room in person — he's pretty sure that she's pregnant, but wants to make certain before distressing or pleasing her.

The following day George is already itching to read his mail: after breakfast he checks the hotel message bank for those forwarded to him from home and leaves a message for a business contact in the Seychelles letting him know of his arrival. If he receives a message or FAX from his contact during his stay, he will place a video call to his office — expensive, but since they've never met face to face, George thinks that a local video call would be worthwhile.

All of the above transactions and scenes are true and happening today. They are not sufficiently widespread to allow the continuous scene outlined above, but to see how this entire set of activities could come about — very soon — consider the technology and processes that are called business automation and how they are, or may be, implemented.

14.3 Myths or reality?

The idea of encouraging staff to work from home, often on a consultancy or retainer basis, is not novel. The use of telephones, PCs, FAX machines and modems linking users by high speed data nets is not new. First on a large scale was Rank Xerox in the UK: they saved an enormous London rent bill and improved productivity. Publishers of all descriptions, advertising agencies and related concerns have long relied on freelance and correspondent staff, but authoritarian organizations have been slow to relinquish the idea of paying for occupied seats in favour of paying for work done.

Automation is not merely the use of clever tools. The integrated fax/copier can be a space and money saver, but this and other devices come into their own when harnessed within a strategic plan, such as that which embraces our hero, George Lee.

The telephone lines (including optical cables, microwave relays and other hidden devices) are in position to serve and link remote users.

The interactive video disks are already in use. In the UK the country-wide survey known as the New Domesday Book is presented to schoolchildren on two disks which allow a child to select areas of interest, zoom in on items and buildings, and generally work his way around a vast compendium of information. While interactive language learning with videodisc technology is not commonplace, a British team has developed such a system which would probably be delivered by interactive cable, whereby the user takes a stroll through a foreign town engaging in conversations with locals. The application mentioned in the text is far simpler and already in use in the US where it is hooked up in travel agencies to 64-jet multi-coloured inkjet printers to produce brochures as described. Howtek Inc., the makers of this printer are manufacturing this and its successors worldwide.

Voice recognition is under development and already incorporated in some systems. Simple commands such as those for lifts are no problem, but voice drive workstations that work are some time away.

Database access is a commonplace for research institutes and should be so for engineering practices, doctors, lawyers and other professionals. These, together with a vast array of publications are accessible through modems as described. It is possible in Hong Kong, for instance, using the Financial Times owned Profile service, to read the Financial Times in Hong Kong before the edition has appeared on the streets of London. Your stockbroker receives daily downloadings of his transactions from the Stock Exchange through minilinks using the public data net, Datapak, and already uses the terminal to send FAX messages.

Point of sale cash transfer is already well established and larger companies are offered direct secure access to their bank accounts. In the UK, the Bank of Scotland already allows individuals to access their accounts, but the availability of a similar service around the world awaits the widespread implementation of cable TV, and standardization of Viewdata services, although modem transmission is possible, should any bank believe that it could make money from being so obliging.

If you make great use of weather reports, airline timetables, foreign exchange rates and such utilities, you should check regularly which new services are provided: these and many other utilities are offered through DataCom or TeleCom services in their FAX and Datapak links.

Such trivia as sound-activated robots are already marketed, while store and forward capacity exists within telephone switchgear as well as in PC cards and as a provision of data and telephone nets. The bar codings on supermarket products are well established for manual reading, but only in the US, so far, are completely automated systems under trial. Kroger supermarkets in Atlanta have been testing out CheckRobot, a system which comprises a laser scanner, touch sensitive video monitor and a security zone designed to detect cheating. The shopper starts by touching the video screen and a computer graphics program then guides him through the process step by step. On an estimated

3% of items, the bar code cannot be read and a 'help' facility summons assistance. The system also has a speech synthesizer which calls out the price as each item is read. After scanning, the items are sent through a security zone which detects whether they have been scanned or not and if not, reverses direction to return the goods to the shopper for re-entry to the system. A typical supermarket will require one cashier for every three self-scanning lanes and CheckRobot claims the system is 40% faster that conventional scanning.

Surveys show about 25% of shoppers prefer the system and feel more in control — typically, these are younger customers. Around 25% have the opposite reaction and the rest really do not care one way or another as long as the shopping gets done.

But are all of these facilities, indeed any of them, necessary for efficient business procedures? Can organizations continue with traditional management practices and be competitive worldwide?

From the USA and the UK come studies indicating strong correlations between investment in information technology and office automation and profitability. Within Hong Kong, a research study by one of the authors shows the emergence of a similar pattern.

Strategic planning which involves the use of automated ticketing and related facilities within the travel industry has boosted profitability of the leading airlines and spurred others to compete, lest they suffer from the facilities and market penetration of their competitors.

While recognizing that different needs and implementation patterns are appropriate to different business sectors, it is agreed by researchers that integrated automation must have as its objectives a mixture of the following: the increased profitability of a business, the reduction of expense, the effective support of business goals, the expansion of management control, effective information integration, and competitive advantage. These objectives will, as implemented, affect four broad groups: clerical/secretarial staff; professional and technical workers; middle and first-line management; and executive management.

Secretarial and clerical staff are the first candidates for automation with accounting procedures, text processing, electronic filing and mail despatch facilities readily and cheaply available. Time and cost savings are readily apparent in this area.

The technical staff who support management functions can speed up their output by the graphics and display capabilities of modern terminals and the speed with which keyboards can retrieve, move and store text and images.

Middle management is the target of much equipment for electronic data processing. Such procedures as inventory control, efficient deployment of resources, on-line information regarding supplies, warehouses, orders in hand and production capability and staff availability allow faster recalculation of the firm's ability to take on orders, staff and resources — material and financial.

Spreadsheets, as we have seen, are a basic tool for any planning activity and the provision of 'What if' calculations. Yet it is this area that things begin to go awry: the *ad hoc* allocation of incompatible resources introduced to replace existing procedures with faster ones can lead to frustration, underuse of equipment and dissatisfaction on the part of management with tools that they perceive as toys — fun for the users, but not affecting the business overall.

For business automation to be successfully introduced and to meet its objectives, this stage requires careful planning and foresight to create afresh the systems whereby the business exists. Such glaring examples as the use of incompatible text processing systems within the office, inability to access mainframes, and failure to include all workers within a system, will render expenditure on these items of marginal utility.

In the case of executive management, the tools needed for business automation must not only give the managers access to and control of the entire office system, they must do so in an easily used way. In addition, many more businesses than realize it would benefit from the introduction of decision-support systems. (That used by the doctor in our scenario is an example of such a system currently in use whereby intelligent choices and paths of analysis are quickly explored by an interactive program.)

14.4 Summary

This chapter was introduced to give a real life perspective to the many possibilities of integrated business automation related to the practicalities and actualities. So what are the trends in business automation from which businesses will profit?

The speed with which new technology is marketed, and the associated drop in cost means that applications rejected as unfeasible a few years ago are now essential. The ease of installation, the ease of usage and increased functions of automation means that the decision to invest should be under continual review.

Furthermore, as stand-alone processing is of limited value, the time taken to check out communication technology repays dividends also.

The use of fourth-generation languages, artificial intelligence and expert systems results in forecasts and advice that is under the control of executives — a competitive advantage ignored at grave peril.

In conclusion, it is apparent that, while no perfect solution exists for each and every business, the complex business and office environment of today and tomorrow demands some level of automation for sheer survival. The merging of traditional automation with networking, personal computing and distributed processing is not a question of 'whether', but rather a question of 'when' for all business activities.

15 Small business systems

15.1 Introduction

The use of IT in a cost-effective and productive fashion can pose greater problems for the owner of a small business than implementing a much larger system in a large organization. The reason for this lies not in comparing the complexities of the two projects but in the capabilities and resources available to each. In a large organization there will probably be more well-defined functional roles for individuals and room for manoeuvre in covering for staff during their absence while training. A large organization is also more likely to be able to afford full-time trained computer staff to do system maintenance and enhancements. In a small business, staff tend to have to help out in a variety of ways according to what needs to be done. There is often a severe problem if one key person is away because there is no reserve or back-up pool of skills to replace him. Training for new systems can severely disrupt daily business and once the system is installed the existing staff will probably have to cope with looking after it and all the minor trouble-shooting which accompanies using any computer. There is unlikely to be a trained computer expert nearer than a phone call away.

For reasons of this sort small businesses have a different set of difficulties to tackle in implementing a good computer system. It might also be said that they stand to gain proportionately more than a large organization in terms of the amount of their work which can be improved through computerization.

15.2 A few warnings

There are drawbacks to using computers which are particular to a small business environment. The most significant of these will be the cost of setting up a computerized system. Such costs are not just in the purchase of the system and its peripherals but in training staff to use the system and in reorganizing ways of working necessitated by the formalization of procedures implicit in computerizing many systems.

Readers will be well aware of the work involved in analyzing information flows within an organization. In a small organization individual idiosyncracies can often be tolerated in operating a manual system. 'Oh, John never fills in his time sheet by Friday — he doesn't like form filling, but we just make up his wages anyway.' John's reluctance to fill in a form may result in him not being paid if it's left to the computer. The point of this example is to show that small businesses often evolve ways of handling their work which achieve the desired results but do not follow formal procedures. This is often felt to be a highly desirable characteristic of working in a small business environment, in contrast to the more bureaucratic methods of working, essential in a larger organization.

Computerizing a system often requires individuals to rethink their operations and their co-operation and willingness to do this will be necessary to the successful implementation of a system.

Once the computer system is in place there is probably no going back. This may not be a bad thing if the new system is reliable and efficient. However small business users should realize that manual ways of working will soon be forgotten and if a difficulty arises with the computer it will probably be impossible to return to the old manual way of working. The company is committing itself to the use of technology, including upgrading to new systems when the time comes to scrap the first computer system.

In a small business it is conceivable that buying a computer is necessary because the staff cannot cope with the amount of work. How then can the staff find the (at first, seemingly unproductive) time needed to help to design and then to learn to use the new system? It is a difficult situation, which often becomes more extreme in a small business with only a few staff, all of whom are key people needed to keep the work flowing.

15.3 Summary

The lesson for management in this chapter is that there can be no prescription for how to use IT best in any organization. The needs of the business, of course, will largely dictate the applications. Equally important is how the senior management sees the business evolving and how the information system can help the business be more efficient while simultaneously allowing it to develop according to the management's style. The cost of setting up a computer system may be proportionately very heavy for a small business but could well serve to cut out the need for subcontracting work, hiring additional staff or compromising on the type of service offered to the client or customer.

Again we see that quality is the key to successful use of IT in an organization — allowing those responsible for running the business to deliver their goods or services on time and to standards of service and quality appropriate to their business philosophy.

16   Information resource management

16.1   Introduction

This chapter deals with information resource management — a topic sufficient for a book in itself. This covers the management of:

> strategic planning for IS/IT, development and use of IS/IT including data administration, information services and facilities and quality assurance and security.

It is also inevitably concerned with the management of the human and physical resources which help provide us with information. These are such large areas, however, that they cannot realistically be discussed in full in the context of this book. They are highlighted here as issues which need considerable planning and merit detailed investigation for those directly concerned with these areas of resource management.

The interplay of technology and management is recursive and multi-dimensional. From one view, technology facilitates management and may improve the processes that must be managed. From another view, the technology itself leads to a set of management problems associated with its own introduction to an organization, with its proliferation throughout the organization and with its operation within the subcultures of an enterprise structure. Technology both solves and presents management problems. Management both solves and creates technology problems.

Unfortunately, the root cause of many of the organizational problems in the management of information resources is an overemphasis on technical factors. The organizational structures of DP departments has been largely determined by technology. The rapid changes in the technological environment often force departments to abandon one organizational model for another. What is required today is an organization which is more concerned with using the technology for the benefit of the business. It must focus on how the technology will be used rather than how it works. The major organizational issues in the management of information resources relate to the way in which information systems serve the business and therefore the ways in which the information systems development function integrates with the organization as a whole.

This chapter does not attempt to provide checklists of do's and dont's.

Rather it explores some of the strategic issues which may impinge on the effectiveness of the information services in an organization.

First we look at the authority structure for IS/IT and where responsibility is centred. The importance which is attached to that role is often a central issue in establishing an information culture in the organization. We then look at a variety of management approaches, emphasizing, yet again, a contingency approach where different management styles are required to cope with many different types of information system and different degrees of technological sophistication. Specifically, we examine some of the operational issues concerned with various styles of resource centres — an information centre and a data centre, and relate this to problems of control.

Finally, we provide an overview of some of the critical issues affecting the human side of IT and the hardware management aspects with a particular emphasis on contingency planning.

16.2   Who's in charge?

16.2.1   The chief information officer or the DP manager?

A key management position emerging today is that of the Chief Information Officer (CIO). In a survey of major Fortune 500 companies in the USA nearly 40% of the respondents stated that they have a CIO. What exactly are they?

Broadly, a CIO may have responsibility in three areas:

> Linking information technology and the business strategy
> Executing the IT interface within the organization
> Overseeing the actual operations of the MIS department

A school of thought exists which see this third area as outside the responsibility of the CIO. One very good reason to support this view is the need to present the CIO as an unbiassed proponent of IT. Too often the MIS or DP manager is viewed with suspicion on the basis that he is empire building or he is too far from the users' perspectives. Another reason is the developing use of distributed processing environments where no one person can normally be in charge of the whole development and operational process.

From a business point of view, the CIO needs to recognize that IT has two fundamental impacts:

> On the product that the business offers
> On the process of producing the product

We have already explored the strategic value of systems for an organization. To enable this to happen the CIO must be a member of the top management team and be part of the decision-making body for both corporate planning and IT planning.

In attempting to assist all parts of the organization to absorb and use IT effectively, the CIO must deal with the history of centralized DP functions and a legacy of poor relations with end-users. He must also recognize that the buyers of systems and technology within the organization have changed and are now spread all over the organization. This means that the CIO becomes a facilitator, providing training, evaluating compatibility of products and defining general standards for consistency of data and overall architecture.

Where does this leave the DP manager? Sometimes he finds himself in the position of being CIO; in other cases he finds himself, together with a telecommunications manager, reporting to the CIO.

16.2.2 Management in practice

British Petroleum (BP) has 30 subsidiaries and about 130 000 employees worldwide. It aims to exercise minimum control over technology policy in its operating divisions. An IT strategy-forming group of only 25 is based at the London headquarters (with half, at any one time representing overseas subsidiaries). A small technical committee of 12 meets regularly and there is a biannual IT conference attended by about 200.

A data transfer system, BP link operating via the PPSS and private data networks connects the 30 divisions to head office. Apart from this, individual companies are left to decide how to run their data communications and how to develop and manage company systems.

A more extreme solution is to devolve responsibility for DP to an external consultancy. Buhrmann-Tetterode, one of the top 20 industrial and commercial organizations in Holland did precisely that, fragmenting systems responsibility and making its DP operation into an independent consultancy. Operations hardware, including twin IBM 4341s and software were even sold to an outside company and leased back on a facilities-management basis. After some years they felt that they needed greater group support and so extended the central core DP staff by bringing in DCE, another specialist consultancy in information management to fill the gaps.

Unilever have a very devolved management style and tend to be even more geographically dispersed than BP. Over the past 20 years the company's management centres have been shifted from a geographical to functional base. Its computing resources have shifted from large national data centres to a wider spread of smaller machines with 500 mini or mainframe systems and upwards of 2000 PCs worldwide.

This reorganization meant dismantling the large data centres that formerly existed to serve the data processing needs of geographical areas. In some cases, the DP staff have been dispersed among the different operating divisions in their region. In others, the data centres have been kept as a single unit and sold off to third parties. This happened in the UK in 1984 with EDS taking over the centre and staff and now looking after all large-scale work for London and Rotterdam.

They find that there is little communication between the different operating companies — soap companies have more in common with other soap companies than they do with margarine producers. A star shaped network has evolved (fig. 16.1).

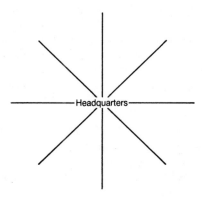

Fig. 16.1 It is common for a star-shaped network of communication to evolve, with the headquarters in the centre.

Phillips until recently used the star network approach. In 1986 they changed this to a matrix arrangement whereby countries could have direct data links with each other — communications between Hong Kong and Singapore no longer needed to go through Eindhoven (fig. 16.2). The company business is more homogeneous than the previous examples but there is another reason for this approach. Phillips is an IT supplier. This has given a more extensive corporate communications infrastructure and a more closely standardized one. With 400 factories and at least 1000 offices worldwide Phillips has had to create an extensive IT planning group. Every Phillips facility has an information systems agency (ISA) group with 6000 people worldwide. The corporate ISA consists of 400–500 and defines strategy and sets guidelines to be implemented in every operating division. In addition, there is a separate corporate communications staff group acting as a resource for the rest of the companies to use if they wish.

Many other different management organizations exist and are tailored to the organizational style of the company as a whole but also to their business. One company who really practice what they preach is Intelligent Environments, a UK-based expert systems software house. At the management level an expert system is ideally suited to network monitoring and control, making informed decisions based on a wide range of changing factors. Intelligent Environments already uses one such system for its internal development, which monitors who is using each file and what they are doing, preventing potential disasters.

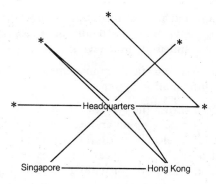

Fig. 16.2 A matrix arrangement whereby different subsidiary companies can communicate directly without going through the headquarters is more efficient.

16.3 A contingency approach to management

The growth in distributed computing and the convergence of computing and communications has undoubtedly provided companies with a powerful business tool. It has also generated an enormous headache for senior management involved in the planning and control of these facilities. In a centralized environment, all control for information processing remains in the hands of a central information services department, including decisions on hardware and software acquisition and their support. In a decentralized environment we find the opposite extreme; decisions are left to the users with no co-ordination from a central group. Distributed processing, in theory, is characterized by shared control but, in practice, has great potential for lack of control and ambiguity.

Most large organizations suffer from a combination of all three environments and have to give careful consideration to where control should be centred. Lucas (1985) suggests possible trade-offs against structure (fig. 16.3).

	Structure		
	Centralized	*Distributed*	*Decentralized*
Coordination and control	Little effort	Heavy demands	Extreme demands
Service	Poor	Good	Good
Support	Market services	Joint effort	Users alone

Fig. 16.3 Control and the tradeoffs against structure.

The contingency approach is a recognition that different information systems and technology environments require different styles and degrees of management. This is expanded at three levels:

> management of user interface, management of IS development and management of information systems.

The diagram in fig. 16.4 shows the type of structure that may be needed and the increasing emphasis on developing an interface with the users which really meets their needs. The development of the information centre has been a particular innovation over the last 5 years and has served to bridge the gap between technology and end-users, providing the user interface. In contrast the MIS or DP centre has increasingly become the Data Centre where the

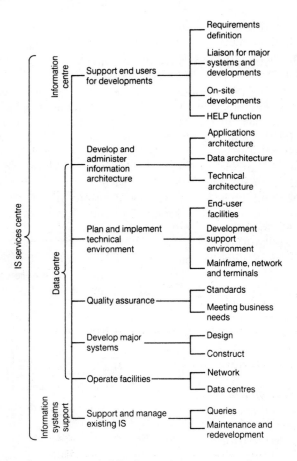

Fig. 16.4   The type of structure needed for the contingency approach.

majority of operational mainframe systems are developed. The maintenance of systems, while seen as a tedious task by any computing professional, is something that will not go away, and the establishment of a system services group who work closely with the users in the operational environment can be a solution to counteract piecemeal redevelopment. It is essential to maintain such a group when strategic systems are developed as they will be required to act as managers of a system which is critical to organizational survival.

16.4 Information centres

Information centres (IC) arose out of an inability within MIS departments to meet the burgeoning demands of information service users. In the mid 1970s IBM began promoting information centres as a means of providing users with the tools to help them meet their own information needs. With the widespread acceptance of the microcomputer, and the accompanying acceleration in computing literacy, information centres have become a dominant factor in organizational information services.

The services of ICs are briefly described below.

User friendly tools
As we have seen throughout this book, a new generation of hardware and software tools exist today which are specifically designed for the non-DP person. Powerful, flexible and easy to learn and use, these tools are non-procedural, normally interactive and very user friendly.

Guidelines in use of tools
The IC will provide formal documentation to act as user guidelines. It will also provide assistance for queries or actual 'handholding' at the keyboard.

User training
This covers: training courses on software products, typically of 1-2 days duration; self-instructional texts; computer-assisted instruction; and tailored reference material. Normally IC staff would become experts in a number of specialized products such as wordprocessing packages, decision-support tools, spreadsheets and integrated software, database and query languages.

Consulting and technical services
Together with training, these activities are the most visible to the users and are essential if users are to achieve full productivity. It covers the provision of advice for the design of new applications to minimize both development and processing time. It may also cover technical services with regard to facilities or access to shared data.

Evaluation and installation of new tools
ICs generally make formal evaluations of products as they are announced and
adopt those which appear to fit user needs best. Given the wide variety of
products on the market, however, most ICs restrict themselves to a certain
range of products or on special user request.

Standards for hardware and software
The IC is normally involved in the development of standards to ensure
compatibility between the users but also to allow for adequate support over a
restricted number of products.

In the early 1980s only a few such centres existed. As the concept evolved their
number has expanded and so too has their role. Increasingly, users want to
integrate with other systems and use other data files. This requires data
administration between the production systems and the user interrogation
systems. It also implies greater levels of standardization, security and control.
In addition, demand for IC services often runs away with itself and growth has
to be managed. Unfortunately, this has paved the way for greater
formalization of procedures for end user computing.
    A further development is the use of IC staff to help user development by
prototyping. With more sophisticated application generators and the unabated
enthusiasm of users for ever more complex information systems, the line
between ICs and DP centres becomes very fuzzy.
    One answer is to keep it so. The proposed contingency approach allows
applications to migrate from one domain to another. Certain users will feel
more comfortable developing their own systems while others prefer
collaboration. Systems which are integrated over a number of functional areas
normally demand professional development but these may use similar tools to
the IC. In such cases it may well be to the organizational advantage to allow
development and support staff to migrate from one environment to another.
Certainly, it can act as a salutory lesson in the development of the
professional's understanding of real user needs.

16.5   Data centres

16.5.1   Quality control issues

Despite the high profile of the PC, the central pillar of modern corporate
computing for most international organizations is still the mainframe. Large
computers are used both for controlling corporate databases and for
developing new corporate applications. Obviously, the American Airlines
system discussed earlier needs mainframe support. This is typical of most new

corporate applications: they are on-line interactive systems with users as drivers rather than engineers.

The major issue in such environments relates to quality control. Many of these installations are multi-vendor environments. A survey of 100 European data centres in 1987 found that 98% were operating in a mixed vendor software environment. Increasingly, to meet individual user needs and match functional requirements data centres are also becoming multi-vendor hardware environments, particularly if this includes PCs. This has emphasized the need for standards — for data, data transfer, systems interfaces. Products such as Uccel's Synova — an environmental integration tool to integrate the plethora of software interfaces — puts a common front on different suppliers' software but is built around IBM concepts. Universal system interfaces are being developed for a number of hardware environments. Data communications products may have to link across a number of different standards and network management can become a nightmare. The only viable solution at present, and in the foreseeable future, is for the data centre manager to develop and maintain in-house standards and effectively create an information architecture which provides for applications, data (with the emphasis on databases) and technology. It may not be possible, or even desirable, to enforce unilateral standardization but the emphasis must be on consistency of data definition both across user levels and within the information systems.

Quality control is also the major issue in application systems development with regard to both producing a bug-free system which meets user needs and to the man hours of development required to produce it. As we discussed in chapter 8, a number of systems development methods have been introduced in recent years which promote effectiveness in both areas. It is noticeable, however, that as organizations move through Nolan's stages of growth there is a need to move away from procedural-driven development towards data driven-methods. Finkelstein (1988) shows the impact of these at each stage of development (figs. 16.5, 16.6). He shows not only that the data model is essential for achievement of stages 4 and beyond, but also that it can free resources at earlier stages and provide organizations with the opportunity to leapfrog stage 3 — the control area where the majority of data centre managers are struggling to survive.

A further operational consideration, however, relates to project control and the use of project management techniques.

16.5.2   Project management

In spite of all the new aids to productivity and the wealth of technological innovation in the information industry, we still hear horror stories of projects which greatly overrun costs and deadlines. In a Datamation survey (1988), the

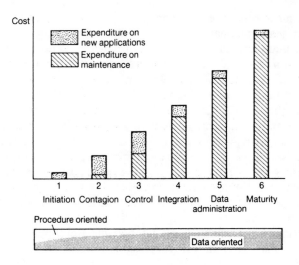

Fig. 16.5 The impact of using procedure-driven methods of analysis and design in the data-orientated stages of automation; Few resources are available for new application development as most are committed to maintenance.

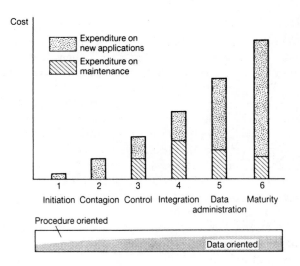

Fig. 16.6 The effects of using data-driven methods of analysis and design in the data-oriented stages of automation. Maintenance drops dramatically and resources are freed for new application development.

top five issues of main concern to IS management are contained in the perennial list headed by project dealines shown in fig. 16.7.

Failure to meet project deadlines is not just to do with the tools used or indeed the professionals who use them, it is also to do with a gross inability to provide realistic estimates.

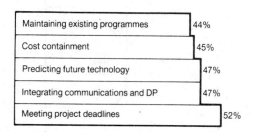

Maintaining existing programmes	44%
Cost containment	45%
Predicting future technology	47%
Integrating communications and DP	47%
Meeting project deadlines	52%

Fig. 16.7   The top five issues of concern to IS management.

Automated development tools such as the information engineering workbench (chapter 8) which include a project management tool may certainly improve the situation but they need to be combined with sound techniques of project management. In addition, the users can play a very important role by being part of the design team and for large-scale projects a project steering committee is essential. There are any number of techniques which can be used as aids to project management but basically, it all comes down to planning, monitoring and controlling — the same skills which must be applied in any management situation. The combination of these talents with respect to the data centre manager's job is shown in fig. 16.8. The combination of the management base with the resource triangle, performance balance and the management cycle means that the manager's lot is not a very happy one.

One final issue of grave concern to the manager is that of data protection and data security with the enaction of a number of acts around the world most notably in Europe and the USA.

16.5.3   Security and control

The basic elements of a security system (illustrated in fig. 16.9) are as follows:

Physical safeguards: locks, fire protection controls, backup and recovery measures, and off-site storage of critical files and programs

Administrative safeguards: company procedures and personnel screening

Hardware safeguards: programmable read-only memory and write-protect tabs and rings

Software safeguards: file access protection, user identification and authorization functions

Communications safeguards: encryption

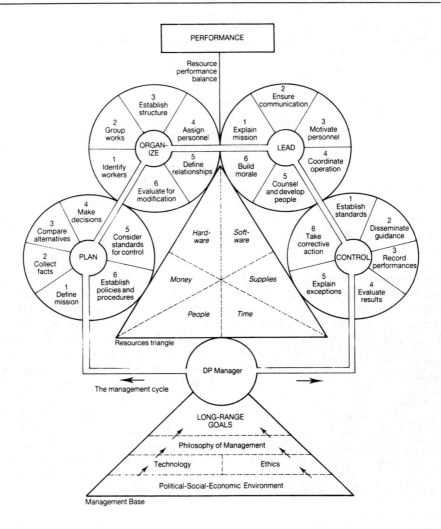

Fig. 16.8 The data centre manager has to combine long-range goals with available resources, management techniques and the resource performance balance.

These have to satisfy the legal requirements for data protection as appropriate to the country of operation. This is, however, becoming a much greater international concern as EDI systems develop across national boundaries. European countries are concerned about the development of EDI systems with Asian countries which do not yet have data protection laws. Even in the USA, Congress has been slow to act, with federal laws in some 15 states only.

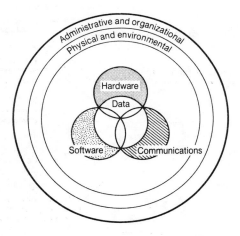

Fig. 16.9 Basic elements of a security system.

To develop an organizational system of security it is necessary to perform a review and evaluation of all current systems to identify security risks and analyze the vulnerability of the systems. Against this we have to identify the relative effects and the acceptability of a certain level of risk — given that there is no such thing as a totally secure system and some risk is always implicit. According to this we should be able to set performance criteria and use these to judge the quality of controls.

One problem, of course is forseeing all possible risks and threats since the controls must guard against intentional and accidental system threats which may be many and various (fig. 16.10).

Security management is similar to all other aspects of control — we have to set the standards in order to identify levels of performance and so allow us to monitor and control the system. Managers cannot leave anything to chance. Finkelstein (1988) provides a model of a decision early warning system which can be introduced to monitor performance in any area of the organization (fig. 16.11). Once again, we are looking at an expert system and its application in the management arena. Let us not forget who the experts are, however. This is simply a model of the management role and without a computer system it represents the actual work we would expect our managers to perform. This is an issue which is too often ignored in the development of information systems — the value of a system is completely dependent on the people who use it and contingent upon the people who develop it.

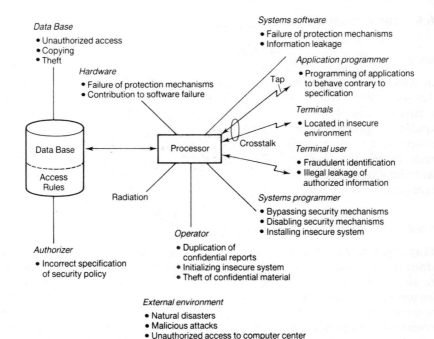

Fig. 16.10 Threats to an information system.

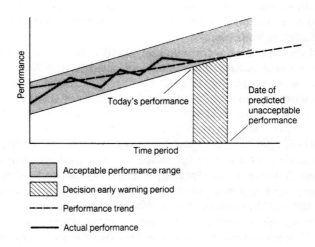

Fig. 16.11 A model of a decision early-warning system: this is an expert business system which monitors defined performance criteria in an organization. It reports unacceptable performance where ever it occurs and also indicates trends towards unacceptable performance.

16.6   The human side of IT

16.6.1   It's people who count

An information system must be designed to meet the needs of those people who will use it. This is a two-way process, the designer has to be able to identify these needs and build a system to satisfy them. The user must also be capable of appreciating how technology can be used to provide information services, and so understand the role it has to play in matching his information needs. In order to develop this mutual understanding, far greater importance has to be attached to human interaction with computers and human resource management issues. This section briefly overviews some of the major issues.

16.6.2   User interfaces

Many organizations still have a them and us syndrome when referring to the information providers, as opposed to the information processors. In fact, we are all information processors and, to some extent, information providers. The problem is a basic one, described in chapter 2: we do not really understand the complexities of information as a cognitive concept or the intricacies of the process of communication. One way to alleviate this is allow for far greater mutual involvement between the two groups. This can take several forms such as dual representation on steering committees, participative development groups, users as members of project teams and implementation teams, using IT specialists as members of other functional groups such as finance, marketing and so on.

The important underlying principle is education and communication. Information centres have broken down the barriers to some extent but this has to be carried through to all IT developments within the organization. To some extent, as we mentioned earlier, the CIO has to be a marketing executive selling IT as a strategic weapon to the organization and developing an appropriate structure for effective user-interface.

16.6.3   Computer people

What about people who work with computers? Work by Couger and others has (Cougar & Zawacki, 1980) confirmed that the average DP staff member has a very different motivational needs profile from the average US working population. DP staff have the highest recorded growth needs from their working environment and the lowest social needs. Work by Hunt (1987) in Australia showed similar results when Maslow's five categories of needs were applied to DP managers (see chapter 4).

It is probably true that this field has attracted a special type of person over the past two decades — much of this may be because of the newness of the profession. It is also true that the profession is changing and hopefully it will continue to attract self-motivated, independent and creative thinkers. It is also to be hoped that their focus will be directed away from a solely technological base towards a socio-technical approach where the human interface with technology poses the real challenge.

16.7   The hard facts of IT

Information systems are an extremely important information weapon for any organization. If the system is running well and performing satisfactorily then its purpose in helping the organization achieve its objectives is fulfilled. However, if things go wrong then the system becomes an inner opponent of progress and efficiency, slowing things down and making the normal functioning of the business difficult if not impossible.

Such questions as how dependent an organization is on its computers, how its computer systems might be put out of action, how much disruption would ensue if the computer system failed and how the organization would cope, are all pertinent and vital. These questions can be collectively addressed through contingency planning. This involves the development of a systematic approach to planning in advance — how staff will deal with problems when or if they arise. Related to this are issues identifying the causes of systems failures. In this section we address the problem of the failure of an information system with a view to helping readers avoid potential disasters both in daily operation and in the longer term. The reliability and robustness of computer-based information systems is closely related to both their security and survivability.

16.7.1   Contingency planning — strategic issues for IT management

In his book *Computer Security*, Garcia (1987) provides a set of extensive checklists designed to allow the information systems user to identify areas in which his system is vulnerable, measure the overall level of systems security and identify appropriate controls. Readers with a particular interest in this are also recommended to read one of the British National Computer Centre (NCC) publications, say on contingency planning.

The IT manager must be able to assess the risk to his organization of various breaches of security. He must identify the various risks, evaluate their possible damage to the organization and then adopt countermeasures which are monitored to ensure continued levels of protection remain adequate. The problem here is in ensuring that protective measures are adequate, and cost justified.

The main purpose of contingency planning is to ensure that the system can recover from something unexpectedly going wrong. Emergency procedures like what to do in the case of fire are common in every organization and do not just apply to information systems. If a general reception area were destroyed by fire, then, assuming that all the staff had safely escaped, the cost to the organization in terms of recovering the losses sustained might be little more than redecoration and replacement of office equipment. If the computer room were destroyed then possible results could easily include bankruptcy to the company if backups of essential data had not been stored in a separate place. Managers have a duty to protect the assets and records of their organization and they must therefore monitor computer security to ensure that effective security measures are being observed.

Emergencies can be aggravated by lack of prior planning. Detailed contingency planning should be a joint effort by all senior managers in an organization. Well-documented contingency plans also help convince insurance companies of the efficient operation of an organization with likely reductions in premiums.

16.7.2   Secure environments

Security is people-dependent

Recruitment of honest staff is a good preventive security measure. Following up of references is obvious good sense. Probationary periods for new employees during which their access to computer files is restricted, and well publicized management policies on the company's ownership of the intellectual property rights to its information, are two other steps which could be adopted. Staff training is critical to the continued operation of information systems. If key areas are identified as crucial to an operation, stand-by staff should be trained and ready to take over in case of illness or resignation of critical personnel.

Systems security training and employees awareness of the importance of security should be regularly addressed. If someone is dismissed he should obviously be immediately deprived of his access to the system and all access codes must immediately be changed to maintain the integrity of the system. Within the organization, the internal management structure should ensure that the responsibility for information systems security is assigned to someone who also has the authority to ensure it is carried out alongside the acknowledgement of the most senior management that they are ultimately responsible for security.

Security is software-dependent

If disaster planning is considered at the systems development stage then security costs can be significantly reduced. Very often systems are designed to perform a specific function and all efforts are concentrated on developing and testing that the system meets the functional specifications. Standards for development should be adopted requiring systems to be developed which include controls to prevent problems. This is much cheaper than adding controls later. Data and program access should be controlled by the definition of specific access privileges for each user and enforced for each of the different parts of the system. Various processing operations can be controlled. For example in a tote betting system the computer system should not allow any more bets to be entered after the start of the race and no override on this should be allowed from any terminal on the system. This prevents racecourse employees entering their own 'winning' bets with 20/20 hindsight.

Security is physical
Physical access to computer systems is necessary. Security of such access is also necessary to prevent damage, destruction or theft. Vast amounts of data of strategic value to an organization (and therefore also to its competitors) can be pocketed by someone lifting a 3-inch diskette. Care should be taken that access to computer systems and data is made physically difficult just as it is to the petty cash which is locked up at night. Remember that data may be worth thousands of dollars to a rival organization.

Data communications through networks should be kept secure through both physical and software protection. Physical backups through the provision of temporary computing facilities by another organization may be a useful stop gap measure. Standard physical security measures such as closed circuit television, fire, smoke and heat detection, infra-red burglar alarms and so on are all commonly used to ensure information systems security.

Finally the old adage 'Garbage in Garbage Out' can be exemplified by data entry operators entering wrong data. Managers should consider whether the physical conditions of their human operators are causing them to make mistakes. Properly designed chairs, no-flicker screens and good lighting are physical considerations which assist in maintaining the integrity of the system.

16.7.3   Learning from others' mistakes

Unfortunately, information systems are often of such importance to an endeavour or an organization that if they go wrong there can be very serious consequences. Analysis of the failure of the W. T. Grant Company, the third largest retail organization in the USA, indicated that the improper use of the available information was a significant factor in that failure.

The ultimate purpose and therefore true measure of effectiveness of an information system is whether the decision-making function in the organization is compatible with the information system structure which is there to support it. System performance, and some measure of the quality of the information it provides, are directly related to the success or failure of the information system. Since an information system is designed to meet specific objectives then, if the information needs of the organization change, the information system must either change or fail to meet the needs of the organization.

The next step therefore is to design the information system in anticipation of failure through lack of responsiveness to the needs of the organization (remember our discussion of planning for change earlier in the book). Certain sound information operating system procedures can be identified including:

An absence of barriers to communication
The presence of several, independent channels to monitor key variables

16.8   Summary

This chapter has looked at some of the issues in information resource management and specifically the organization structure which can support this activity. This will vary according to the individual organization but should reflect the business needs rather than being technology driven. Within the overall IT structure there are also several possible models for information resource management and the devolution of responsibility over a number of centres such as an information centre and data centre is increasingly becoming the accepted model. More and more the emphasis is on the user and end-user computing. This relieves some of the pressure on the data centre and with other tools now available for increased productivity the backlog and maintenance load can be considerably reduced.

The pressure is still on management, however, to improve quality control both in the information centre and data centre environment. Faced with multi-vendor environments and constantly changing software, the problem is often one of just not being able to keep up. One research development which may, in time, provide the solution is in the area of expert systems and DSS. Nunamaker and his team at the University of Arizona are working on the development of a knowledge-based systems support for information centres. This system attempts to provide support for consultation, distribution and help-services and assists the users with the process of software selection.

Other suggestions have been made to introduce expert systems for performance monitoring into IT management. Nevertheless, it is the manager, himself, who must ultimately be responsible for effective control of efficient services.

The social impact of IT and the rapid changes in available technology mean that future trends are far from determined. IT is changing the nature of work, and thus creating understandable social concern. However technology is under human control. Its impact depends on management competence and foresight and the adoption and integration of those particular aspects of the available technology which help that particular organization carry out its plans most effectively.

Amin Rajan put this concisely when discussing the future impact of IT on our society: 'With foresight and effective management the threats could be minimized and the opportunities realized.'

Part III   Summary

This section has been concerned with the management of IT. Too many organizations believe that this is solely concerned with hardware and software management. In fact, it is all about selecting appropriate corporate strategies for IT and then applying the appropriate management style to match these strategies to the overall business of the organization and the structure which supports it. The type of approach required for successful office automation within an organization requires a different management style from strategic systems planning and development where the major impacts will be on the organization's external relations.

There are specific technical considerations related to particular systems approaches and different modes of systems development. Systems which span a number of functional areas within an organization or which have a direct strategic impact on it will need far more formal development methods and professional development skills. End-user computing undoubtedly has a place in organizations but is generally more appropriate for internal departmental systems. A growing use is being made of collaborative user/specialist development and such different development modes require different management styles and service units.

A specific issue is one of people management — information systems are all about people. It is people who need them, people who will design them, people who will manage them, and people who will benefit from them. There is little point in designing a computer-based order entry system for customers if customers find the system more difficult to use than the existing one. The problem is often one of lack of communication between the users and designers. More and more the study of human interaction with computers is the focus of current research. This is a large area and we have tried only to outline some of the major issues and give some direction for those readers who would like to follow up this issue in depth. In recent years the focus has been on motivation of personnel involved in the department of information systems. Their great concern for technical environments may well prove a mismatch with the easy-to-use system generators available today. The rise of end-user computing may have been promoted to combat unfriendly technically oriented systems. Finally, the continuing lack of professional staff forces the organization to review the needs of such staff and the appropriate management styles to ensure their development and continued job satisfaction.

We will now look at a specific organization which represents the kind of growth and change rate typical of many Asian businesses. It shows the kind of opportunities which were presented and the type of information support which was required. It also illustrates a success story. Not every organization is successful in its use of IT and we have tried to point this out and show how to learn from mistakes. There is also much to be learned from success.

Case study: Collect-Calls

This company was set up only 5 years ago as a courier service for local deliveries in Hong Kong — a city densely populated with over 5 millon people and an amazing number of business enterprises. The company was specifically geared to fast delivery of urgent documents. It solved the traffic problem by using messengers with bicycles for delivery in the central business area. Costs were low, delivery fast, and the company secured a steady base of customers, mainly from larger businesses who could affort to pay a premium over their own messenger services in order to cope with extra work or urgent delivery needs. This covered work such as legal or financial transactions.

The company also secured a number of contracts from larger international courier companies for the local delivery of international courier packages.

The average turnover climbed to US $1 million within 2 years. A staff of 75 was employed. The company operated on an anticipated profit figure of 40% (in fact, this worked out at 25% in reality due to the lack of sophisticated estimating techniques).

During this time, a number of smaller organizations also approached Collect-Calls for delivery of product designs to their factory outlets and return delivery of product samples. This involved travel over a longer distance and led to the upgrading of the transportation to light scooters. It also required the opening of two further delivery/collection offices closer to the main factory areas.

The company also secured the deliveries contract for a large international book and magazine publisher which, being a less time-critical delivery schedule, allowed them more fully to utilize their messengers' time around the urgent but erratic delivery requests.

Three years after starting the business the owners were asked to tender for the contract to act as sole distribution agent for one of the major banks. This involved the collection of computer printouts from the central offices and distribution to over 380 branches with deliveries and pick-up services for each per day. The bank insisted on a computerized tracking service for the documents and extensive security and control. The company secured the contract which was worth over US $1.5 million per annum with expectations of further expansion. Obviously, there was initially a high investment cost to the company.

A network of five additional distribution offices had to be set up as shown

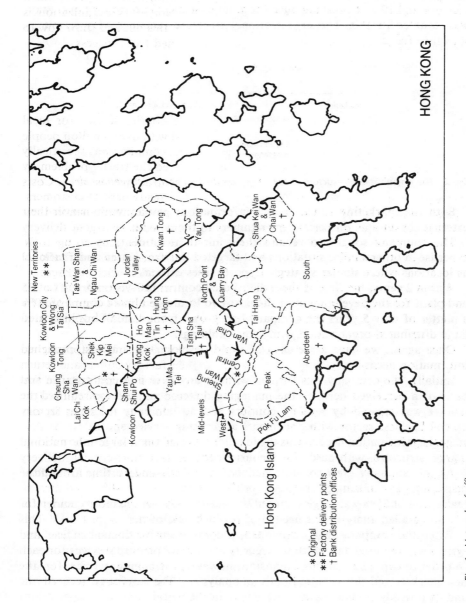

Fig. 1 Network of offices.

in fig. 1. Each of these had to be in a high security area and each had to have a manager and staff operating a control system. The offices were linked by a network and 10 multi-tasking micro-computers installed on the network. Staff was doubled to 150. The organizational structure remained very simple as shown in fig. 2.

Fig. 2   The organizational structure of the bank's distribution agent remained simple.

Both the marketing function and information services were handled by external consultants on permanent retainers to the company.

The company sought to recoup their initial investment, by using their expertise in other similar situations and targeted Taiwan, Korea and Thailand as locations where similar strategic opportunities existed.

Within 2 years, the first of these distributed companies was on profit target and plans for the development of the next two locations almost completed. In a matter of only 5 years the company had grown from a small business to a large distributed organization with group holdings.

Once again, we have a scenario of rapid development and fast changing information needs.

Initially, the company was formed without any customer contracts on the basis of a perceived need by the managing director and a lot of faith. The market was created by sending couriers around company locations in the central business sector with documents advertising service and rates. At this stage the information needed was the location of customers, within the existing market structure, with needs for a courier service.

As the company grew so did scheduling problems and costing for urgent deliveries. The mismatch between profit expectation of 40% and actual realization of 25% was largely caused by underquotes for the more tricky jobs and so detailed analysis was needed of profit breakdown.

When the company really expanded, a comprehensive document tracking system was required and far more security and control procedures introduced. In order to capitalize on this expansion, however, the company had to create new markets and this required both an analysis of the current customer base and of possibly similar markets elsewhere in the world.

Collect-Calls expanded by growing in their chosen market sector — local courier delivery service — but by increasing the customer base and the number of markets.

Information systems applications

The company have a number of opportunities for strategic systems development which arose from analyzing some of their threats.

One might ask how a fast delivery service can be required in a world increasingly being dominated by electronic transmission such as EDI and especially FAX. But, as we mentioned in chapter 11 there will probably always be a need for paper especially contracts and legal documents. Collect-Calls also realized, however, that not every company could justify their own FAX services and so they offered a local FAX delivery service to their customers.

The company set up a simple accounting record of customers and deliveries. Both for standard and FAX deliveries they built up a mailing list of deliveries where consignees were not current customers. These were targeted for a special marketing promotion.

The delivery schedules also allowed them to build up selective marketing mailing lists for other companies such as industry magazines, financial advertising and legal services. These were used to secure the delivery contracts for such material and also as part of their own promotional base.

When the decision was made to develop identical local delivery services in a number of other Asian cities, it also opened up the possibility of a network of distribution between these cities. In order to do this they would have to select the cheapest carrier services operating internationally. This led them to consider an expert decision-support system which was in time extended to cover all the delivery services outside the city boundaries in these regions. The system was developed using an IKBS- DSS generator and part of it is shown in fig. 3.

Sample consultation

What type or package is it?
> Box
How much does the package weigh in pounds?
> 4
Please tell me the city where you wish to send this package.
> Bangkok
What delivery service is required — same day, overnight, anytime?
> overnight
What is the combined length and width of package? I only need to know if this exceeds 80 inches otherwise press RETURN.
> <RETURN>
ATTN Ms Barnett
After careful consideration I have selected ODT as your best alternative at a cost of 300$ HK. This selection was based on sending a 4lb parcel with a delivery requirement of overnight from Hong Kong to Bangkok.
Other alternatives rejected:
DAL   400$
Fast freight   360$
Oversee express 500$
Please let me know if I can be of any further service to you.

Fig. 3 Sample consultation.

The development of electronic trade networks in the region created a specific opportunity for Collect-Calls such that they invested in an EDI interface to these. This was then marketed as a service to local delivery services and smaller shipping agents and other trade customers. Collect-Calls took care of the EDI and then proceeded to hand deliver the documents to these groups.

All of these services, of course, did not just happen. They developed within the overall IT strategy which had started with their first steps into office automation for a small business.

References

Aktas A.Z. (1987) *Structured analysis and design of information systems*. New York: Prentice-Hall.

Anthony R.N. (1965) *Planning and control system*. Boston: Harvard University.

Benjamin R.I., Scott Morton M.S. (1988) Information technology, integration and organizational change. *Interfaces*, **18**, May–June.

Bair H.J. & Nelson J.K. (1985) User needs as the basis of strategic planning. In *Advances in office automation*, Ch.1. London: Heyden.

Bariff M.L. & Galbraith J.R. (1978) Intraorganizational power considerations for designing information systems. *Accounting, Organisations and Society*, **3**, no. 1.

Baron N. (1989) Apple's new computer Mac IIX. *Byte Magazine*, May.

Blake R. & Mouton J. (1964) The management goal. *Advanced Management Journal*.

Boddy D. & Buchanan D. (1986) *Managing new technology*. Oxford: Blackwell.

Brillouin L. (1964) *Scientific uncertainty and information*. New York: Academic Press.

Burn J. & O'Neil M. (1987) *Information analysis*. London: Paradigm.

Butler & Cox (1987) *Electric data interchange*. London: Butler & Cox Foundation.

Churchill C. (1979) In *A systems approach*, West, ed. New York: Del Publishing Co.

Conrath D.W. (1985) Office automation: the organization and integration. *Office Automation Conference Digest*. AFIPS.

Couger J.D. & Zawacki R.A. (1980) *Motivating and managing computer personnel*. New York: Wiley.

DeMarco T. (1978) *Structured analysis and systems specification*. New York: Yourdon.

Doll W.J. (1989) Information technology's strategic impact on the American air travel industry. *Information and Management*, **16**.

Doll & Torkzadeh (1987) Relationship of MIS steering committees to size of firm and formalisation of MIS planning. *ACM*, **30**, no. 1.

Druker P.F. (1985) *Innovation and entrepreneurship*. London: Heinemann.

Drucker P.F. (1988) 'The coming of the new organization.' *Harvard Business Review*, **66**, no. 1.

Duffy L. (1989) Printers — the state of the art. *Practical Computing Magazine*, June.

Dykstra D. (1989) Integrated excellence. *PC World Magazine*, April.

Feeny D. (1987) *Creating and sustaining competitive advantage from information technology*. Oxford: Institute of Information Management.

Finkelstein C. (1988) Achieving competitive advantage through expert systems and automated development. *Proc. 10th annual Hong Kong computer conf.*

Foulkes W.E & Parizek M.L. (1985) Successful office automation: for the people, by the people. In *Office Automation Conference Digest*. AFIPS.

Gaffney C.T (1983) The impact of office automation on power in organizations. In *Office Automation Conference Digest*. AFIPS.

Gane C. & Sarson T. (1977) *Structured systems analysis: tools and techniques*. Improved Systems Technologies.

Garcia A.A. (ed.) (1987) *Computer security — a comprehensive controls checklist*. New York: Wiley.

Gilbert L. (1988) Battle for supremacy. *Asia Computer Weekly*, 15 February.

Grindley K. (1975) *Systematics, a new approach to systems analysis*. New York: McGraw Hill.

Hackathorn R.D. & Keen P.G.W. (1981) Organizational strategies for personal computing in decision support systems. *MIS Quarterly*, September.

Handy C.B. (1985) *Understanding organisations* (3rd edn). London: Penguin.

Harris S.E. & Katz J.L. (1988) Profitability and information technology capital intensity in the insurance industry. *Proc. 21st annual Hawaii conference on systems science*.

Herber M. & Hartog C. (1986) MIS rates the issues. *Datamation*, November.

Huber G.P. (1984) The decision making paradigm of organizational design. *Management Science*, **32**, no.5, May.

Huber G.P. & McDaniel R.R. (1986) The nature and design of post-industrial organizations. *Management Science*, **30**, no.8.

Hunt J. (1987) Reported in Brodley C. A new breed of DP manager. *Hong Kong Computer Journal*.

Jackson M. (1983) *Systems development*. New York: Prentice-Hall.

Kearney A.T. (1985) *The barriers and opportunities from information technology — a management perspective*. London: Department of Trade and Industry and the Institute of Administrative Management.

Keen P.G.W. (1981) Information systems and organizational change. *Communications of the ACM*, **24**, no.1, 24–33.

Konstans C. (1982) Financial analysis for small businesses. *Business*, **34**, April.

Leavitt H.J. (1964) *Managerial psychology*. Chicago: University of Chicago Press.

Lehman J.A. & Wetherbee J.C. (1989) A survey of 4gl users and applications. *Journal of Information Systems Management*, Summer.

Lind M.R., Zmud R.W., Fisher W.A. (1989) Microcomputer adoption — the impact of organizational size and structure. *Information and Management*, **16**.

Lucas H.C. (1985) *Managing the revolution in information technology*. CRIS Working Paper no. 103, New York: Center for Research in Information Systems.

Lucas H.C. & Turner J.A. (1981) *A corporate strategy for the control of information processing*. CRIS Working Paper no. 28. New York: Center for Research in Information Systems.

Mandelbrot B. (1953) An informational theory of the statistical structure of language: In *Communication theory*, Jackson W. (ed.) Sevenoaks, Kent: Butterworth.

March J.G. & Simon H.A. (1958) *Organizations*. New York: Wiley.

Martin J. (1981) *Managing the environment*. Savant Research Studies.

Martin J. & Finkelstein C. (1981) *Information engineering*. Savant Research Studies.

Maslow A.H. (1954) *Motivation and personality*. New York: Harper and Row.

Mattison R.M. (1987) The organisational and informational content of large business systems integration projects. *Sigmod Record*, **16**, no. 2, September.

McFarlan F.W. & McKenney J.L. (1982) The information archipelago — gaps and bridges. *Harvard Business Review*, **60**, no. 5.

McFarlan F.W. & McKenney J.L. (1983) *Corporate information systems management: the issues facing senior executives*. Richard Irwin.

McKeen J.D. & Guimares T. (1985) Selecting MIS projects by steering committee. *Communications of the ACM*, **28**, no. 13.

Methlie L.B. (1984) *Knowledge based DSS for financial diagnostics*. Working paper A-84.005. Norwegian School of Economic and Business Administration.

Miller J.G. (1960) Information input overload the psychopathology. *American Journal of Psychiatry*, **116**, 695–704.

Mintzberg H. (1973) *The nature of managerial work*. New York: Harper and Row.

Mintzberg H. (1979) *The structuring of organizations*. New York: Prentice-Hall.

Nadler D.A. & Tushman M.L. (1977) *A congruence model for diagnosing organizational behaviour*. Research paper no. 40a. Graduate School of Business, Columbia University.

Naumann J.D. & Jenkins A.M. (1982) Prototyping: the new paradigm for systems development. *MIS Quarterly*, September.

Newell A. & Simon H.A. (1972) *Human problem solving*. New York: Prentice-Hall.

Nolan R.L. (1974) Managing the four stages of EDP growth. *Harvard Business Review*, **52**, no. 1.

Nolan R.L. (1979) Managing the crisis in data processing. *Harvard Business Review*, **57**, no. 2.

Nolan R.L. (1981) DP must be run as a business within a business. *Stage by Stage*, **1** no. 1.

Nolan R.L., *et al.* (1986) Creating an information utility. *Stage by Stage*, **6**, March.

Nosek J.T. (1989) Organization design strategies to enhance information resource management. *Information and Management*, **16**.

Nunamaker J.F. Jr, *et al* (1988) Knowledge-based systems support for information centres. *Proc. 21st annual Hawaii conference on systems science*.

Orr K. (1977) *Structured systems development*. New York: Yourdon Press.

Orr K. (1981) *Structured requirements definition*. K. Orr and Assoc.

Paradice D.B. (1988) The role of memory in intelligent information systems. *Proc. 21st annual Hawaii conference on systems science*.

Parker M.M. & Benson R.J. (1988) *Information economics*. New York: Prentice-Hall.

Parker M.M. & Benson R.J. (1989) Enterprise information management state-of-the-art strategy planning. *Journal of Information Systems Management*, Summer.

Parsons G.L. (1983) Information technology: a new competitive weapon *Sloan Management Review*, Fall, 3-14.

Porat M.U. (1977) *The information economy*. US Dept of Commerce, Office of Telecommunication Policy.

Porter M.E. (1985) *Competitive advantage: creating and sustaining superior performance*. New York: Free Press.

Raho L.E., *et al.* (1987) Assimilating new technology into the organization: an assessment of McFarlan and McKenney's model. *MIS Quarterly*, March.

Rockart J. (1979) Chief executives define their own data needs. *Harvard Business Review*, **57**, no. 2.

Sencker P. (1984) Implications of CAD/CAM for management. *Omega*, **12**, no. 3.

Shannon C. & Weaver W. (1962) *Mathematical theory of communication*. Urbana: University of Illinois.

Simon H.A. (1976) *Administrative behavior*. New York: Free Press.

Sprague R.H. & Carlson E.D. (1982) *Building effective decision support systems*. New York: Prentice-Hall.

Sprague R.H. & McNurlin B.C. (1986) *Information systems management in practice*. New York: Prentice-Hall.

Sprague R.H. & Watson H.J. (1986) *Decision support systems: putting theory into practice*. New York: Prentice-Hall.

Strassman P.A. (1985) *Information payoff: the transformation of work in the electronic age*. New York: Free Press.

Suppe F. (1977) *Structure of scientific theories*. Urbana: University of Illinois.

Synott W.R. (1987) *The information weapon: winning customers and markets with new technology*. New York: Wiley.

Tozer E.E. (1986) The Information factory. In *Information management*, Griffiths P.M. (ed.) Oxford: Pergamon Infotech.

Tricker R.I. (1982) *Effective information management*. Beaumont Press.

Turner J.A. (1983) *Organizational performance; size and the use of data processing resources*. CRIS Working Paper no. 58. New York: Centre for Research in Information Systems.

Warnier J.D. (1981) *Logical construction of systems*. New York: Van Nostrand Reinhold.

Wong K.K. (1977) *Risk analysis and control*. London: National Computer Centre.

Yourdon E. & Constantine L. (1979) *Structured design*. New York: Prentice-Hall.

Zipf G.K. (1949) *Human behavior and the principle of least effort*. Cambridge: MIT Press.

Further Reading

Very few references given in this book are specific to one chapter as throughout, we take an integrated approach to the development of information systems. We therefore present suggestions for further reading under global subject areas.

Many writers are mentioned in the text because of their 'classic' contributions to the field — and although it is fitting that they should be given due mention they do not necessarily form the basics for further study as more recent writers build on these theories and develop them in a more appropriate manner for the overall topic.

We particularly recommend regular perusal of the many excellent journals in the field. Subscriptions to these are invaluable for anyone who wants to keep up with the subject.

Information and Organizations (chapters 1,2,4,7,8,13)

Information

Although there is growing interest in information science, it has existed for quite some time and many of the papers critical to an understanding of the related psychology, philosophy and sociology are dated although not out-dated. *I/S Analyser* and *Decision Sciences* are both apropriate journals and *Librarian Sciences* is also an excellent source.

For a comprehensive and concise coverage consult:

Stamper, R. (1973) *Information in business and administrative systems.* London: Batsford.

Lawler, E.E. & Rhokle, J.G. (1976) *Information and control in organizations.* Goodyear.

The AAAS selected symposium series has been published since 1977 by the American Association for the Advancement of Science. The volumes on information science examine the various aspects of the science as an emerging discipline.

The Special Interest Group on the Foundations of Information Science (SIG/FIS) of the American Society for Information Science also publish volumes on papers presented at their annual sessions and offer a cross-sectional and longitudinal view of the development of thought in the science.

Organization

For those whom the subject is totally new, two excellent primer books review organizational theory development. Between them, they cover most of the theories supporting management and organizational studies and summarize the work of many of the writers discussed in chs 4 and 5.

Handy, B. (1985) *Understanding organisations* (3rd edn). London: Penguin.

Child, J. (1984) *Organizations — a guide to problems and practice*. New York: Harper and Row.

For a more in-depth view of the decision-making in an organization see:

Porter, M.E. (1980) *Competitive strategy*. New York: Free Press.

We also advise regular reading of the *Harvard Business Review* or *Sloan Management Review*.

Information systems strategies (chapters 1,3,4,5,11)

As an introduction to the subject a primer can be selected from the following:

Davis, G.B. & Olson, M.H. (1985) *Management information systems: conceptual foundations, structure and development*. New York: McGraw-Hill.

Watson, H.J., Caroll, A.B. & Mann, R.I. (1987) *Information systems for management: a book of readings*. Business Publications.

Zmud, R.W. (1983) *Information systems in organisations*. Scott Foresman.

An excellent introduction to Part II of this book is:

Martin, J. (1985) *An information systems manifesto*. New York: Prentice-Hall.

For a more advanced view, state-of-the-art reports are regularly produced by Pergamon Infotech, and consultants such as Butler and Cox. Again, journals provide some of the most in-depth and up-to-date papers: *Harvard Business Review; Information and Management; Interfaces; Journal of Information Systems Management; Journal of Management Information Systems; Journal of Systems Management; MIS Quarterly; Sloan Management Review.*

Information technology

This area is changing so rapidly that any one text rapidly becomes out-of-date. For those who have little or no knowledge of the field then a general introductory text can be very useful:

Long, L. (1988) *Introduction to computers and information processing* (2nd edn). New York: Prentice-Hall.
An associated computer assisted learning package accompanies the text.

Other useful texts relate specifically to business communications:

Fitzgerald, J. (1984) *Business data communications: basic concepts, security and design*. Chichester: Wiley.

Green, D. (1987) *Business guide to communications systems*. London: Pitman.

A classic of its kind is still:

Martin, J. (1985) *Telecommunications and the computer*. New York: Prentice-Hall.

A number of guides to Office Automation exist and particularly recommended is:

Hirschtim, R. (1985) *Office automation: a social and organisational perspective*. Chichester: Wiley.

The *International Journal of Future Computing Systems* links the applications of the future to the technology and provides a forum for high level research on future computing systems.

In order to keep abreast of developments it is essential to read a number of magazines and journals such as: *Byte; Computerworld; Datamation; Data Communications; IEEE Software; IEEE Computer; IEEE Spectrum; Communications of the ACM.*

Information systems development (chapters 5,7,8,16)

Several texts provide a good foundation for this area:

Sprague, R. and McNurlin, B. (eds) (1989) *Information systems management in practice* (2nd edn). New York: Prentice-Hall.

Wilson, B. (1984) *Systems concepts, methodologies and applications.* Chichester: Wiley.

Couger, Colter & Knapp (1982) *Advanced system development/feasibility techniques.* Chichester: Wiley.

For those who want to grasp a specific methodology then the following title gives a comprehensive coverage of the UK government standard method.

Cutts, G. (1987) *Structured systems analysis and design methodology.* London: Paradigm.

A further source comes from the International Federation for Information Processing. Conference reports and working papers are published under the North Holland imprint. Finally, there are a number of journals providing research support and up-to-date systems development evaluations: *MIS Quarterly; Journal of Systems Management; Information Management; EDP Analyser; Datamation.*

These are supported by local journals and magazines such as those published by the professional computing societies around the world.

Information management (chapters 5,8,9,10,13,11,12,15,16)

This is a very broad area and within this book we have grouped competitive systems, management support systems and management of systems and information under this heading. For comprehensive coverage of these three areas as specialist subjects the following are recommended:

Synott, W.R. (1987) *The information weapon winning customers and markets with technology.* Chichester: Wiley.

Sprague, R.H. & Watson, H.J. (1989) *Decision support systems: putting theory into practice* (2nd edn). New York: Prentice-Hall.

Griffiths, P.M. (ed) (1985) *Information management.* Oxford: Pergamon Infotech.

A number of specialist journals exist and the following are recommended:
Behaviour and Information Technology; Communications of ACM; Decision Sciences; Decision Support Systems; Harvard Business Review; IEEE Expert; IEEE Transactions on Systems, Man and Cybernetics; Information and Management; Interfaces; International Journal of Resource Management; Journal of Information Systems management; Journal of Management Information Systems; Journal of Systems Management; Management Science; MIS Quarterly; Sloan Management Review.

Index